THE IRISH FREE STATE

ITS GOVERNMENT AND POLITICS

by

NICHOLAS MANSERGH
B.A., B.Litt.

With a Foreword

by

W. G. S. ADAMS, M.A., Hon. D.C.L.
Warden of All Souls College, Oxford

LONDON
GEORGE ALLEN & UNWIN LTD
MUSEUM STREET

TO
THE MEMORY OF
MY FATHER

PREFACE

It is a commonplace to say that Democracy is on its trial. If this statement is true—as I believe it to be true—then it is well to examine in the light of more than twelve years of practical experience the peculiar virtues and vices which Representative Government has displayed in our country. This book is an attempt to carry out such an analysis. It is not its purpose to give an exact photographic reproduction of the Government and Politics of the Irish Free State at any precise moment. Rather has it been my aim to discover the underlying principles at work in our political structure. The task was rendered the more interesting, on the one hand by the vitality of the political issues in this country, on the other by my belief that in our generation we are creating a new democratic State. This State, the offspring of a Revolution very real even if not sensational, will make it quite evident that Democracy cannot be subjected to one final interpretation, but must prove itself the form of government best fitted to solve the changing problems of our ever-changing political outlook.

It is in no spirit of conventional formality that I wish to thank all who have so kindly helped by criticism and advice during the preparation of this work, for without the encouragement so generously given by leaders and thinkers of all political parties, by civil servants, and by the members of the Staff of both Houses of the Oireachtas, this book had been very much the poorer. My gratitude for their unfailing patience and courtesy in answering series of frequently obscure and rather trying questions is deep and sincere. My inquiries were spread over a large field, so it is perhaps rather invidious to mention certain names. But I would like to convey my especial thanks to Professor Michael Hayes, ex-Chairman of Dáil Eireann; Mr. J. J. Hearne, Legal Adviser to the Department of External Affairs; Mr. D. Coffey, Assistant Clerk of Seanad Eireann;

Mr. E. Mansfield, Commissioner at the Land Commission; and to Mr. E. J. Riordan, the Controller of Prices, who read over parts of my MSS. and made most valuable suggestions. Further, my thanks are due to Professor A. Zimmern for the opportunity of a most helpful conversation.

I cannot conclude this acknowledgement without paying a tribute, inadequate though it be, to Mr. W. G. S. Adams, Warden of All Souls College, Oxford, under whose kindly aegis this work has grown. His experience of the many-sided problems of modern government made his advice an inspiration. I am very grateful that he should do me the honour of writing the Foreword.

Needless to say, neither he nor anyone else is in any sense responsible for any statement or opinion whatsoever appearing in this book.

NICHOLAS MANSERGH

GRENANE HOUSE
TIPPERARY
July, 1934

FOREWORD

IN British-Irish relations, however perverse and difficult, there is only one direction which is worth exploring, and that is the way of good understanding and of friendship between the British and Irish peoples.

There has been hatred, and there has been misunderstanding, and each of these begets unhappiness and ill-will. There can be no real friendship unless it is built on the desire to be friends, and on the will to preserve friendship and to remove whatever divides and breeds distrust and misunderstanding. Within Ireland all men and women of good will must work patiently and with determination for better understanding between North and South. It is easy to sow division, it is slow and difficult to build up confidence and co-operation. But friendship between the British and Irish peoples—within these islands and overseas—depends mainly on the growth of mutual confidence and co-operation between North and South within Ireland. Every step, however small, on the road of understanding and co-operation makes the next step easier. The way may be slow but it is sure. The means of co-operation may be different from the forms and symbols of the past and even of the present. But the world is changing rapidly and new forces are creating new forms and even new ideals. This book is an honest and thoughtful effort to interpret the growth of institutions and of ideas to-day in the realm of the Free State.

Mr. Mansergh provides much interesting material for the student of comparative politics. The history of the system of government in the Irish Free State is full of instruction in many of the main problems of political organization. The relations of the Legislature, the Executive, and the Judiciary, the Cabinet system and the question of "extern" or non-party ministers, the growth of delegated legislation and of administrative tribunals, the organization of local government and its relation to the central authority, the place of Proportional Representation; these and many other questions are being worked out again in the Irish Free State of to-day.

Despite appearances, Ireland, North and South, has set her face to realizing a democratic form of government. The love of liberty is very deep in Irish nature; and Representative Government has a safer future in Irish than in most hands. The student of Mr. Mansergh's pages will find many evidences of the growth of the executive power both in central and in local government. But democratic control is not wanting. Self-government has shown also that the Irish people are ready to experiment. But experience has brought out the caution and common sense of the Irish nature. The system of "extern" ministers has been allowed to fall into abeyance. The methods of the Referendum and the Initiative have been set aside, at least for the present. The procedure of the Legislature has followed much more closely British than Continental methods. Proportional Representation in the Free State has not produced the multiplicity of groups which has been its bane in some other countries. The weapon of the dissolution, so important in the system of responsible democratic Cabinet government, has been made a part of the working constitution. Mr. Mansergh, an Irishman with a wide outlook over the field of comparative politics and with a deep appreciation of the significance of historical development, has given us a calm, well-planned, readable survey of the Constitution and Government of the Free State. We may not always agree with his views; we may think, for example, that the contrast between English and Irish methods of political thought is drawn more sharply and deeply than it is in fact, and that Irishmen to-day have as much of the spirit of Burke as of Rousseau. But Mr. Mansergh's reflections provoke serious thought.

To all who are concerned with the future of the British Commonwealth this book is timely and of peculiar value, but especially to the peoples of the Free State, of Northern Ireland, and of Great Britain. We have to "know ourselves," and to try and get a view, *sine ira aut studio*, of the way in which we can prepare for better understanding and true co-operation among our peoples. This book helps all to know the Free State.

W. G. S. ADAMS

CONTENTS

		PAGE
	PREFACE	7
	FOREWORD	9

CHAPTER
- I. THE EVOLUTION OF THE IRISH FREE STATE — 15
- II. THE ANGLO-IRISH TREATY — 26
  (I) THE NEGOTIATIONS (II) THE SETTLEMENT
- III. THE WORK OF THE CONSTITUENT ASSEMBLY — 43
  (I) THE CONSTITUENT COMMITTEE (II) THE CONSTITUTION AND THE TREATY (III) THE CONSTITUENT POWER
- IV. THE STRUCTURE OF THE CONSTITUTION — 50
  (I) THE DECLARATION OF RIGHTS (II) THE FRAMEWORK OF GOVERNMENT
- V. THE ELECTORAL SYSTEM — 58
  (I) DÁIL EIREANN (II) SEANAD EIREANN
- VI. THE LEGISLATURE — 86
  (I) STRUCTURE AND COMPETENCE (II) THE CROWN (III) SEANAD EIREANN (IV) DÁIL EIREANN
- VII. THE PROCEDURE OF THE LEGISLATURE — 105
  (I) THE SPHERE OF PARLIAMENTARY PROCEDURE (II) PRIVILEGE (III) THE CHAIRMAN (IV) PROCEDURE ON BILLS (V) LEGISLATIVE COMMITTEES (VI) THE PARLIAMENTARY TIME-TABLE (VII) FINANCIAL PROCEDURE
- VIII. THE REFERENDUM AND THE INITIATIVE — 137
- IX. THE EXECUTIVE — 147
  (I) THE CROWN (II) THE EXPERIMENT OF THE "EXTERN" MINISTRIES (III) THE FAILURE OF THE EXPERIMENT
- X. THE MINISTERS. THEIR POLITICAL RÔLE — 172
  (I) THE PRESIDENT (II) THE FORM AND STATUS OF THE EXECUTIVE COUNCIL (III) THE POWER OF DISSOLUTION (IV) MINISTERIAL AUTHORITY
- XI. THE MINISTERS. THEIR ADMINISTRATIVE RÔLE — 190
  (I) DISTRIBUTION OF THE FUNCTIONS OF GOVERNMENT (II) THE EXTENT OF MINISTERIAL DISCRETION (III) DELEGATED LEGISLATION (IV) ARE THERE ADEQUATE SAFEGUARDS? (V) JUDICIAL FUNCTIONS OF THE EXECUTIVE (VI) ADMINISTRATIVE TRIBUNALS (VII) MINISTERIAL TRIBUNALS (VIII) POWERS OF INQUIRY (IX) THE DICTATORSHIP OF THE DEPARTMENTS

CHAPTER		PAGE
XII.	INTERNAL ADMINISTRATION	217
	(I) THE CIVIL SERVICE (II) THE DEPARTMENTS OF STATE (III) CONSULTATIVE COMMITTEES (IV) UNIFICATION OF FUNCTION	
XIII.	LOCAL GOVERNMENT	225
	(I) LOCAL GOVERNMENT IN TRANSITION (II) RECONSTRUCTION AND REFORM (III) POOR RELIEF (IV) THE LOCAL COUNCILS AND THEIR OFFICIALS (V) LOCAL FINANCE (VI) THE GROWTH OF COLLECTIVE BARGAINING (VII) THE CONTROL OF THE MINISTER (VIII) THE CITY MANAGERS (IX) THE INTRUSION OF THE POLITICAL PARTY (X) THE DECLINE OF CIVIC PATRIOTISM	
XIV.	FINANCE AND FINANCIAL RELATIONS	251
	(I) THE FINANCIAL AGREEMENTS WITH GREAT BRITAIN (II) THE DEPARTMENT OF FINANCE (III) REVENUE AND EXPENDITURE	
XV.	EXTERNAL AFFAIRS	259
	(I) INTER-IMPERIAL RELATIONS (II) INTERNATIONAL AFFAIRS	
XVI.	POLITICAL PARTIES	276
	(I) POLITICAL ISSUES (II) THE UNITED IRELAND PARTY (III) THE FIANNA FAIL PARTY (IV) THE SMALLER PARTIES (V) CONCLUSION	
XVII.	THE JUDICIAL SYSTEM	292
	(I) THE JUDICIARY IN TRANSITION (II) THE NEW SYSTEM (III) THE COURTS (IV) THE JUDGES (V) THE JURY SYSTEM (VI) THE MINISTRY FOR JUSTICE (VII) THE LAW (VIII) MARTIAL LAW (IX) THE PUBLIC SAFETY ACTS (X) THE JUDICIAL REVIEW OF LEGISLATION (XI) THE APPEAL TO THE PRIVY COUNCIL	
XVIII.	THE POLITICAL AND CONSTITUTIONAL DEVELOPMENT OF THE FREE STATE	328
	APPENDIX—LIST OF AUTHORITIES	335
	INDEX	341

THE IRISH FREE STATE
ITS GOVERNMENT AND POLITICS

CHAPTER I

THE EVOLUTION OF THE IRISH FREE STATE

REPRESENTATIVE Government is more than an abstract conception of polity. Its vitality is inspired, not by the dictates of an unchanging doctrine, but by the readiness of its response to the changing needs of political life. No conformity to existent thought, no common conception of its ideal of government, can level out differences created by physical environment and inherited institutions. In every country it displays distinctive characteristics. Thus it is absurd to seek for a typical democracy. No nation can pursue the path to self-government free from all external considerations and untrammelled by intellectual influences descending from the past. A political theory, a certain form of government, may have (as happened in 1919) an almost universal support, yet it cannot be successfully transplanted unless due attention is paid to the prejudices of its adoptive country. The emphasis on the historical development of institutions is the debt which political philosophy owes to the *scienza nuovo* of Vico, and to the writings of Montesquieu. Their teaching on the organic unity and growth of the State was deepened and strengthened by Burke. In no country, least of all in Ireland, can this truth be neglected. In history there can be no such thing as a decisive breach with the past. Fundamentally, even in the most violent of revolutions, a remarkable continuity is preserved. Of this De Tocqueville's analysis of the French Revolution is a striking (and even exaggerated) endorsement. And no study of the Irish Free State Constitution would be complete which did not make some reference, however brief, to the events which led to its creation. Political theory, after all, can decide no more than the forms of political institutions. It is the history of the people which determines the spirit in which those institutions are to be worked.

The history of the Irish Question has shown that the difference between the settlement proposed by the Unionists and that proposed by the supporters of Home Rule was one only of degree. The principle underlying both was the political unity of the British Isles. The validity of this principle was not accepted in Ireland. The Irish solution differed from the English in kind. Its basis was the national and inalienable sovereignty of Ireland. The motive power behind the separatist movement in Ireland was Nationalism. Since the Union, despite superficial fluctuations of opinion, there has been a powerful undercurrent of resentment against English rule. It was not, broadly speaking, a demand for better government. It was a demand for national government. So it was that from the American Declaration of Independence to the revolutions which followed the Great War, every nationalist movement abroad gave a fresh impetus to Irish aims. The Irish claim to national sovereignty has been stated by a long line of philosophers and politicians. In the last century the Repeal Movement brought out three men of real genius—Davis, Mitchell, and Lalor. Of these Thomas Davis was the most influential. His knowledge, as R. M. Henry[1] suggests, was too wide for him to be able to consider that the Repeal of the Union was the ultimate end of Irish political life. "The prophet I followed throughout my life, the man whose words and teachings I tried to translate into practice in politics, the man whom I revered above all Irish patriots," said Arthur Griffith[2] in a well-known speech in the Treaty debate "was Thomas Davis." And Thomas Davis was thoroughly representative of the Irish separatist idea. Its central postulate, accepted by all thinkers alike, was

[1] *The Evolution of Sinn Fein.*
[2] *Treaty Debate*, Official Report, col. 23.

the Independence of Ireland. This was the objective of Tone, whose aim was to secure the independence of Ireland under any form of government, leaving "to others better qualified for the inquiry the investigation and merits of the different forms of government," as it was a century later the goal which Pearse[1] aspired to reach. Later, the conception of a republican form of government became interwoven with the revolutionary thought of Sinn Fein. But, as R. M. Henry writes, "it will be noticed that the status of an independent republic is claimed, not because republicanism is the ideal polity but because such a status will leave Ireland free to choose either that or any other form of government."[2] The central issue, the rock upon which policies so divergent as the Home Rule Acts and Balfour's aim of "killing Home Rule by kindness" alike were doomed to founder, was the claim of Ireland to independent national sovereignty. The position was plainly stated by the Nationalists in 1918. "Ireland is a Nation," they said, "and it is upon a like foundation that we believe the Irish Constitution should now be built. There is room for compromise on details and even on secondary questions of principle, and there is abundant room for compromise of the wisest kind in the form of safeguards for the minorities inside Ireland, without limiting the powers of Ireland as a whole."[3] To this claim the British Government consistently refused to accede.

Economic nationalism was an important aspect of the thought of Sinn Fein. It was not sufficient that the State should be politically independent; it must also be economically self-supporting. Arthur Griffith, who emphasized the need for industrial development and the benefits which would accrue from a system of protective tariffs, was an acknowledged debtor to the doctrines of Friedrich List. It was the emphasis on economic nationalism which provoked the severest criticism of the Home Rule Acts. "We think," declared the Nationalist

[1] From P. H. Pearse, *Collected Essays*, p. 273.
[2] Op. cit., p. 242.
[3] Report of the Irish Convention 1918, Cmd. 9019.

members of the Convention, "it is essential to abide by the principle that Irish affairs, including all branches of taxation, should be under the Irish Parliament."[1] Griffith's economic nationalism went hand in hand with his political programme. In a series of articles, of a frankly propagandist character, entitled the "Resurrection of Hungary," he outlined the history and objectives of the Magyar national movement. A consequent familiarity with the constitutional structure of the Dual Monarchy led to its frequent proposal as a means whereby the Anglo-Irish question might be settled. It was not till after 1916 that Republicanism became in the eyes of Sinn Fein the only acceptable status.[2]

The attempts of the British Government to solve the Anglo-Irish dilemma were handicapped by an unwillingness to understand the nature of the Irish demands. Nothing is more remarkable than the contrast between the complexity of the Home Rule Acts and the simplicity of the Treaty settlement. Moreover, despite the precision of their detailed draughtsmanship, it was only too apparent that the former did not meet in any way the claims of the Irish Opposition. They represented a compromise between differing systems of thought and satisfied neither. The last of the Home Rule Acts[3] was enacted in 1914. It was neither more nor less than a scheme of devolution. It set up an Irish Parliament, whose legislative powers were carefully restricted. It was to be expected that external affairs would be considered outside its scope, but the reservation of internal services, such as the collection of taxes, postal services, police, land purchase, and national insurance diminished to a dangerous extent the competence of the Irish Legislature.[4] Moreover, it was reduced to a state of tutelage by the power of absolute veto retained by the British Government, and by the right of the Imperial Parliament to legislate on matters within the competence of the Irish Parliament. The right of fiscal

---

[1] Cmd. 9019, p. 37.   [2] Cf. R. M. Henry, op. cit., p. 242.
[3] Government of Ireland Act 1914, 4 & 5 Geo. V.
[4] Several of these were reserved for only a limited period.

legislation was permanently reserved. At Westminster, Ireland was to be represented by forty members. The Lord-Lieutenant was to be aided and advised by a Ministry responsible to the Irish Legislature, whilst in respect of the powers reserved, he was to be advised by the British Cabinet.

The dualism of this remarkable constitutional experiment was intended to preserve the political unity of the British Isles. It bears a striking similarity to the schemes proposed in the Conference on Devolution Report[1] of 1920. The manner of its practical working may be estimated by a consideration of the Government of Northern Ireland under the Act of 1920,[2] for both depend upon a devolution of function and repudiate a claim to national sovereignty. In Northern Ireland to-day the Act of 1920 provides a practical basis for government solely because of the frozen political conditions which prevail there. And even in spite of this the dual source of authority and administrative direction has prevented a concentration of political interest. The retention, in effect, of the control of Finance by the Parliament of the United Kingdom destroys the reality of parliamentary government in Belfast. The difficulties, however, which are noticeable in the Constitution of Northern Ireland are insignificant in comparison with those which confronted the practical operation of the Home Rule Act of 1914. On the one hand it was extremely doubtful whether Ulster would have accepted an all-Ireland Parliament without coercion, and on the other whether the Act would have received that minimum of popular support without which no constitution can survive.

The outbreak of the Great War in 1914 shelved this proposed solution of the Irish Question. Under the leadership of John Redmond the Nationalist Party actively supported the forces of the British Crown. For the moment the policy was well received in Ireland. But it was proposed and accepted upon the then prevalent assumption that the War would not last for more than two years at the outside. Whatever may have

[1] Cmd. 692.   [2] Government of Ireland Act, 10 & 11 Geo. V.

been the possibilities of success contained in Redmond's policy, they disappeared with the prolongation of the World War. Leadership in Ireland passed from those who aspired to attain their ends by co-operation to those who relied on a policy of revolution. The revolt in Ulster, the outbreak of the Great War, had revived a policy dependent for its execution upon physical force. The evolutionary policy of internal reconstruction, supported by the Sinn Fein Party, was to make way for the decisive act of revolution, prepared and planned by the Irish Republican Brotherhood.

The Easter Insurrection of 1916 was the most significant and the most dramatic of the events which led to the creation of the Irish Free State. The Irish Republic was proclaimed. The Proclamation of the "Provisional Government of the Irish Republic to the People of Ireland" indicates the trend of Irish thought. "We declare," it read, "the right of Ireland to the ownership of Ireland, and to the unfettered control of Irish destinies, to be sovereign and indefeasible. The long usurpation of that right by a foreign people and government has not extinguished the right, nor can it ever be extinguished except by the destruction of the Irish people. In every generation, the Irish people have asserted their right to national freedom and sovereignty; six times during the past three hundred years they have asserted it in arms.

"Standing on that fundamental right and again asserting it in arms in the face of the world, we hereby proclaim the Irish Republic as a Sovereign Independent State, and we pledge our lives and the lives of our comrades-in-arms to the cause of its freedom, of its welfare, and of its exaltation among the nations."[1]

The words of this Proclamation show how wide was the gulf between what the British Cabinet was prepared to offer and what the Nationalists of the Left were prepared to accept.

---

[1] The Proclamation was signed on behalf of the Provisional Government by Thomas Clarke, Sean MacDiarmada, Thomas McDonagh, P. H. Pearse, Eamonn Ceannt, Joseph Plunket, and James Connolly.

In one direction the Proclamation indicated a decisive breach both with past and future attempts at compromise. A stand was taken on national right—the right of the Irish people to the unfettered control of Irish destinies was declared "sovereign and indefeasible"—and such a stand rendered compromise exceedingly difficult, if not impossible.

From a military standpoint the rising was not a success. Its instigators had realized that such success was impossible. But they hoped that the blood-sacrifice of the men of 1916 would revive the cause of Irish independence. In that they were not mistaken. The manner in which the British Government suppressed the rising was exceptionally ill-advised. "If they had laughed at it, tried the promoters before a magistrate," writes Mr. O'Hegarty,[1] "and ridiculed the whole thing with no general arrests and no long, vindictive sentences, they could have done what they liked with Ireland. But the completeness of their victory . . . took away their political sanity." While it is difficult to accept this view without modification it contains at any rate this truth, that the manner of the suppression of the rising of 1916 materially hastened a breach that was in any event inevitable.

The task of the National Convention, which assembled in 1917, was rendered exceedingly difficult because of the rising of 1916. Its object was to secure a compromise at a time when the atmosphere of compromise had passed from Irish affairs. The convention was summoned by the British Government; it was composed of "representative Irishmen in Ireland" and its purpose was "to submit to the British Government a constitution for the future government of Ireland within the Empire."[2] The entire proceedings were boycotted by Sinn Fein. It was not therefore representative of the most significant aspect of Irish opinion. Moreover, the Ulster Unionists dissented profoundly from the recommendations of the Convention. Thus it was that two sections of opinion, which were

[1] *Victory of Sinn Fein.*
[2] Report of the Proceedings of the Irish Convention, p. 9.

later to exercise the most profound influence upon the political development of Ireland, were in opposition to the proposals put forward by the Convention.

"The difficulties of the Irish Convention," wrote[1] the Chairman, Sir Horace Plunkett, "may be summed up in two words—Ulster and Customs." It was indeed one of the more remarkable commentaries on the recent development of Irish thought that the Customs question came to be one of vital principle. The central feature of the statement of the Nationalist minority was the emphasis placed upon the principle of nationality. Fiscal independence was held to be a necessary preliminary to any realization of this principle in constitutional fact. "We think it essential to abide by the principle that Irish affairs, including all branches of taxation, should be under the Irish Parliament."[2] So reads the Report of the Nationalist Group, and it indicates that this was a question upon which compromise was impossible. The Nationalist Group, moreover, protested against Irish Representation at Westminster, declaring it to be an influence disturbing the balance of English parties, and entirely ineffectual for the promotion of Irish interests.[3]

The Nationalist position was embodied in the statement:[4] "We regard Ireland as a nation, an economic entity. Self-government does not exist where those nominally entrusted with the affairs of government have not control of fiscal and economic policy." The Ulster Unionists strongly opposed this view, maintaining that the "fiscal unity of the United Kingdom must be preserved intact." Fiscal independence was, so the Nationalists hoped, the first step on the road to political independence. That was exactly what the Ulster Unionists feared. To resist the menace of political separation it was imperative to maintain the fiscal unity of the United Kingdom, with its implication of the sovereignty of the Imperial Parliament and its consequence of continued Irish representation at Westminster.

[1] Report of the Proceedings of the Irish Convention, p. 5.
[2] Ibid., p. 37.   [3] Ibid., p. 40.   [4] Ibid., p. 32.

The Evolution of the Irish Free State

The failure of the British Government to give practical effect to the recommendations of the Convention prepared the stage for the catastrophic climax of British rule in Ireland. The rising of 1916 had destroyed the old Irish party system. Within two years the Nationalist Party had lost all claim to speak for the Irish people. Sinn Fein was everywhere triumphant. The results of the General Election, held under the new franchise in 1918, indicated the extent of their power. The election was fought on the issue of independence. Outside the north-eastern counties of Ulster, Sinn Fein was uniformly successful. Its candidates were pledged not to take their seats at Westminster. The elected members assembled in Dublin on January 21, 1919, and constituted themselves the first Dáil Eireann. A Declaration of Independence was promulgated, reiterating the principles of 1916. "We the elected representatives of the Irish people in National Parliament assembled," it read, "do in the name of the Irish Nation . . . ordain that the elected representatives of the people alone have power to make laws binding on the Irish people, and that the Irish Parliament is the only Parliament to which that people will give its allegiance. . . ." A Constitution was drawn up and a Ministry appointed responsible to Dáil Eireann. It was this Ministry which developed an internal administration functioning in opposition to that of the British Government. In the sphere of local government and in that of the judiciary the new administration was remarkably successful. An active external policy directed by Dáil Eireann presented the hope of settlement through international arbitration. Such hopes, however, disappeared with the failure to secure a discussion of the Irish situation at the Peace Conference at Versailles. The last possibility that any real measure of the Sinn Fein claims would be acknowledged without an appeal to arms thereby vanished.

The division of opinion within Ireland itself was becoming an insuperable problem in the way of a settlement on the basis of a United Ireland. The position of the industrial and Unionist North was one of peculiar difficulty. On the one hand, its inhabitants were resolutely opposed to the demand for an independent Ireland, in which their interests might be neglected and in which they would certainly be a minority; on the other the apostles of Sinn Fein had made it a cardinal point in their creed that the struggle was for a united as well as independent Ireland. "So long as the Irish question remains unsettled there can be no peace either in the United Kingdom or in the Empire," wrote Mr. Lloyd George and Mr. Bonar Law in a joint manifesto,[1] "and we regard it as a first object of British statesmanship to explore all practical paths towards the settlement of this grave and difficult question on the basis of self-government. But there are two paths which are closed; the one leading to a complete severance of Ireland from the British Empire, and the other the forcible submission of Ulster to a Home Rule Parliament against their will."

It is possible that the Government of Ireland Act[2] might have provided a temporary solution at the end of the War. In the event it satisfied none of the parties concerned. It proposed to set up in Ireland two Parliaments, one for the counties of north-east Ulster, the other for the rest of Ireland. Unity was to be preserved by a Council of Ireland nominated by the two Parliaments. Provisions were inserted which would enable a future reunion of North and South to take place without difficulty. The fiscal restrictions were more severe than in 1914. The scheme, from the first, suffered from the handicap of paying no attention whatever to existing Irish opinion. "The 'Act of 1920,'" Captain Redmond some time later remarked,[3] "was condemned in every corner of Ireland, and and it had not even the support of a single Irish member whether he came from the North or the South." It is important in that it heralded the future partition of Ireland.

Meanwhile, since 1919 the country was devastated by internal warfare. The machinery of the Dáil Government was pro-

---

[1] November 28, 1920, per Alison Philips' *Revolution in Ireland*, p. 150.   [2] 1920, 10 & 11 Geo. V.
[3] *House of Commons Debates*, 1922, vol. 151, col. 1408.

scribed. In May of 1921 a General Election was ordered by Proclamation for the return of members to serve in the Parliaments of Northern and Southern Ireland. Dáil Eireann decreed that these elections should be treated as elections to itself and candidates duly elected should be regarded as deputies of Dáil Eireann. It was the deputies thus elected who eventually ratified the Anglo-Irish Treaty.

CHAPTER II

THE ANGLO-IRISH TREATY

THE NEGOTIATIONS

In the early months of 1921 the urgent need of a lasting peace was felt both in England and in Ireland. Public opinion demanded that every avenue which might lead to a settlement should be explored. It demanded that a compromise should be made between conflicting principles and ideals, rather than that open hostilities should continue. The military situation was not decisively in favour of either combatant. The Lord Chancellor declared[1] in the House of Lords: "Everyone remembers that the problem became more and more formidable. ... We were not, with the resources which at the given time were at our disposal, successfully coping with the forces of disorder." Michael Collins declared in the debate on the Treaty, "We had not beaten the enemy out of our country by force of arms."[2] It was in these circumstances that on June 2nd the Prime Minister opened a correspondence with the leader of the Irish forces. The letter was addressed to Mr. de Valera as "the chosen leader of the great majority in Southern Ireland." These preliminary negotiations resulted in a truce which came into force on June 11, 1921. In a document July 20, 1921, Mr. Lloyd George, the Prime Minister, outlined the "Proposals of the British Government for an Irish Settlement."[3] The Act of 1920, as anticipated, was shelved, and the basis of the new proposals was Dominion status. The British Government "are convinced that the Irish people may find as worthy and as complete an expression of their political and spiritual ideals within the Empire as any

[1] *Parl. Debates, Lords,* vol. 49, p. 614.
[2] *Treaty Debate,* p. 32.
[3] Proposals of H.M. Government for an Irish Settlement, Cmd. 1502.

of the numerous and varied nations united in allegiance to His Majesty's Throne...." "... They propose that Ireland shall assume forthwith the status of a Dominion, with all the powers and privileges set forth in this document." To this new status certain conditions, peculiar to Ireland, were appended. They dealt with the rights to be enjoyed by the British Army, Navy, and Air Force, with Ireland's share of the national debt, and, most important, with an agreement that no protective tariffs were to be imposed upon "the flow of transport, trade, and commerce between all parts of these islands." Only the broad outline of a settlement was set forward, but "the British Government propose that the conditions of settlement between Great Britain and Ireland shall be embodied in the form of a Treaty, to which effect shall in due course be given by the British and Irish Parliaments." Such were the proposals of the Prime Minister. It was their weakness that what was given with one hand was taken away with the other. The "conditions" directly diminished the privileges of Dominion status. As Mr. de Valera quite rightly replied, "the outline given in the draft is self-contradictory, and the principle of the pact not easy to determine."[1] The more positive aspect of the proposals is to be found, on the one hand, in the offer of a modified form of Dominion self-government—in itself a very great advance in principle on the Home Rule Acts—and on the other, in the proposal for a settlement in Treaty form. That the British Government should suggest an agreement on a Treaty basis, is an indication of a profound change in attitude toward the Irish Question since 1914.

The Dáil Ministry based their case on a belief in an inalienable national sovereignty. "Ireland's right to choose for herself the path she shall take to realize her own destiny," replied Mr. de Valera, "must be accepted as indefeasible.... Dominion status for Ireland, everyone who understands the conditions, knows to be illusory.... The most explicit guarantees, including the Dominion's acknowledged right to secede, would

[1] Cmd. 1502.

be necessary to secure for Ireland an equal degree of freedom." The Prime Minister's reply[1] on August 10th reiterated the British standpoint. "In our opinion nothing is to be gained by prolonging a theoretical discussion of the national status which you may be willing to accept, as compared with that of the great self-governing Dominions of the British Commonwealth, but we must direct your attention to one point upon which you lay some emphasis, and upon which no British Government can compromise; namely, the claim that we should acknowledge the right of Ireland to secede from her allegiance to the King. No such right can ever be acknowledged by us." In his reply Mr. de Valera informed[2] the Prime Minister that the proposals for a settlement had been rejected by the unanimous vote of Dáil Eireann. "On the basis," he wrote, "of the broad guiding principle of government by consent of the governed, peace can be secured."

On August 26th the correspondence was continued. The Prime Minister emphasized[3] "that we can discuss no settlement which involves a refusal on the part of Ireland to accept our invitation to free equal and loyal partnership in the British Commonwealth. . . ." Mr. de Valera,[4] whilst refraining "from commenting on the fallacious historical references" of the Prime Minister's letter, re-affirmed the rejection of the proposals. "They were *not* an invitation to Ireland to enter into a free and willing partnership with the free nations of the British Commonwealth." On August 30th the Prime Minister proposed[5] a conference at Inverness "to ascertain how the association of Ireland with the community of nations known as the British Empire can best be reconciled with Irish national aspirations." Mr. de Valera declared[6] his willingness to enter a conference, but "in this final note we deem it our

---

[1] Letter of August 10th, Cmd. 1502.
[2] Letter of August 24th, Cmd. 1502, p. 6.
[3] Letter of the Prime Minister, August 26th, Cmd. 1502.
[4] Letter of Mr. de Valera, August 31st, Cmd. 1539.
[5] Letter of August 30th, Cmd. 1539.
[6] Letter of September 13th, Cmd. 1539.

duty to re-affirm" our position. "Our nation has formally declared its independence and recognizes itself as a sovereign State. It is only as representatives of that State" that we negotiate on behalf of the people. This statement of the Irish position nearly caused a breakdown of the negotiations. The Prime Minister[1] declared a conference on that basis would constitute an official recognition "of the severance of Ireland from the Empire." "We cannot," he declared in a later reply,[2] "consent to any abandonment however informal of the principle of allegiance to the King." In his final letter[3] the Prime Minister issued a new invitation. This invitation was accepted.

Thus the prolonged correspondence ended in the assembly of a Peace Conference. Throughout the controversy neither side had abandoned its original position. The conflict was one between an unvarying dogma of national sovereignty and an appeal to the dictates of political expediency. It was a conflict which re-emerged in a later discussion on the legal aspect of the Anglo-Irish settlement. The British Government refused to recognize the Irish Republic. They had, however, signed a truce with, what they claimed to be, a section of their own citizens. They had entered into negotiations with a part of their own State. With it they were to sign an Agreement. These actions were inconsistent with the pretension that they were a Government dealing with their own subjects. But except for its bearing on the character of the Treaty, it was a question of no importance. The ministry of Dáil Eireann on the other hand did not abandon their claim to be the legitimate Government of the Irish State. Thus it was that the "Irish Treaty" was, from the point of the British Government, a Settlement which terminated a state of rebellion. But on the theory of the other party, it was an international engagement between the Irish Republic and the British Empire.[4] The drafting of

---

[1] Telegraphed Reply of September 12th.
[2] Telegraphed Reply of September 17th.
[3] Of September 19th, telegraphed.
[4] Cf. Zimmern, *Third British Empire*.

the Irish Constitution was influenced by these opposing theories.

In the meantime the Prime Minister had been engaged in correspondence with Sir James Craig, Prime Minister of Northern Ireland, with a view to exploring the possibility of reviving a United Ireland. The course of this correspondence does not concern us here, save in the one respect, that it showed that for the moment, at any rate, any question of a United Ireland was outside the bounds of possibility. Sir James Craig wrote, "as a final settlement and supreme sacrifice in the interests of peace, the Government of Ireland Act, 1920, was accepted by Northern Ireland although not asked for by her representatives. An all-Ireland Parliament cannot under existing circumstances be accepted by Northern Ireland. Such a Parliament is precisely what Ulster has for many years resisted by all the means at her disposal, and her detestation of it is in no degree diminished by the local institutions conferred upon her by the Act of 1920."[1] So uncompromising a standpoint virtually settled the future of Ulster. It was evident that neither the Nationalists nor the British Government could or would apply coercion.

The British representatives at the Peace Conference were the Prime Minister; Mr. Austen Chamberlain, Leader of the House of Commons; Lord Birkenhead, the Lord Chancellor; Mr. Winston Churchill, Secretary of State for the Colonies; Sir L. Worthington Evans, Secretary of State for War; Sir Hamar Greenwood, Chief Secretary for Ireland. On the Irish side the plenipotentiaries were nominated by the Dáil Ministry. The credentials were issued by Mr. de Valera, and they read: "In virtue of the authority vested in me by Dáil Eireann I hereby appoint Arthur Griffith, T.D., Minister for Foreign Affairs, Chairman; Michael Collins, T.D., Minister for Finance; Robert C. Barton, T.D., Minister for Economic Affairs; Edmund T. Duggan, T.D., and George Gavan

[1] Letter from Sir J. Craig to the Prime Minister, November 11, 1921, Cmd. 1561.

The Anglo-Irish Treaty

Duffy, T.D., as envoys plenipotentiaries from the elected government of the Republic of Ireland to negotiate and conclude on behalf of Ireland, with the representatives of His Britannic Majesty George V, a treaty or treaties of settlement, association, accommodation between Ireland and the Community of Nations known as the British Commonwealth. In witness hereof I hereunder subscribe my name as President.

"Signed, EAMON DE VALERA"[1]

The first session of the Conference was held at Downing Street on October 11th. The negotiations lasted for nearly two months. The Irish delegates returned to Dublin from time to time to keep the Dáil Ministry informed of the progress of the discussions. On December 3rd the draft Treaty was presented by the Irish delegation to the Dáil Ministry. It was regarded as unacceptable and rejected. Negotiations were resumed on Sunday, December 4th, but ended in a definite breakdown. The following day the Prime Minister asked for a further discussion before the breakdown was announced to the public. An altered draft was finally agreed upon on the night December 5th–6th, and these Articles of Agreement between Great Britain and Ireland were signed by the respective Delegations.

THE SETTLEMENT

The extent to which the Treaty affected the framework of the Constitution will be estimated in dealing with the several parts of the constitutional machinery. Here we need only indicate the broad principle of the settlement. Its all-important feature was the grant of Dominion status to the Irish Free State. Ireland was to have the same Constitutional status in the British Commonwealth of Nations "as the Dominion of Canada, the Commonwealth of Australia, the Dominion of New Zealand, and the Union of South Africa, with a Parliament having powers to make laws for the peace, order, and

---

[1] Quoted by M. Collins, *Treaty Debate*, p. 11.

good government of Ireland, and an Executive responsible to that Parliament,[1] . . ." Ireland was thus invested with the constitutional status enjoyed by the five self-governing Dominions of the British Empire. The Dominion of Canada was selected as the model, by reference to which this new status was to be more precisely defined. Subject to certain conditions "the position of the Irish Free State in relation to the Imperial Parliament and Government and otherwise" was declared[2] to be "that of the Dominion of Canada, and the law, practice, and constitutional usage governing the relationship of the Crown or the Representative of the Crown and the Imperial Parliament to the Dominion of Canada shall govern their relationship to the Irish Free State." Canada was selected because it was held to be the *primus inter pares* among the communities composing the British Commonwealth of Nations.

There was one inevitable distinction between the position of the Free State and that of the Dominions. The former was *legally* invested with a status which the latter enjoyed by practice and constitutional convention. This difference constituted one of the great difficulties confronting the negotiators. The transformation of Dominion status into positive law led to the later creation, in the Free State Constitution, of an Executive and Legislature designed so as to reconcile "the association of Ireland with the Community of nations known as the British Empire" with "Irish national aspirations." The reconciliation thus attempted has not proved successful. In substance, as we shall see, acceptance by the Free State of Dominion status has resulted in a conclusive recognition of Irish internal sovereignty. But this end has been achieved in a manner quite alien to the theoretic conceptions of the Irish revolutionary movement. As the correspondence prior to the Settlement had indicated, the Irish claim was based upon the positive dogma of national sovereignty. The form of government achieved owed its essential virtue to an adapta-

[1] The Treaty, Art. 1.   [2] Ibid., Art. 2.

bility derived from its characteristic lack of definition. So it was that the advance in status, secured by the Treaty, was not fully recognized in Ireland. After all it was an advance along a different constitutional road than that which Irishmen had intended to travel.

Certain conditions, stipulated in the Treaty, modified the Dominion status of the Free State. Of these the imposition of the Oath attracted most attention. The Oath, which was to be taken by all members of the Parliament of the Free State, was in the following form:[1] "I . . . do solemnly swear true faith and allegiance to the Constitution of the Irish Free State as by law established and that I will be faithful to H.M. George V, his heirs and successors by law, in virtue of the common citizenship of Ireland with Great Britain and her adherence to and membership of the group of nations forming the British Commonwealth of Nations."

In the British and Dominion Parliaments the Oath taken is one of unqualified allegiance to the King. In this respect the Oath prescribed in the Treaty differs considerably. Its import was stressed by Professor Keith, when he wrote:[2] "The adoption of a new form of Oath emphasizes that the fidelity and allegiance of the members of the Parliament of the Free State are primarily to the Constitution and only secondarily to the Crown." A review of the Treaty Debate will reveal the origins of the controversy to which the Oath gave rise.

The proximity of the Free State to Great Britain was held to necessitate Treaty provisions respecting rights of naval and military defence. British naval control over Irish coastal defence was maintained, pending subsequent arrangement between the British and Irish Governments.[3] In time of peace the Government of the Irish Free State was to afford to the Imperial Forces such harbour and other facilities as were

[1] The Treaty, Art. 4.
[2] *Journal of Comparative Legislation*, vol. 14, p. 105.
[3] The Treaty, Art. 6.

specified in the Annexe to the Treaty, while in time of war or strained relations these facilities might be extended to anything required for defensive purposes by the British Government.[1] It was further provided, "with a view to securing the principle of international limitation of armaments," that the military forces of the Free State should not exceed "in size such proportion of the military establishments maintained in Great Britain as that which the population of Ireland bears to the population of Great Britain."[2] These provisions were keenly criticized in the debate on the Treaty.

The Treaty furthermore defined the manner in which power should be transferred to the Provisional Government of the Free State, certain matters of administrative importance, and finally the manner in which the Settlement itself should be ratified. The concluding article provided that "this instrument shall be submitted forthwith by His Majesty's Government for the approval of Parliament, and by the Irish signatories to a meeting summoned for the purpose, of the members elected to sit in the Commons of Southern Ireland, and if approved shall be ratified by the necessary legislation."[3] To the Irish delegation it was essential that the ratification should be bilateral. In the correspondence prior to the Treaty this was acknowledged by the British Government.[4] It is noticeable, however, that direct recognition of the status of Dáil Eireann is evaded. It is to "members elected to sit in the House of Commons of Southern Ireland" that the Treaty is to be submitted for ratification. It was quite evident, none the less, that the approval or rejection of the Articles of Agreement would be determined by the Dáil. It was to that assembly, on December 14, 1921, that Mr. Arthur Griffith, Chairman of the Irish delegation, moved their acceptance. The debate was protracted, and nearly every member spoke before the final vote was taken on January 7th. The issue between the two parties was clearly defined. Mr. Griffith said, "he had

[1] The Treaty, Art. 7.   [2] Ibid., Art. 8.   [3] Ibid., Art. 18.
[4] Cf. Letter of Prime Minister, July 20, 1921.

signed that Treaty, not as the ideal thing, but fully believing, as I believe now, that it is a Treaty honourable to Ireland, and that it safeguards the vital interests of Ireland."[1] "I am once more asking you to reject this Treaty," declared President de Valera, "for two main reasons; . . . it gives away Irish independence, it brings us into the British Empire, it acknowledges the head of the British Empire, not merely as the head of an association, but as the direct monarch of Ireland as the source of executive authority in Ireland."[2] Later Mr. de Valera added, "I am against this Treaty on one basis only; that we are signing our names to a promise we cannot keep."[3] Every matter of importance in the Treaty was discussed in the course of the debate, but undue attention was attracted by the question of the Oath to be taken by members of the Dáil. In insisting on its imposition the British Government provided the republicans with a focal point for their opposition. Of far more practical significance was the second clause of the Treaty, which defined the status of the new Dominion, stating that the position of the Irish Free State "in relation to the Imperial Parliament and Government and otherwise, shall be that of the Dominion of Canada. . . ."[4] Mr. Erskine Childers[5] attacked this clause on the ground that in the issue the law would override the practice and usage of the Constitution. On the other hand Mr. Kevin O'Higgins held that the words " 'practice' and 'usage' neutralize and nullify 'law.' "[6] While Mr. Collins was justified in claiming that the references to the constitutional status of Canada and South Africa were introduced "as guarantors of our freedom," yet a lack of definition is apparent in these clauses. Mr. Churchill in the debate in the House of Commons on the same question, said he did "not think we would be well advised to define that

---

[1] *Treaty Debate*, p. 20.
[2] Cf. *Treaty Debate*, Official Report, p. 26. [3] Ibid., p. 380.
[4] Cf. December 1921 *Parl. Debates*. The Prime Minister: Dominion Status "is something that has never been defined by Act of Parliament, even in this country, and yet it works perfectly."
[5] *Treaty Debate*, p. 38. [6] Ibid., p. 47.

(Dominion) status more precisely than is done in these articles .... What the British Empire exhibits more than anything else is the result of freedom of growth. No one has laid down carefully beforehand the exact conditions limiting its action." From these extracts the difficulty which confronted the signatories of the Treaty becomes apparent. In an agreement of the nature of the Anglo-Irish Treaty precise definition alone could satisfy the opposing claims. Precise definition was unfortunately a contradiction of the spirit of inter-imperial relations. So it was that the Imperial Government appealed to established law and practice rather than venture to define the status of the Dominions in a formal document. To the Irish people unversed in Imperial relations such references were capable of varying interpretation. It was therefore round the question of interpretation that the debates in the Dáil revolved. It was maintained by the Opposition that adequate definition alone would be secured by some form of external association. In Document No. 2 (then confidential, but subsequently made public) it was suggested "that for purposes of common concern Ireland shall be associated with the States of the British Commonwealth,"[2] and that "for the purposes of the Association Ireland shall recognize his Britannic Majesty as head of the Association."[3] It was also suggested that the source of all authority in Ireland "shall be derived solely from the people of Ireland."[4] Thus while the fiction of the authority of the Crown was to be formally destroyed its actual position was to be freely acknowledged. But the conception of the "associate State" was quite alien to the thought and structure of the Empire, it might have necessitated modifications which would have affected the status of the older Dominions; in the question of the exercise of external sovereignty by the States of the Empire acting in concert, a new problem would at that time have been raised, which might have become more acute than the problem which Document No. 2 was intended to solve.

[1] *Parl. Debates*, 1922, vol. 151, p. 686.
[2] Document No. 2, Art. 2. [3] Ibid., Art. 6. [4] Ibid., Art. 1.

The possibility that Ulster would become part of a National Irish State had been, since the events of 1914, extremely remote. But it was a question which could be omitted from none of the negotiations which preceded the Settlement. In the Articles of Agreement several clauses were devoted to a solution of the burning issue of the position of Ulster. For a month after the ratification the powers of the Free State Parliament were not to extend to Northern Ireland, where the Act of 1920 was to remain in force. Within this month the Parliament of Northern Ireland was empowered to opt out of the new State. It was evident that, in the existing state of public opinion, she would do so, and therefore Article 12 defined the method by which the boundary was to be determined. The Act of 1920 was to continue to apply to Ulster, but "a Commission consisting of three persons, one to be appointed by the Government of the Irish Free State, one to be appointed by the Government of Northern Ireland, and one who shall be Chairman to be appointed by the British Government, shall determine in accordance with the wishes of the inhabitants, so far as may be compatible with economic and geographic conditions, the boundaries between Northern Ireland and the rest of Ireland, and for the purposes of the Government of Ireland Act, 1920, and of this instrument, the boundary of Northern Ireland shall be such as may be determined by such Commission."[1] In the event the method of arbitration adopted was not satisfactory. Such, however, were the difficulties which had led to a divided Ireland that it was perhaps not possible to secure a solution agreeable to both North and South. Boundary rectification in any shape was regarded as a breach of the Act of 1920 by the Ulster Unionists. The Prime Minister, dealing with the more "vexed question of Ulster," reaffirmed his pledge of no coercion, but held it did not "preclude him from endeavouring to persuade Ulster to come into an all-Ireland Parliament."[2]

[1] The Treaty, Art. 12.
[2] *Parl. Debates*, 1921, vol. 149, p. 38.

Before narrating the formal ratification of the Treaty it is well to mention the manner in which it was viewed by the Dáil. From the debate it seems apparent that while the majority approved the settlement, it was a minority, and probably a very small minority, which regarded it as permanent. Mr. Erskine Childers detected[1] the difference on this question among the supporters of the Treaty. Mr. Griffith declared: "It did not mean that they would not go beyond the Treaty . . . but they would move on in comfort and in peace towards an ultimate goal. There is no more finality than that this generation will be the final generation on earth." Mr. Michael Collins declared the Treaty "gave Ireland freedom—not the ultimate freedom that all nations hoped for and struggled for, but freedom to achieve that end."[2] Mr. Milroy later declared, "this Treaty is no more a final settlement than this is a final generation. A time will probably come when a revision of this Treaty will be required."[3] These are the opinions of three supporters of the Treaty, of which two were members of the delegation. This repudiation of the conception that the signatures were appended to a final document is important. It emphasized that the Treaty could not be regarded as incapable of amendment. Its value would depend rather on its capacity to supply a basis upon which Anglo-Irish relations might peacefully develop. The very conception of Dominion status presupposes development. Fixity of relations is alien to its nature. Perhaps Mr. Kevin O'Higgins put this side of the issue most plainly, when he said in the Dáil: "I hardly hope that within the terms of this Treaty there lies the fulfilment of Ireland's destiny, but I do hope . . . what remains may be won by peaceful political evolution."[4]

The acceptance of the Articles of Agreement by the Dáil led to the resignation of President de Valera. Mr. Griffith was

---

[1] *Treaty Debate*, p. 37.
[2] *Arguments for the Treaty*, M. Collins, p. 3.
[3] *Dáil Debates*, September 20, 1922.
[4] *Treaty Debate*, p. 47.

elected in his place.¹ The new President expressed his intention of carrying out the decision of the Dáil in respect of the ratification of the Treaty. As Chairman of the Irish Delegation it fell to President Griffith to summon the members "elected to sit in the House of Commons of Southern Ireland" as defined by the Act of 1920, and as prescribed by the concluding Article of the Treaty. The Assembly thus summoned had two duties to perform; namely, the ratification of the Treaty and the appointment of a Provisional Government. The meeting took place in the Mansion House, Dublin, on January 14, 1922. The Treaty was formally ratified, and a Provisional Government, with Michael Collins as Chairman, duly constituted.²

In the Treaty the status of Dáil Eireann is not acknowledged. In reality, it is true, approval or rejection lay in the hands of that assembly. But the concluding Article specified a certain form of ratification. The assembly there mentioned differed constitutionally from Dáil Eireann. The former contained representatives only from Southern Ireland, whilst the latter was (in theory) an assembly representing all Irish constituencies. By the British signatories it was no doubt intended that the Irish ratification should be sanctioned by a body identical in composition to the House of Commons of Southern Ireland, as prescribed by the Act of 1920. Apart, however, from the fact that a second Chamber was not called into existence, there were important differences. In the Act of 1920 it was laid down "that the Lord Lieutenant shall in His Majesty's name summon, prorogue, dissolve the Parliament of Southern Ireland. . . ."³ More important "Treaties or any relations with

---

[1] The new Dáil Ministry: President, Arthur Griffith; Minister of Finance, Michael Collins; Minister of Foreign Affairs, Gavan Duffy; Minister of Home Affairs, E. Duggan; Minister of Local Government, W. T. Cosgrave; Minister of Economic Affairs, Kevin O'Higgins; Minister of Defence, Richard Mulcahy.

[2] The Provisional Government: M. Collins, Chairman; W. T. Cosgrave; E. Duggan; P. Hogan; F. Lynch; J. McGrath; Eoin MacNeill; Kevin O'Higgins.   [3] 10 & 11 Geo. V, Art 11.

Foreign States or relations with any of His Majesty's dominions"[1] were *ultra vires* and among the powers reserved to the Imperial Parliament. It is also noticeable that no Oath was taken, as prescribed in this Act, by the representatives assembled at the Mansion House.[2] The ratification of a Treaty was, however, the *raison d'être* of the meeting at the Mansion House. The issue is one which is of juridical but of little constitutional significance. Ratification of an agreement may take any form which is acceptable to both signatories. The form adopted might be unusual, but the validity was not thereby affected. It was to the Provisional Government that the machinery and powers of State were to be transferred. The actual authorization did not take place till March 31, 1922, when the Irish Agreement Act received the Royal assent. Mr. Winston Churchill, remarking on the urgency of the measure, asked if it were "not fatal to peace, social order, and good government to have power wielded by men who have no legal authority." "A provisional government," he said, "unsanctified by law, yet recognized by His Majesty's Ministers, was an anomaly unprecedented in the history of the British Empire." In agreement with the Irish representatives this Act also provided that "as soon as may be, and not later than four months after the passing of this Act, the Parliament of Southern Ireland shall be dissolved," and there shall take place "an election of members for the constituencies which have been entitled to elect members for that Parliament (of Southern Ireland), and the members so elected shall constitute the House of Parliament to which the Provisional Government shall be responsible."[3] It was essential that the Provisional Government should be supported by a national mandate. The view of the Irish signatories of the Treaty was that the Irish Republic was set up by the Irish people at the elections which took place in 1918, and that this Republic could only be converted into an Irish Free State by the decision of the Irish

---

[1] 10 & 11 Geo. V, Art. 4.   [2] Ibid., Art. 18.
[3] 12 Geo. V, c. 4, Art 2.

people. Such was not, of course, the view of the British Government, but it is much to be regretted that the Provisional Government did not insist on an immediate election. A decision by the people in the early Spring of 1922 would have been invaluable. That it was not asked for cannot but be accounted a grave blunder. The Irish Agreement Act did not, be it noted, supply the necessary ratification of the Treaty by the Imperial Parliament. In the final clause it is expressly stated "this Act shall not be deemed to be the Act of Parliament for the ratification of the said Articles of Agreement. . . ."[1]

The legal character of the Articles of Agreement has been the subject of dispute. They were, Professor N. Baker[2] remarks, "an Agreement between the British Cabinet on the one side and the representatives of a *de facto* revolutionary Government on the other. The *de facto* revolutionary Government had never established its authority over the territory it claimed to rule, still less had its independence of the British Empire received formal recognition by any foreign Power." On that ground, it would therefore appear that, in International law, the word "Treaty" was a concession to Irish sentiment rather than the statement of an actual fact. This view, not surprisingly, was that held by the British Government. "The use of the word (Treaty) has a great sentimental advantage" . . . declared Mr. Churchill. "When you come to choose what words you will use, and when your actual position is not affected thereby, you should surely use the words most likely to help you to secure the good will, support, and agreement which you seek."[3] Certainly the Treaty was not a normal example of an inter-Commonwealth Agreement. That, however, does not necessarily suggest it was less, it might (according to the point of view) be maintained that it was more definitely international than the ordinary inter-Commonwealth Agreement. President Cosgrave described it to the League as an "international Treaty," and his description

---

[1] 12 Geo. V, c. 4, Art. 5.
[2] *The Present Juridical Status of the British Dominions in International Law*, p. 319.   [3] *Parl. Debates*, 1922, vol. 151, col. 602.

42   The Government of the Irish Free State

was not challenged. Also long before its present status was determined Ireland was a kingdom governed by its Lords and Commons, and the ultimate judicial tribunal of which was the Irish House of Lords, and not, as in the case of the other Dominions (which were then colonies), the Privy Council.[1] This differentiates its status from that of the Dominions. The Attorney General (Sir Gordon Hewart), in defending the use of the word "Treaty," declared, "In my opinion this is not an occasion for constitutional pedantry." In reality it seems that it was an important practical issue. For the controversy about the Treaty raises two questions. The first is whether the Irish Republic, which in Ireland is considered to have been one of the parties to the Treaty, was an international entity and would therefore come into existence again were the Treaty abrogated. The second is whether treaties made between members of the British Commonwealth are international or domestic documents.[2] An ultimate solution of these issues has not yet been attained. It is to be hoped that it will not long be delayed. For the need for some form of super-national tribunal, accepted by both parties, to arbitrate on differences arising out of the interpretation of the Settlement of 1921 is daily becoming more apparent.

[1] Cf. Hughes, *Judicial Autonomy in the British Commonwealth of Nations*, pp. 36–37.
[2] Cf. Zimmern, *Third British Empire*, pp. 36–37.

CHAPTER III

THE WORK OF THE CONSTITUENT ASSEMBLY

A COMMITTEE to draft the new Constitution of the Free State was appointed by the Provisional Government a short time after their accession to office. The increasing difficulties of the task confronting this Committee is indicated by a brief review of the course of political events. A minority, but a very large minority, it will be remembered, had opposed the ratification of the Treaty in the Dáil. The actual voting was 64 in favour and 57 against. The issue was not referred at once to the people for decision. The election was postponed. It was not till May 27, 1922, that a Proclamation declaring "the calling of a Parliament in Ireland" was promulgated. The assembly of the new Parliament was fixed for July 1st. The elections, held in the previous month, materially strengthened the supporters of the Treaty. But the assembly of the new Legislature was postponed till September 9th, owing to the outbreak of the Civil War. The Republican Deputies, under the leadership of Mr. de Valera, refused to take any part in its deliberations.

In the Treaty debate the question was raised, whether "this assembly shall, or even can, surrender its own independence."[1] The Act of Union between Scotland and England had provoked the same question. The destruction of the Scots Parliament was held, by the Opposition, to be the usurpation of a power neither created by nor within the power of the constituencies to create.[2] The basic conception invoked by this argument is that of an inalienable national sovereignty. It is supplemented by the doctrine of Rousseau, who emphasized the purity of the *volonté générale*. He declared that the community could not will any injustice to itself. The surrender of national independence is an injustice. If, therefore, the community wills this surrender,

[1] *Speech of Erskine Childers*, p. 37.
[2] Cf. Leadam, *Political History of England*, vol. ix, pp. 105-106.

its will is no longer pure.[1] It is no longer the *volonté générale*. It is the *volonté de tous* governed by sectional and sinister interests. Therefore it is the duty of citizens to reassert the supremacy of the *volonté générale*. Such would be the theoretic standpoint of those who opposed the Treaty. Even allowing that such a line of argument is irrefutable, two grave assumptions were involved: namely that the Treaty did, in fact, surrender national independence; and secondly, that its opponents were in a position to interpret the purity of the national will.

THE CONSTITUENT COMMITTEE

The framing of a Draft Constitution was undertaken shortly after the Treaty had been ratified by the Irish Parliament. The Constitution Committee, appointed by the Provisional Government, was composed of: Michael Collins, Chairman; Darrell Figgis, Vice-Chairman and Secretary; James Douglas; Hugh Kennedy, K.C., Law Adviser to the Provisional Government; James Murnaghan; James MacNeill; Alfred O'Rahilly; C. J. France; Kevin O'Shiel, and John O'Byrne. The Committee first met in January 1922. In accordance with the instructions of the Provisional Government the Committee submitted a draft within a month. Later two further drafts were produced by the Committee. None of these three drafts have been made public. On the basis of the schemes thus evolved, a final Draft Constitution was prepared by the Provisional Government. This Draft was taken to London and shown to the British Government.

It is important to remember that the framers of the Final Draft Constitution anticipated future consultation on its contents with the British Cabinet. Consequently in it national sovereignty was emphasized so far as possible, at the expense of the legal formalism of a Dominion Constitution. In London, it would appear, the balance was redressed. The Cabinet, it

---

[1] Cf. Rousseau, *Du Contrat Social, livre* ii, chap. iii.

The Work of the Constituent Assembly 45

is to be remarked, were shown the Final Draft as of courtesy and not as of right.[1] This Draft, amended in certain of the points to which the British Government took exception, was issued for publication by the Provisional Government on June 15, 1922.

THE CONSTITUTION AND THE TREATY

The Constituent Assembly did not meet until September 9th. Civil War, which broke out at the end of June, was still raging. The two most prominent supporters of the Treaty, Arthur Griffith and Michael Collins, were dead. The Final Draft, in the form of a Constitution Bill, was introduced by the new President, Mr. W. T. Cosgrave, on September 18, 1922. The debate was not concluded till October 25th. The Bill was conducted through its various stages, with remarkable ability, by Mr. Kevin O'Higgins, then Minister for Home Affairs. It was not, in its entirety, regarded as a Government measure. The Assembly was informed that certain articles,[2] namely those implementing the Treaty and those introduced to safeguard the rights of minorities, were regarded as vital, and that their rejection would involve the resignation of the Ministry. With these exceptions voting was free. The Draft Constitution was discussed article by article. It was considerably amended. In respect of its provisions outlining the structure of the executive, it was radically revised.

The Constitution was brought into operation on December 6, 1922, by Proclamation.[3] It had been preceded by the passage of the Irish Free State Constitution[4] Act through the Imperial Parliament. This Act ratified the Treaty, the Free State Constitution being incorporated in a schedule.

The Irish ratification of the Treaty is to be found in the

[1] This was expressly admitted by the Colonial Secretary on June 15, 1922. *Hansard*, vol. 155, col. 512.
[2] These Articles were: Articles 12, 17, 24, 36, 40, 41, 50, 58, 65, 67, 77, 79.
[3] As prescribed in Art. 82.   [4] 13 Geo. V, c. 1, Session 2.

Constitution Act.[1] It is entitled, "an Act to enact a Constitution for the Irish Free State and for implementing the Treaty between Great Britain and Ireland signed at London on the 6th Day of December 1921." It is therein declared that "Dáil Eireann sitting as a Constituent Assembly in this Provisional Parliament, acknowledging that all lawful authority comes from God to the people and in the confidence that the National life and unity of Ireland shall thus be restored, hereby proclaims the establishment of the Irish Free State and in the exercise of undoubted right decrees . . ." the new Free State Constitution. As Kohn has remarked,[2] "the sovereignty as well as the continuity of the native Parliament could not have been expressed more emphatically."

In the Free State the Treaty is invested with the force of law. The second article of the Constitution Act provided that:—

"The said Constitution shall be construed with reference to the Articles of Agreement for a Treaty between Great Britain and Ireland . . . which are hereby given the force of law, and if any provision of the said Constitution or of any amendment thereof or of any law made thereunder is in any respect repugnant to any of the provisions of the scheduled Treaty, it shall, to the extent only of such repugnancy be absolutely void and inoperative and the Parliament and the Executive Council of the Irish Free State shall respectively pass such further legislation and do all such other things as may be necessary to implement the Scheduled Treaty."

This, the much disputed Repugnancy Clause, invests the Treaty with the highest legal status. Its provisions override both the Constitution and all subsequent legislation. An international agreement is thereby invested with the force of municipal law. The intention was to maintain that the basis of the Free State rested upon the instrument which called it into being. But, while the assertion of the legal sovereignty of the Treaty was definite, the manner in which it was to be

[1] No. 1 of 1922.
[2] *The Constitution of the Irish Free State*, p. 97.

legally enforced was obviously inadequate. Under the Constitution[1] the question of repugnancy would be decided by the Central Courts. But while the latter might declare legislation inoperative because it conflicted with the Treaty, they would be in no position to coerce "the Parliament and Executive Council to pass such further legislation . . . as may be necessary to implement the Treaty."

There exist several instances in which the provisions of the Treaty conflict with those of the Constitution. Under the former, the position of the Free State in relation to the Imperial Parliament and Government was to conform to that of Canada. But, for example, in that the Governor-General of the Free State is not granted any discretionary power in respect of the dissolution of Parliament; in that an appeal from the Courts of the Free State to the Judicial Committee of the Privy Council was not as of right, but only by special leave; and most important in that the Free State Parliament is empowered to amend its Constitution, there exists a notable deviation from Canadian practice. Since the Constitution was shown to the British Cabinet, and approved by them as being in accordance with the Treaty, it would appear that a literal adherence to the practice of Canada is not intended.[2] In respect of the amending power the deviation from Canadian practice is of great significance. The Free State Legislature possesses full powers of amendment, with the proviso that any amendment repugnant to the terms of the Treaty is void. A provision to this effect was inserted in the Constitution.[3] In 1933, however, the Constitution (Removal of Oath) Act deleted the repugnancy clause in the Constituent Act and the restrictive clause in the Constitution, which permitted the Constitution to be amended only "within the terms of the scheduled Treaty." Subsequent to the passage of this Act it is no longer open to the Irish Courts to declare Irish legislation invalid on the ground that it contravened the

---

[1] Art. 65.
[2] On the other hand, cf. Keith, *The Sovereignty of the British Dominions*, pp. 209–215.
[3] Art. 50.

terms of the Treaty. The latter is divested of its force as municipal law, and is placed in the position of ordinary international agreements.

THE CONSTITUENT POWER

Amendments to the Constitution, it is provided,[1] may be made by ordinary legislation, within a period of eight years from the date of its coming into operation. After the expiration of that period the proposed amendment must first pass through the ordinary channels of legislation and then be submitted to a Referendum. The provisions governing this constitutional Referendum are not identical with those governing the ordinary Referendum. In the former case a simple majority of those voting is not sufficient. Unless a majority of the registered voters record their votes and either the votes of the majority of the voters on the register or two-thirds of the votes recorded are in favour of the constitutional amendment, it does not become operative.[2] The whole process appears excessively complicated, but it has as yet received no practical trial. In the Constituent Assembly it was felt that the experimental and somewhat eclectic form of Constitution evolved would necessitate a considerable number of constitutional amendments within a short period. Consequently it was decided that the provision, requiring that every constitutional amendment should be submitted to a Referendum, should not apply for the first eight years after the enactment of the Constitution. During that period such amendments were passed by the Oireachtas in the same manner as ordinary legislation. Subsequently, the term of amendment by ordinary legislation was extended for a further period of eight years, that is till December 5, 1938.[3] Whether the Oireachtas will permit itself to be deprived of full constituent power is open to doubt. It seems at any rate that the constitutional Referendum is too cumbersome for

---

[1] The Constitution, Art. 50.   [2] Ibid.
[3] Constitution (Amendment No. 16) Act.

frequent use. During the first eight years of its existence the Constitution was amended by sixteen Acts. It is not to be anticipated that it will be amended less often in the future.

It remains to remark on the nature of the Constituent Assembly. It was summoned by the Provisional Government as "a House of Parliament to which we, the said Provisional Government, shall be responsible."[1] It functioned as the third Dáil Eireann, and is so described in its own official publications. It acted as a Constituent Assembly. Finally, having enacted a Constitution, it continued its existence for a period of not more than one year under the provisions of that Constitution,[2] functioning as the Lower House in the new bicameral Legislature. This confusion of status reflects the anomalies of the constitutional position. It will be noticed, however, that this assembly considered itself purely as a Constituent, and not as a Legislative Assembly. Though it was termed both "Dáil Eireann" and "Parliament," it did not perform a single act of ordinary legislation.[3] All matters of immediate importance were dealt with by decrees or orders of the Provisional Government. This rigid separation of the Constituent and Legislative Power emphasized the more important issue, namely that, unlike the Dominion Constitutions, that of the Free State emanated from a national Constituent Assembly.

[1] Proclamation of May 27, 1922.   [2] Art. 81.
[3] Cf. B. O'Brien, *Irish Constitution*, p. 54.

CHAPTER IV

THE STRUCTURE OF THE CONSTITUTION

POLITICAL institutions have become cosmopolitan, in the sense that (generally speaking) they owe their existence, not to national history, but to international thought. In the Constitutions which emerged as a result of the Great War, democracy was regarded as the inevitable form of government. Its phenomena were not remarked upon, its merits were not reckoned in comparison with those of other political institutions; it had become part of the established order of things. A century ago only one country in the Old World could boast democratic self-government. Now the whole position is reversed. The peak point of paper democracy was attained in the years following the Great War. But a universal triumph dims enthusiasm. There was no longer a challenge to a hostile world. With the passing of the heroic age of continental democracy, Constitutions were no longer prefaced by an enunciation of the Rights of Man. As early as 1790 Mirabeau had thrown his influence in the Constituent Assembly against this proclamation, and posterity has endorsed his judgment. Most of the new European Constitutions contain a detailed list of the rights, not of man, but of the citizen. Sections in Constitutions are devoted to defining these rights, but at the same time the corresponding duties are emphasized. In the Constitution of Germany the title of the second section runs "The fundamental Rights and Duties of the German people." In those of Yugoslavia[1] and Poland[2] an almost identical section is inserted. But the Constitution of the Irish Free State has in this respect more in common with pre-War than post-War democratic constitutions. For while the rights of citizens are proclaimed, their duties are assumed. In the Polish Constitution, it is declared[3] "the first duty of a citizen is fidelity to the Polish Republic."

[1] Yugoslavia, Sec. 2.   [2] Poland, chap. 5.   [3] Art. 89.

To explain the omission to counteract Rights with Duties, we need only remind ourselves of the inevitable influence of English individualist thought.[1] The idea of duty toward the State, as an obligation imposed by a constitutional sanction, was alien to English political practice till at any rate the closing years of the last century. Now it is true that the Irish Constitution is by no means an individualist Constitution. There are clauses which show plainly an acceptance of the conception of social and economic duties of government. But in general the declaratory articles, coming in the Final Draft Constitution under the heading of Fundamental Rights, are the product of an individualist philosophy. In a non-industrialized community this is not, perhaps, surprising. In Germany, for example, the framers of the Constitution, whilst creating the husk of a formal democracy, were unable to escape from the traditional organic view and so, while accepting the Western conceptions of individualist democracy, they reinforced and amended them, on the one hand in proclaiming Socialist principles, on the other in aligning the new juridical mechanism of the Reich to the organic conception of the State.[2] In the case of the Free State the influence of its historical background is shown in the weakening of the rights of individual citizens by the grant of extensive powers to the State.

THE DECLARATION OF RIGHTS

The individual is safeguarded by a translation of the English guarantees into constitutional right. "The liberty of the person is inviolable" (Art. 6); he cannot be detained or imprisoned except in accordance with law (Art. 6), his dwelling is inviolable and may not be forcibly entered except in accordance with law (Art. 7), freedom of conscience and free profession and practice of religion are, subject to public order and morality,

[1] The phrase "obligations of such citizenship" in Art. 3 has no general application within the meaning of the antithesis.
[2] Cf. Mirkine-Guetzevitch, *Les Constitutions de L'Europe Nouvelle*, p. 10.

guaranteed to every citizen. The right of free expression of opinion as well as the right of peaceable assembly are guaranteed (Art. 9) and no legal distinction is to be drawn between classes or Churches. During a state of war or armed rebellion the guarantee of the liberty of the individual may not prohibit, control, or interfere with any act of the military forces. These guarantees may well be compared with the more flamboyant phrases of earlier times. "We hold these truths to be self-evident, that all men are created equal, that they are endowed by their Creator with certain inalienable Rights, that among these are Life, Liberty, and the pursuit of Happiness, that to secure these Rights Governments are instituted deriving their just powers from the consent of the governed" (American Declaration of Independence). "Men are born and continue equal in respect of their rights. The end of political society is the preservation of the natural and imprescriptible rights of man" (Declaration of the Rights of Man, August 1791). It will be seen at once that the difference is not merely one of verbiage. The earlier Declarations were extremely, anarchically, individualist in tone; the Free State Declaration, though no less democratic, is more balanced. Fear of the executive inspired the earlier constitutionalists, the later, profiting by experience, realize that a promulgation of democratic doctrine alone will not secure good government. The executive must be given adequate powers.

There are, however, on the issue of fundamental rights two clauses alien to individualist democracy. We read (Art. 10): "all citizens of the Irish Free State have the right to free elementary education." It is true this clause is phrased so that it carries the appearance of an individual right. In practice it is not a right. It is an obligation. The English Education Act of 1870 is rightly regarded as a decisive turning-point in her political practice. For compulsory education (though it may secure the support of extreme individualists as J. Stuart Mill on other grounds) means essentially a recognition of the moral duties of the State. It is a direct defiance to individualist

The Structure of the Constitution 53

philosophy. As such it was accepted, either directly or indirectly, by the majority of post-War constitutions. In Poland it is prescribed (Art. 118) that "elementary education is obligatory for all citizens." In the Weimar Constitutions it is set out with elaborate detail in four articles (142–146). In the Free State Constitution the principle is laid down; the practice is prescribed in subsequent legislation. But if universal education is a striking feature of the declaratory articles of the Constitution the most potential for future changes is that (Art. 12) in which the right of the State in and to natural resources is asserted. These resources, it is declared, shall not be alienated and their exploitation by private individuals must be "in the public interest" and under State supervision. At the same time it confirms the title of the Free State to the rights in lands and waters, mines and minerals, within its territory which were previously vested in the hands of the British Government. The vagueness of the verbiage defies precise definition. It might be interpreted as providing a constitutional sanction for nationalization of natural resources; it might be held to assert a very considerable measure of State control over property to imply that the duty of the State is to prevent a use of property inconsistent with the public interest, or as Deputy Johnson declared, "property is held in trust for the public welfare."[1] On the other hand it may be read as a confirmation of the *status quo*. In any event the article was held to be purely declaratory.[2] It does seem, however, to bring the Free State Constitution in a certain measure into line with the economic (as distinct from the political) declaratory articles in post-War Constitutions.[3]

The counterpart of the relation of the individual to the State is to be found in the relation of the State to other States. Many of the post-War constitutions, being the product of an alliance between constitutional and national movements, begin with a

---

[1] *Dáil Debates*, vol. 1, col. 719.   [2] Deputy Blythe, col. 720.
[3] Subsequent legislation affected by this article has thrown little light on its interpretation as a whole. Cf. State Lands Act, 1924.

a preamble to the effect that the people of the country have given themselves a Constitution. In the case of the Free State its status in the British Commonwealth was of first importance. The opening clause runs therefore: "The Irish Free State is a co-equal member of the community of nations forming the British Commonwealth of Nations." But if in this respect the Irish Constitution differs from post-War continental Constitutions, yet in the proclamation of the sovereignty of the people it differs yet more profoundly from those of the Dominions. "All powers of government and all authority, legislative, executive, judicial, in Ireland," it is declared,[1] "are derived from the people of Ireland and the same shall be exercised in the Irish Free State through the organizations established by or under and in accord with, this Constitution." The principle of popular sovereignty is here as plainly expressed as in contemporary European Constitutions. There is only one distinguishing feature, and that is the implied recognition of the exercise of popular sovereignty through representative assemblies. In Finland[2] this idea is expressed in a somewhat old-fashioned form. "Sovereign power in Finland," it is declared,[3] "belongs to the people represented by their delegates assembled in the chamber of Representatives." The insertion of the initiative and Referendum forbids the supposition that a delegated authority of the people in Ireland was contemplated. In the issue, however, the constitutional practice has approached that laid down in the Finnish Constitution.

THE FRAMEWORK OF GOVERNMENT

The declaratory articles would lead one to expect a balanced and somewhat eclectic Constitution. In them individualism is tempered with a recognition of extensive State powers, nationalism is counteracted by the qualified recognition of an international constitutional basis, democracy whilst extreme

[1] Art. 2.
[2] Cf. Headlam-Morley, *The New Democratic Constitutions of Europe*, p. 90.   [3] Art. 2.

The Structure of the Constitution

does not (as in Esthonia[1]) charge the people with executive functions. The broad outline of the constitutional structure follows nineteenth-century practice, but in detail there are some remarkable features. The Irish Free State Legislature consists of two Houses. The Senate or Upper House has sixty members. Though a bicameral Legislature was favoured by the Constituent Assembly, the method of election for the Senate has presented certain difficulties. Originally elected by the suffrage of all citizens over thirty years of age, it is now elected by Proportional Representation by the members of both Houses of the Legislature. A citizen, to be eligible for membership of the Senate, must have reached the age of thirty years. One-fourth of the members of the Senate retire every three years. Its abolition is now proposed. The Lower House, or Dáil Eireann, is the more important Chamber. Its membership is determined on a population basis, subject to decennial revision, and at present stands at one hundred and fifty-three.[2] The deputies are elected by Proportional Representation under the system known as the transferable vote. Every citizen who has reached the age of twenty-one years is eligible as a deputy. Universal suffrage is in practice. The term of the Dáil Eireann is six years, subject to the power of earlier dissolution exercised by the Governor-General on the advice of the ministers. Members of both Houses receive a salary.

Executive power resides nominally with the Governor-General as the representative of the Crown, but in reality with the ministry of the Dáil. This ministry, termed the Executive Council, is nominated by a President, elected by the Dáil. The Council is declared to be responsible to the Dáil.[3] The ministers who form the Executive Council must all be members of the Legislature.[4] The Council acts as a collective body and

---

[1] Art. 27.
[2] It is proposed to reduce this number to 136. Vide Electoral (Revision of Constituencies) Bill, 1934.   [3] Art. 51.
[4] Art. 52. By subsequent amendment (Act No. 9 of 1929) one minister may be a Senator.

is collectively responsible. It must resign should it cease to retain the support of a majority in the Dáil.[1] When that support is lost it cannot advise the dissolution of the Lower House. Besides the ministers who compose the Council, approval is given to the general principle of "extern" ministers. These ministers are to be nominated by the Dáil and are individually responsible. They are not to be members of the Executive Council. This introduction of Swiss executive practice into the machinery of the English Cabinet system will be discussed later. Here it is sufficient to remark that, in general, party feeling has been too strong for a serious attempt to give it practical or prolonged trial. Subordinate officials are appointed by the Executive Council, and they compose a permanent civil service. While the ministers and a small minority of the high officials are changed with the fall of the Executive Council, in a large majority offices are held during good behaviour. There is nothing in the nature of a "spoils system" in the American sense of the term.

The Executive Council being responsible only to the Dáil it is evident that the influence of the Senate is considerably less than that of the Lower House. The framers of the Constitution gave to the Senate inferior powers, not only in financial, but in all legislation. A contest between the two houses is, therefore, always improbable.[2] It is possible, however, when one party comes into power after its opponents have enjoyed a long period of office, in which the latter have been able to secure a majority in the Upper, by their voting strength in the Lower House. Such conflicts would be in time adjusted by the election of new Senators. In the framework of the Constitution provision is made for the direct action of the people on legislation. The Referendum is optional save in case of constitutional amendment. There is no other legislation for which its sanction is demanded. The Initiative was never a part of the machinery of the Constitution. It was, however,

[1] Art. 53.
[2] The Oath Bill 1932 provided a noteworthy exception.

permissible to set up such machinery as would be necessary for direct legislation by the people.

The most remarkable contribution of the Constitution of the United States to political theory was the conception of the Judiciary, as an independent branch of Government side by side with the Executive and the Legislature. The existence of a written Constitution led the Constituent Assembly to establish a Judiciary competent to give legal interpretation. It is empowered to decide the question of the validity of any law having regard to the provisions of the Constitution. The judges of the Supreme Court, of the High Court, and of all other Courts are to be appointed by the Governor-General acting on the advice of the Executive Council.[1] In all cases affecting and arising out of the provisions of the Constitution the High Court alone exercises original jurisdiction.[2] In the United States the place assigned to the Judiciary turned out to be greater than its founders foresaw.[3] In the Irish Free State the tendency is in the opposite direction. Critics in America claim that the judges are legislating under the guise of enactment; in the Free State that the Executive unduly subordinates judicial control.

[1] Art. 68. [2] Art. 65.
[3] Bryce, *Modern Democracies*, vol. ii, p. 89.

CHAPTER V

THE ELECTORAL SYSTEM

DÁIL EIREANN

IT has become increasingly evident that the modern democratic State has no alternative to universal adult suffrage. This does not imply a tribute to the inherent virtues of universal suffrage, but rather suggests that no practicable test of exclusion is available which would eliminate its evils, without (and to greater extent) diminishing its benefits. An educational qualification, supported by the powerful advocacy of J. S. Mill, is perhaps the least open to objection. It has, however, the practical defect that no technique is known whereby an educational qualification can be made synonymous with political fitness.[1] In 1922 the framers of the Free State Constitution were in no position to adopt an experimental franchise. The difficulties confronting the emergence of the new State were so great that, in matters of secondary importance, an adoption of the existing system was the obvious course to be pursued. Dáil Eireann is elected by universal suffrage. The voting qualifications are by no means complex: (i) Citizenship of the Irish Free State, (ii) the age of twenty-one years, (iii) enjoyment of civil and political rights. The first two qualifications are laid down in the Constitution,[2] it being added that compliance with the prevailing Electoral Laws is also necessary. The Electoral Act[3] by which the system of election was regulated, maintained, broadly speaking, the existing disabilities. One exception perhaps deserves mention. The receipt of poor relief was no longer regarded as a fit ground for disqualification. This is a definite advance on the previous law. To exclude a man on the ground that he has been in receipt of public

[1] Cf. Professor Laski, *Grammar of Politics*, p. 311.
[2] Art. 14.   [3] No. 12, 1923.

The Electoral System

relief is merely, in the words of Professor Laski, "to stigmatize economic misfortune as a crime."[1] Exclusion on the ground of a judicial conviction or of imbeciles and persons of unsound mind rests on a different basis and is perfectly logical. Additional restrictions were imposed in 1923[2] disenfranchising all persons found guilty of corrupt and illegal practices at elections. Our hereditary ingenuity in outwitting electoral officers might well, without some such deterrent, establish an extensive system of plural voting quite alien to the intentions of the Electoral Act. To secure fair representation strict measures were necessary, but in general it seems wise to diminish rather than to increase the bases of exclusion from the poll. For theory apart, the fewer the exclusions, the greater will be the confidence in the equality of the system.

If universal suffrage has passed from the sphere of acute political controversy yet its acceptance has involved a discussion, a minute discussion, on the method by which votes should be recorded. And it is not without significance that attention is directed rather to an elimination of the evils of electoral systems than to the more positive goal of securing the benefits that may be inherent in any one of them. For that type of political thinker, to whom legislative ingenuity makes all things possible, is becoming increasingly rare. In the field of the Legislature, however, he may still attract attention by evolving second chambers as chimerical as the subtle creations of the Abbé Siéyès, whilst the field of representation is ever open for the compilation of the pedantic absurdities of the fancy franchise. For what, after all, is the purpose of representation? It is not only that Parliament ought to be in Mirabeau's phrase "a reduced map" of the country in its political aspect. It is also for the purpose of providing a government. The latter object is the more important, in that mathematical accuracy should always be sacrificed to stable government. To say that one must choose either

[1] Laski, *Grammar of Politics*, p. 312.
[2] Electoral Abuses Act, No. 38, 1923.

mathematical accuracy or stable government is to state a dilemma which is non-existent. But once confident of the stability of the government, one would then prefer the system which secures the greater mathematical accuracy.

It does not seem probable that the difficulties of the modern State are such as can, to any appreciable measure, be remedied by electoral machinery. For those difficulties are largely of a moral character. They are to be met rather by an elevation in the popular standard of education, by an elimination of economic injustices, than by making men choose in proportion to the neatly graded volume of opinion.[1] None the less, for the elections to the popular representative assembly the vast majority of the new Constitutions all prescribe direct election on the principles of Proportional Representation or with "representation of minorities."[2] Nothing, in fact, is more remarkable than the almost universal acceptance of Proportional Representation. Before the War it was applied only in a few of the smaller States in Europe. Now, not only is it generally adopted, but it has been included in most of the new Constitutions almost without discussion.[3] It is tending rapidly to become a part of the accepted machinery of the modern State. This is a tribute, not merely to its logical symmetry, but also to its carefully analysed effects. These effects, as the history of the Irish Free State has abundantly illustrated, are of remarkable diversity, and only show that it is the spirit of the electors, not the mechanism of the electoral system, which determines the nature of the Legislature.

In one respect the history of representation in Ireland gave an exceptional opportunity for judging the merits of different electoral systems. Till the open conflict between the British and Irish forces, the simple majority system had been in practice. For a short period, however, previous to the signature of the Treaty, Proportional Representation had been introduced.[4]

[1] Cf. Laski, *Grammar of Politics*, p. 317.
[2] Yugoslav Constitution, Art. 69.
[3] Cf. Headlam-Morley, op. cit., p. 101.
[4] Under the Government of Ireland Act, 1920.

The Electoral System

The framers of the Irish Constitution had therefore, in appearance at any rate, an exceptional advantage in that they had seen both systems in force. This advantage was more illusory than real. Not only did the tide of public opinion flow strongly in favour of Proportional Representation, but also a promise given by the Chairman of the Irish Peace Delegation to the spokesman of the Unionist minority guaranteed that the latter would be assured of a fair mode of representation. The majority system tended to eliminate all representation of a small minority, so the adoption of Proportional Representation remained the obvious means of fulfilling that guarantee.

The more general reasons for the abolition of the single-member constituency deserve to be mentioned. The system, indeed, entails obvious disadvantages. Since the voters in any given district are grouped into several antagonistic parties only a fraction of them can be represented by the single deputy who is elected. In a contingency, which can hardly be altogether eliminated, the simple majority system promotes the return of the least popular candidate.[1] This phenomenon is liable to occur as soon as more than two candidates contest one seat. But unequal representation is not the only ground of complaint. There are others which apply with peculiar force to particular countries. It has been said that little districts make little deputies, men whose horizon is bounded by the frontiers of their constituency. Their conception of office, it is held, tends to go no further than service to the intriguing politicians who secured their return. Instead of occupying themselves with legislative questions of national importance the deputies are engaged in playing the rôle of mendicants for their districts. They solicit favours from ministers, and the latter, dependent on their votes, are unwilling to offend. The evils of "deputantism," as it was termed, were in no small degree responsible for the abolition in 1919 of single-member constituencies in France.[2] The play of local influence has perverted American

---

[1] *Report Royal Commission on Electoral Systems*, p. 5.
[2] Sait, *Government and Politics of France*, p. 149.

assemblies in the same manner, and one is tempted to place the responsibility on the single-member constituency. On the other hand the Members of Parliament in England, elected by the majority system, are almost entirely free from local control. This makes it evident that the electoral system cannot be held responsible. In the Irish Free State the dangers of "deputantism" are very real. Under the existing system they are by no means eliminated. But under a simple majority system the evil would be much intensified.

There is a further objection to the single-member district. Government pressure is easily applied. In a large constituency this is more difficult. In France the whole weight of a centralized administration can be thrown into an electoral campaign, and this explains "in some degree why cabinets, though hurried to execution by the Chamber of Deputies every eight or ten months, have never been driven from office by the voters."[1] Now administrative influence would have, admittedly, freer play in a small district electing one member. The administrative centralization that has taken place in the Free State since its inception augments the possibility that pressure might be applied. But these aspects of the case for Proportional Representation in Ireland are no more than negative. Justly or unjustly the single-member constituency has fallen into disrepute. And whatever opinion one holds as to its merits, it is plain that its abuses are liable to exaggeration in the Irish Free State.

To claim that the limitations of the simple majority system were responsible for the introduction of Proportional Representation would be but to state one half of the case. In post-War Europe the adoption of this system of representation tended to become axiomatic. It was not discussed. It was accepted.[2] This was to a large extent what occurred in the Free State. Proportional Representation secured a large number of adherents in the Universities. In Ireland it was the idol of the student before it became the idol of the market place. But

[1] Sait, op. cit., p. 150. [2] Headlam-Morley, op. cit., p. 101.

by 1922 its popularity was assured. In the event the will of the people was reinforced by the demands of statesmanship. It was generally understood that the guarantee of a fair mode of representation, given to the spokesman of the Unionist minority, involved the introduction of Proportional Representation. Moreover, apart altogether from this guarantee, the form of government, envisaged by the framers of the Constitution, demanded a full representation of minorities. To this we shall recur. Here it is sufficient to remark that Proportional Representation was intended to secure not merely a different (and higher) type of candidate, but also to modify the rigidity of the two-party system. In both of these aims the hopes entertained have been largely falsified. But in any event the inclusion of a provision in the Constitution enacting the precise form of the electoral system seems unfortunate. "The members shall be elected," it is declared, "upon the principles of Proportional Representation."[1] The Constitution is intended to be rigid. To preserve its rigidity only essentials should be included. While there is at present no serious alternative to the simple majority system, other than some mode of Proportional Representation, yet with changing conditions and varying needs it is probable that new systems of election will come to the fore. A return to the simple majority system may even be desired. In either event a constitutional amendment will be required. Apart altogether from the difficulty of the amending procedure it is undesirable that the Constitution should be changed unnecessarily. In the Yugoslav[2] alone, of post-War Constitutions, is this mistake avoided. In it, "representation of minorities" is prescribed, but the actual system by which this is to be provided is left to ordinary legislation.

The form of Proportional Representation, adopted by the Irish Free State, is laid down in the Electoral Act of 1923. It is the system known as the Single Transferable Vote. It represents a modification of the original proposals of Mr.

[1] Art. 26.   [2] Art. 69.

Thomas Hare[1] both in the method of counting the votes and in the size of constituency. The Transferable Vote system, as in practice in the Free State, is as follows. Constituencies return several members. The elector, in voting, places the figure 1 opposite the name of the candidate he likes best, and is invited to place the number 2 opposite the name of second choice, the number 3 opposite his third choice and so on, numbering as many candidates as he pleases. The Returning Officer ascertains the result of the election in the following manner. He counts each ballot paper as one vote to the candidate marked 1 thereon. He also counts the total number of votes. He ascertains the quota. This figure is obtained by dividing the votes cast by the number of seats to be filled plus one, and adding one to the result. If there are 100 votes cast and two seats to be filled the quota will then be $\frac{100}{2+1} + 1 = 34$, a number which can be obtained only by two candidates. The candidates who have received the quota are then declared elected. The surplus votes of those candidates who have received more than the quota are transferred in strict proportions, and credited to the unelected candidates indicated by the figures 2, 3, and so on as the next preferences of the electors whose votes are transferred. Then those candidates who after the transfer of surplus votes have obtained the quota are declared elected. The candidates lowest on the poll are now eliminated one after another by transferring their votes, in accordance with the wishes of their supporters, to the candidates indicated as next preferences. This process is continued until either the required number of candidates having each obtained the quota, is elected, or the number of candidates not eliminated is reduced to the number of seats still vacant. In the latter event the candidates not eliminated are declared elected.

The assertion that the actual mechanism, the method of counting the votes, is so complicated as to be incapable of cor-

[1] *Treatise on the Election of Representatives*, 1859.

rect and expeditious application under the conditions of political elections is proved to be without foundation. From the point of view of the electors the system has proved reasonably simple. The percentage of spoiled votes has been remarkably small. In county Dublin, where in 1932 there were eighteen candidates for eight seats, the number of spoiled votes was 1·07 per cent. In the scattered rural constituency of Galway the percentage was 1·6. It cannot therefore be claimed that from the point of view of the elector the system is too complicated. The published transfers of votes showed that many took full advantage of the freedom which this method of voting gives. The electors were free to vote on party or non-party lines. Two to five days elapse before the results are known—a delay which has occasioned criticism. It must, however, be remembered that in the large county divisions a day or more may elapse before the ballot boxes are collected at the polling booth. The voting is by secret ballot.[1] Under the system in practice till 1934 each constituency in the Free State, generally a single county, elected several deputies. The county of Louth elected three, the county of Galway elected nine, whilst the largest county, Cork, was divided. Each University elected three members, but it is proposed to abolish University Representation.[2] The number of deputies is fixed from time to time by the Oireachtas, whose powers in this respect are limited by the Constitution. It is prescribed[3] therein that the number shall be fixed at not less than one member for each thirty thousand of the population, or at more than one member for every twenty thousand. The constituencies are revised every ten years, and the most noteworthy features of the Bill introduced for that purpose in 1934 are the reduction of the number of deputies from 153 to 136, and the abolition of the larger and more unwieldy constituencies. No constituencies would return more than five or less than three deputies.[4]

[1] Constitution, Art. 14.
[2] Constitution (Amendment No. 23) Bill 1934.   [3] Art. 26.
[4] Electoral (Revision of Constituencies) Bill, 1934.

The accuracy of the Single Transferable Vote system must first be considered. How great an element of chance is involved by the processes of elimination and transfer? The Proportional Representation Society maintain that with their system of transfers it is negligible,[1] and further that the order in which

GENERAL ELECTION, JUNE 1927[2]

Parties	Votes	Seats Won	Seats in Proportion to Votes
Cumann na nGaedheal	314,684	46	42
Fianna Fail	299,626	44	40
Labour	143,987	22	19
Independents	139,679	14	19
Farmers	109,114	11	14
Nationl League	84,048	8	11
Sinn Fein	41,436	5	5
Ind. Republican	9,215	2	1
Clann Eireann	5,567	0	1
Totals	1,147,356	152	152

GENERAL ELECTION, SEPTEMBER 1927[3]

Parties	Votes	Seats Won	Seats in Proportion to Votes
Cumann na nGaedheal	453,064	61	57·2
Fianna Fail	411,833	57	52·0
Labour	105,271	13	13·3
Independent	104,059	9	13·1
Farmers	74,723	6	9·4
National League	19,000	2	2·4
Ind. Labour	12,473	1	1·6
Totals	1,180,423	149	149·0

candidates are eliminated can make no difference. The former claim appears accurate, but it does appear probable that there is some element of chance involved in the order of elimination. It is apparent in very rare contingencies. From these rather

[1] With the Tasmanian refinement it disappears.
[2] One uncontested seat not included.
[3] Four uncontested seats not included.

The Electoral System

minute criticisms of the mechanism one may pass to the general accuracy of the system. Here an examination of votes cast for the respective political parties proportionate to the number of seats secured places its substantial accuracy beyond all question.

In the 1933 election the issue was sufficiently clear-cut to permit of the division of all the parties into two opposing

GENERAL ELECTION, 1932[1]

Parties	Votes Polled	Seats Won	Seats in Proportion to Votes
Fianna Fail	566,475	72	66
Cumann na nGaedheal	449,810	56	53
Labour	98,285	7	11
Farmers	41,302	5	5
Independents and others	117,333	9	14
Totals	1,273,205	149	149

GENERAL ELECTION, 1933

	Votes Polled	Seats Won	Seats in Proportion to Votes
Fianna Fail and Labour	770,968	85	85
Cumann na nGaedheal, Centre and Independ.	615,358	68	68
Totals	1,386,326	153	153

camps. The results reveal the remarkable accuracy of the Single Transferable Vote. On the whole the figures quoted show a close approximation to equality in the value of the votes recorded for the two largest parties. These parties, however, gained in comparison with the smaller parties. The system, it would appear, whilst giving an opportunity to small parties, does not favour them. The Labour Party in 1932 nominated candidates in many constituencies, but in the majority failed to poll a quota of votes. But it did secure

[1] Four uncontested seats not included.

68   *The Government of the Irish Free State*

seven seats. Under the simple majority system it would not in all probability have secured any representation at all. Moreover, in the figures tabulated above, it must be remembered that the Independents are not, as their name implies, a party at all. Hence their preferences, when distributed, frequently favoured one of the larger parties. But in contrast with the simple majority system, the accuracy of the Transferable Vote is beyond reproach.

GREAT BRITAIN AND NORTHERN IRELAND—GENERAL ELECTION, 1931

Party	Votes Polled	Seats[1]	Seats in Proportion to Votes
Government Parties (Cons., Lib., Nat., Lab.)	14,531,925	493	368
Labour	6,648,023	46	168
Independent Liberal	106,106	4	3
Others	371,252	5	9
Totals	21,657,306	548	548

The Single Transferable Vote system secures fair representation. In no constituency does one party monopolize representation. In Ireland this is consequence of no little importance. It prevents an exaggeration of the difference in political opinion between the inhabitants of various parts of the country. Under the simple majority system, Kerry, Clare, Limerick, and other western counties (in 1932) would have been solid for Fianna Fail; some of the eastern counties for Cumann na nGaedheal. An emphasis of this geographical division of opinion could not but have had harmful results.

Some of the more positive benefits may be mentioned. Not only is national representation comprehensive and fair, but also, with very rare exceptions, the leaders of the parties have been returned. The Cumann na nGaedheal Government were

[1] Not including 67 uncontested seats (61 Government, 6 Labour).

defeated at the General Election held in 1932, after ten years of office. None the less every member of Mr. Cosgrave's Executive Council was returned. The contrast with the defeat of the Labour Party in England in 1931 could scarcely be more pronounced. There the leaders of the Opposition were, with but one single exception, all defeated. In general this may not be an issue of great significance. In Ireland it is a matter of supreme importance. A fully manned Opposition front bench alone is likely to secure an adequate debate on legislative proposals.

Under the Single Transferable Vote system the electors have the fullest freedom in determining who should be returned from among the candidates of each party. They are not bound in any way by a party list. It is interesting to observe how the choice is exercised. Two tendencies are clearly marked. Those who have distinguished themselves in the public life of the country are not summarily dismissed from service, but are generally re-elected; the local candidate has an advantage where his policy or record is acceptable.[1] This is not to suggest that the local candidate is inevitably preferred. But candidates are selected by local party conventions, and these are apt to favour those who are well-known in the district. This suggests one of the more fundamental criticisms against Proportional Representation. Does it favour the representation of interests at the expense of the *volonté générale*? There can be but little doubt that the tendency of modern democracy is towards functional representation. It has not, as such, been introduced; but Continental parties frequently represent, not general political opinions, but the particular interests of certain classes or of certain professions.[2] The multiplication of parties is in part both the cause and the effect of this movement. From its influence the Free State has not escaped. The Labour Party, the Farmers' Party, the Centre Party have (or had) at heart the interests of certain sections of the community. It is to

[1] Cf. *Representation*, journal of Proportional Representation Society, 1927. [2] Cf. Headlam-Morley, op. cit., p. 131.

that they owe their existence. The Centre Party (first known as the Farmers and Ratepayers League) was a good example. It based its electoral appeal on its determination to further at all costs the interests of the farmer. Is this functional representation due to the electoral system? Whilst it is a question that does not permit of a categorical reply, it does seem that any system of Proportional Representation tends to encourage its growth in normal circumstances. A classification of the occupational interests of the deputies of successive Dála is instructive.

Dáil	Farmers	Business	Small Tradesmen	Journalists
1932	39	24	18	5
1927 (Sept. election)	45	19	19	5

Dáil	Learned Professions	Teachers	Engaged in Local Government
1932	27	8	40
1927 (Sept. election)	26	7	43

It will be seen from the above figures[1] that the rural constituencies favour representation by farmers. The latter are to be found in all parties, and form a large and constant element in the successive Dála. It is also remarkable how frequently service in Local Government paves the way to a seat in the National Legislature.

While Proportional Representation may, in some measure, favour functional representation, it is also held to promote a multiplicity of parties. This criticism has no doubt been exaggerated, partly indeed owing to the erroneous impression that Proportional Representation was introduced in France in 1919. The French Electoral Act of that year provided for Proportional Representation on a list system. It was a Proportional Representation measure as introduced, but as it was passed no trace of Proportional Representation, except the

[1] There is no claim that the statistics are absolutely accurate. There is considerable difficulty in placing certain occupations in any definite category and a certain discretion must therefore be allowed.

title, remained. It cannot therefore be claimed that Proportional Representation is responsible for the group system in France. Moreover, in Germany the introduction of Proportional Representation considerably reduced the number of parties. In the Irish Free State the tendency has been in the same direction. There has been a gradual elimination of the smaller parties. This, however, is due rather to a concentration of interest on the Treaty issue than to the electoral system. The chief criticism to be directed against the present system is that it may give undue influence to a small party holding the balance of power.[1] This party, if it represents functional interests, may use its power to secure concessions for its supporters. But when the very Constitution is a political question it is evident that this criticism is small compared with that likely to be aroused by a violent swing of the political pendulum. In Ireland no danger is greater than that of the disproportionate majority.

It is the aim of Proportional Representation to create a multiplicity of parties. In so far, therefore, its aim is to destroy the Cabinet system. For the Cabinet system of government depended on the existence of two, and only two, parties. It is a tribute to the adaptability of this system that the introduction of many parties has not seriously diminished its stability. In the Free State, however, alone of European countries, can the Constituent Assembly claim to have been severely logical. In introducing Proportional Representation they also introduced an executive form of government peculiarly suitable to a multiplicity of parties. By a strange irony their logic was wasted owing to an artificial division of parties on the Treaty issue. Thus the whole system of Extern ministries collapsed and the Cabinet system emerged.

The function of the Legislature is twofold: to deliberate and to decide. Under the majority system it is claimed that deliberation is unprofitable since one section of opinion is vastly over-represented. In practice, Proportional Represen-

[1] E.g., Labour Party, 1932.

tation, as a result of the power it gives to party organizations, makes deliberation as unprofitable. The large constituencies can be canvassed only by the party organization. As a result the deputy is neither free to express his opinion nor open to conviction by the arguments of others. He is tied by the decision of his party. He must vote with it. All the new Constitutions (the Irish is an exception) contain clauses which state that the deputy must not receive any *mandat impératif*. He must vote as he personally sees fit. He must receive no instructions. In practice these provisions are ignored. Deputies are instructed by their parties. The party conclave is the deciding factor. A deputy who votes against his party is expelled by the party organization.[1] In many cases this terminates a political career. It is a natural development of modern democracy that the individual should become dependent on the party. It is exaggerated in some measure by Proportional Representation, if only on account of the size of the constituency.[2] There is not in these large districts, as in the single-member area, any tie binding the member to his constituency. He tends to become the party's delegate. Candidates of the larger parties are required to sign a declaration promising obedience to the Party Whip. The personality of the candidate tends to be pushed into the background. The tendency is increased when the electorate votes directly for the Government it would desire to see in office. The party man then becomes desirable. Independence only serves to confuse the issue. As Lord Palmerston remarked, the Independent member is the member on whom nobody can depend.

One difficulty Proportional Representation has failed to solve. That is the question of by-elections. Under the present system the whole constituency votes as if returning a single member. This involves considerable expense. It is also inequit-

[1] As were Deputies Morissey and Anthony in 1931 from the Labour Party.
[2] The criticism is modified by the proposed abolition of the largest constituencies.

The Electoral System

able. For the largest party in the constituency will secure the seat irrespective of whether it held it before or not. Thus, if representation in a six-member constituency were Fianna Fail 3, United Ireland 2, Labour 1, and a United Ireland seat is vacated, then representation will become (the voting strength remaining the same) Fianna Fail 4, United Ireland 1, Labour 1. The inequity is not perhaps of great importance, but it does eliminate the only real value that attaches to by-elections. They are a means of testing opinion in the constituencies. But cumbersome and unsatisfactory though the present machinery remains there appears to be no more attractive alternative.

In general we may say that the system of Proportional Representation is peculiarly suitable to the Irish Free State. Political conditions and the course of events have combined to eradicate evils which, under its aegis, are commonly supposed to flourish. To the critics who claim that group government is the inevitable offspring of Proportional Representation, no more decisive refutation is to be found than in a statement as to its effect in the Free State. In the first place since the inception of the new State every Government has been a party Government. In the second place there is no multiplicity of parties. Since 1922 the number of parties has steadily dwindled, and the consummation of this decline was reached in September 1933 when a merger of the sections of the Right left only three parties—Fianna Fail and United Ireland and Labour—in the field.[1] Lastly, Governments have been remarkable, not for instability, but stability. Only once has a Government been defeated during its term of office.[2] Thus the benefits of the English system have been secured with the added advantage of accurate representation. Moreover, and it cannot be repeated too often, the merits of the simple majority system would be diminished, its disadvantages considerably exaggerated, in the prevalent political life and organization of the Free State.

[1] Labour returned only eight deputies in 1933.
[2] The Cosgrave Administration in 1930.

SEANAD EIREANN

The Legislature of the Irish Free State is a bicameral body,[1] composed of the Dáil (or Lower House) and the Senate. This bicameral system is hardly in accord with Republican tradition. Till the signature of the Anglo-Irish Treaty Dáil Eireann had functioned as a unicameral Legislature, in opposition to the established British Government. In effect this was as much a matter of convenience as of principle. It has, however, left a heritage of hostility among the more extreme Republicans towards the Second Chamber. Moreover, the establishment of the latter was determined, not merely by balancing the merits of a uni- and a bi-cameral Legislature, but also in accordance with an assurance given by the Chairman of the Irish Peace Delegation, both to the Southern Unionists and to the British Government. It was thereby guaranteed that a Second Chamber was to be included in the Legislature, and that, in this Chamber, the Unionists were to be assured of full or even special representation. The framers of the Constitution had therefore a circumscribed area in which to work. In reality, however, though the Second Chamber might be mistrusted, it was only a small minority which would have opposed its creation. And that opposition would seem to rest on political rather than on constitutional grounds.

We are not concerned here with the functions of the Second Chamber. We are concerned with its composition. While the creation of a bicameral Legislature showed that extreme democracy found no favour with the framers of the Irish Constitution, the mode of election adopted for the Second Chamber was based on a faith in the electorate, which has not been justified. The composition of the Second Chamber has proved one of the great testing points of the Constitution. For the Senate had to reconcile two opposing influences. It had to guarantee full representation to the Unionists. It had

---

[1] Art. 12. By Constitution (Amendment) (No. 24) Bill, it is proposed to abolish the Senate.

The Electoral System

also to conform with the democratic trend of the Constitution. The Unionists demanded an Upper House, sheltered from the direct play of universal suffrage, which would provide an essential barrier to democratic nationalism, and which would safeguard their interests. It would be hardly too much to say that for the Unionists the Constitution of the Irish Free State was first of all a Senate. Certainly a Conservative Senate was to them a *sine qua non* for the acceptance of the new order. It was guaranteed to them by the Chairman of the Peace Delegation. Ultimately it proved no easy task to reconcile this guarantee with the demand of other interests for a democratic Senate. And strangely enough opinion was more divided on the question of the composition than on that of the powers of the Second Chamber.

The alternative methods of composing Second Chambers have been the subject of much discussion, from which it has emerged that in federal States alone does the problem present a comparatively simple solution. In a unitary State no form of regional representation would seem to be practicable. The alternatives consequently remaining to the framers of the Constitution were nomination, election by universal suffrage, or some form of indirect election. The former presented abundant attractions as well as insuperable difficulties. It provided the simplest method of fulfilling the guarantee for Unionist representation. It provided a method by which persons of experience and distinction might be enabled to wield a proper influence in national affairs. The objections were equally formidable. Not only is nomination plainly opposed to the precepts of democratic theory, but also, theory apart, it tends to strengthen the Executive at the expense of the elected Chamber, and ultimately of the electorate itself. Moreover, in the modern State there seems no practicable alternative to the Executive as a nominating authority. Other proposals have been made, but for adoption in a new State they would be dangerously experimental. It was possible, then, to have a purely nominated Second

Chamber, chosen by the Executive. But such a Chamber, undemocratic and almost certainly partisan, could command but little confidence. The Canadian Senate is an example and a warning. It shows the tendency for the Executive to fill a nominated Second Chamber with its own supporters. But nomination, owing to the peculiar circumstances existent in the Irish Free State in 1922, presented a ready loop-hole for escape. The Senate was originally composed of thirty members nominated by the President of the Executive Council and thirty elected by the Dáil.[1] In respect of the nominated members the President was expected to consult other than political interests. The Dáil resolved,[2] "that it is expedient that the President of the Executive Council, in nominating the nominated members of the Senate should, with a view to the providing of representation for groups of all parties not adequately represented in the Chamber, consult with representative persons and bodies, including the following: The Chamber of Commerce, the Royal College of Physicians of Ireland, the Royal College of Surgeons in Ireland, the Benchers of the Honourable Society of King's Inn, Dublin, the Incorporated Law Society of Ireland, Councils of the County Boroughs of the Irish Free State."[3]

The provisional method of composing the Senate is of interest, in that the resolution of the Dáil shows the trend of Irish political thought in its evolution of a Second Chamber. It exposes the strong influence exercised by the idea of vocational or functional representation, which is evident in frequent and recurring suggestions for a Second Chamber constituted on those lines.[4] Moreover, had it been mandatory (and not optional) for the President to nominate the Second Chamber according to the advice of these vocational bodies, the essential weakness of the system would not have disappeared. It was obviously not desirable that the Executive

[1] Art. 82 (provisional).   [2] October 25, 1922.
[3] Resolution of Dáil, October 25, 1922.
[4] Cf. Proposals of Senator Johnson, *Dáil Debates*, vol. 1, col. 1141.

The Electoral System

should have an unrestricted field of choice. But if that field were confined to men who had won distinction in specified spheres, such as industry, agriculture, the professions, and the public services, the difficulties would still remain. For a Chamber thus composed would lack authority from the mere fact that it was nominated and not elected. Mr. Johnson, the leader of the Labour Party, in his proposals to the Dáil countered this criticism by suggesting that the members of the Senate should be the representatives of the principal economic groups in the country, and that they should be directly elected by the citizens. Each elector was to choose the vocational group in which he would desire to be registered. Apart from particular objections (Mr. Johnson proposed one hundred and fifty members, which would make too large a Chamber), the solution of the problem on these lines raises as many difficulties as it eliminates. For, apart altogether from the organization of these vocational bodies, an interest in political affairs is demanded of the elector, which in Ireland does not yet, at any rate, exist. The lack of enthusiasm displayed on the single occasion when the Second Chamber was elected by universal suffrage would scarcely disappear with the introduction of vocational representation. Moreover, there remains the apparently insoluble problem of how to weight each trade and profession, relative to one another, so as to secure an adequately proportioned Assembly. And the objections to vocational representation are not merely of a practical nature. There is also, as Professor Laski suggests,[1] "the difficulty of seeing why a man elected, say, as a doctor to represent doctors should have any special virtue in the opinions he expresses on problems of currency and banking. If he does not possess that virtue, he is valueless to the assembly; if he does, it is not by reason of his relation to his profession that he possesses it."

The objections to nomination being so great the framers of the Constitution were left two practicable alternatives;

[1] *Grammar of Politics*, p. 330.

namely, direct election by the people, or some form of indirect election. The former with certain limitations was that sanctioned by the Constitution as promulgated in 1922.[1] It was therein provided,[2] that all citizens of the Irish Free State who had reached the age of thirty years, and who complied with the electoral laws, should have the right to vote for members of Seanad Eireann. The whole country was to be treated as one constituency, and the election was to be held under the principles of Proportional Representation. The Senate was to be composed of sixty members, of whom one-fourth retired every third year. An election was to be held to fill these fifteen vacancies, as well as any other vacancies caused by death or resignation or disqualification since the previous election.[3] Before each election a panel was to be prepared.[4] This panel was to consist of a list comprising three times as many candidates as there were vacancies to be filled, as well as the names of Senators submitting themselves for re-election. The list of candidates was obtained in the following manner. Dáil Eireann, voting according to the principles of Proportional Representation, nominated twice as many qualified persons as were to be elected, whilst the Senate, voting on the same principle, nominated a number equal to the number to be elected. It was from the full panel that the electorate was to select the members of the Senate. No qualification for membership of the Senate is required except the candidate must be eligible for election to the Dáil and must have reached the age of thirty years.

The method of direct election for composing the Second Chamber has many advantages, and under the system adopted in Ireland those advantages were exploited to the full. Direct election produces a Chamber at once homogeneous and directly responsible to the people. It has (or should have) the full weight of popular approval behind it. The danger that a House, so elected, might become a rival of the Lower House, was

---

[1] Art. 32.   [2] Art. 14.   [3] Art. 32.   [4] Art. 33.

carefully eliminated. The higher age limit, demanded both of candidates and of electors, ensured that the Second House would be no mere repetition of the First. Moreover, the Triennial elections provided both a continuity of personnel and a certain conservatism in outlook. To secure deliberative calm the membership was fixed at sixty. On the other hand the powers of the Senate were such as to preclude any possibility of prolonged controversy with the Dáil. The functions of the Second Chamber were not purely deliberative. It was created also in order to provide a guarantee to the Southern Unionists against the rash enthusiasm of a democratic nationalism. The second purpose is reflected in the mode of election. The method of forming the panel, the age required of the electorate, the term of Senatorial office as well as the national constituency, were safeguards agreed upon with the representatives of the minority. But when all is said it yet appears that these safeguards are only incidental and do not represent the *raison d'être* of the system evolved.[1] It is almost a dogma of political science that the Legislature should consist of two chambers.[2] This dogma was accepted in Ireland. If a uni-cameral Legislature was not felt to be the very apotheosis of democratic temerity, it was at least considered that a revising chamber supplied a very necessary element of deliberation upon legislative proposals. Moreover, the system of election adopted is explained by the popular enthusiasm for Proportional Representation. Its mechanism is based on the original proposals put forward by Mr. Thomas Hare[3] in his book on *The Machinery of Representation*. The object most dear to the author was to secure the return, not of parties or of interests, but of the persons most desired by the electorate as a whole. Indeed, in so far as this system (already described) known as the Transferable Vote, owes its peculiar merits and defects to the fact that, subordinating as it does the party to the persons, it is not a system of Proportional Representation at

---

[1] Cf. B. O'Brien, *Irish Constitution*, p. 86.
[2] Laski, op. cit., p. 328.
[3] In 1859.

all.[1] With considerable modifications it is used in the elections for the Dáil. But for the elections to the Senate, in which the whole country was to be treated as one constituency, it was used in substantially the same form as that in which it was originally propounded. It will be remembered that Thomas Hare and his powerful advocate J. S. Mill[2] aimed above all to secure to the nation the services of men of national fame, who would be able to muster a quota of supporters in the whole country, but who would have no local strength or political backing. This was precisely the aim of the Constituent Assembly in devising the mode of election for the Senate. It was provided that,[3] "Seanad Eireann shall be composed of citizens who shall be proposed on the grounds that they have done honour to the nation by reason of useful public service or that, because of special qualifications or attainments, they represent important aspects of the nation's life."[4] It was also required that each proposal should state the qualifications of the person proposed.[5] This elaborate system of checks was introduced, not primarily to safeguard Unionist interests, but rather to secure a Senate composed of distinguished national figures.

The mode of election prescribed by the Constitution was used only once.[6] Its progress and result were considered to have proved the impracticability of the system. The cumbrous machinery of the electoral system was not responsible for the failure. It laboured under the unequal handicap of a boycott by the second largest political party in the State. Fianna Fail declined to take any share or part in the election. Voters were bewildered by the list of candidates, and rarely exercised more than a few preferences. But it was apathy rather than confusion which destroyed the value of the election. Less than one quarter of the electorate voted. The behaviour of the

---

[1] Cf. *Report of Royal Commission on Electoral Systems*, 1910, p. 16.
[2] *Representative Government*, chap. 7.   [3] Art. 30.
[4] The phrasing of this article has been much admired.
[5] Art. 33.   [6] Triennial Election, 1925.

The Electoral System

Executive Council was partly responsible. The electorate required guidance. It required stimulated interest. But neither the President nor his colleagues gave the required lead. They treated the election as though it were of no importance.

The many attractions of the system have led to the proposal of numerous remedies. Compulsory voting has aroused but little enthusiasm, and would clearly be opposed to the democratic individualism of the Constitution. The proposal for smaller constituencies has received more support. It is probable that it would diminish the difficulties of the electorate. On the other hand regional or provincial election in an essentially unitary country is somewhat artificial. Moreover, the congregation of distinguished men in the capital infers that provincial election would defeat the object envisaged by the Constituent Assembly. It is perhaps a problem only soluble by the introduction of the party into Senatorial elections. For the large constituency is at the mercy of the well-organized party machine.

After the first Triennial election a Committee of both Houses was appointed to consider the system of Senatorial election. Its abolition was recommended. The old method was accordingly changed by a series of constitutional amendments all passed in 1928. Indirect election was now adopted. One-third of the members of the Senate were to retire every three years and their successors were to hold office for nine years. Provisions of a transitory character were passed to effect this change. The new system of election was to be by members of the Dáil and Seanad voting together according to the principles of Proportional Representation. The panel[1] was to be composed of twice as many candidates as there were vacancies to be filled. One-half of these candidates was to be nominated by the Dáil and Senate respectively. Casual vacancies, which had been filled by co-option under the old system, were now to be filled in the same manner as in the Triennial elections. This new system of Senatorial election, which is still in force,

[1] Seanad Electoral Act, 1928.

required a comprehensive amendment of three Articles of the Constitution.[1]

Under the system of indirect election thus adopted, two[2] elections have been held. On neither occasion has the full panel of twice the number of candidates been formed. In 1928 there were 19 vacancies, but only 27 candidates. Both the Dáil and the Senate formed the requisite panel of 19 names. The Senate panel, however, duplicated 11 names which had already appeared on that of the Dáil. In 1931 there were 23 vacancies. The Senate nominated the 23 outgoing Senators as its panel. The Dáil, however, only nominated 16, and of these 11 had already appeared on the panel submitted by the Senate.[3] There were thus only 28 candidates for 23 seats. This is contrary to the intention of the 1928 Seanad Electoral Act. The scarcity of suitable and willing candidates is, no doubt, responsible. Moreover, the method of composing the Senate has increased the rôle of the party machine. Since 1928 (when the new Act came into force) party affiliations have become more rigid. The panel is now almost entirely composed of party nominees. The party as an official entity, nominates and sponsors the various candidates. For the number of candidates to be nominated requires careful calculation of voting power. Each party nominates a number of supporters equivalent to the number of seats it may reasonably hope to secure. Inaccurate calculation would diminish the party's representation. This is an important consideration in accounting for the small panel of nominated candidates. It also eliminates in a large measure the possibility that men who have done honour to the nation by reason of useful public service or who represent important aspects of the nation's life, will be elected to the Senate. It is the formation of the panel which determines the personnel of the Second Chamber. Under the system adopted it was inevitable that the party executives should nominate. The Senate tends

---

[1] Arts. 31, 32, 33.   [2] 1928 and 1931.
[3] For these figures see Flynn, F. S., *Parliamentary Companion*, p. 91.

therefore to become a refuge for the elderly politician, a reward for the party hack.

The Joint Committee appointed in 1928 to consider the reform of the Second Chamber recommended the method of voting subsequently adopted.[1] It did not, however, recommend the method of forming the panel. The Joint Committee suggested that the task of forming the panel should be entrusted to a nominating college, subject to the right of the Dáil and Senate to add a limited number of names. The Committee could not reach agreement upon the manner in which this college was to be constituted. They recommended, however, that persons representing Agriculture, Labour, Commerce, Education, and "National Development" should compose it. The suggestion was not peculiarly helpful as it in no way solved how this functional nomination was to be equitably provided. In broad outline the proposal approximates to that approved by Lord Bryce[2] as a means of making the Second Chamber strong and respected, mainly by the quality of its members. He envisaged a small Selective Committee of men generally respected and trusted by the best opinion of their fellow-citizens to be specially appointed by the Legislature for the purpose of selecting persons fitted by ability, experience, and knowledge of affairs to sit in a Second Chamber. This proposal is more practicable and more simple than that put forward by the Joint Committee, but it would entail a certain sacrifice of democratic principle. Moreover, where party feeling runs so strong it is questionable whether the material for such a selective Committee exists.

A further criticism of the system in force is that the Triennial elections renewing one-third (twenty members) of the Senate every three years make it as a whole representative of no body of opinion. It renders, moreover, minor conflicts between the two Houses a frequent and recurring event. In these circumstances a Second Chamber on the Norwegian model would

---

[1] 10th Amendment to Constitution.
[2] *Modern Democracies*, vol. ii, p. 455.

seem preferable. The Chamber then, while functionally limited, would be coterminous with the Dáil. It would be a purely revising body. This model received much attention during the framing of the Constitution, and it may well come under serious consideration again.

Arthur Young wrote contemptuously of the Constituent Assembly of the French Revolution, "they make the Constitution as though the Constitution were a pudding to be made from a recipe." The gibe was not unmerited and has by no means lost its force to-day. It is peculiarly applicable to the systems devised for the formation of Second Chambers. It is a dogma of political thought that a well-framed Constitution should contain some check on the popularly elected assembly. This has usually been found in the creation of a Second Chamber. The latter are all the more acceptable in that they preserve the appearance of historical continuity. In reality, however, the modern Second Chamber is of a very artificial nature. Only in name is it the heir of the Medieval Estates.[1] For the special influence given to an hereditary aristocracy, in which we find the historical origin of the Second Chamber, is antagonistic to democratic principle. It is because of that antagonism that the twentieth century has seen the abolition or radical transformation of two of the last remaining hereditary Chambers—the Prussian Herrenhaus and the Hungarian House of Magnates. The continued existence of the House of Lords is due to the difficulty of creating an alternative agreeable to differing shades of opinion. It is because of this lack of historical continuity that so many difficulties are encountered in composing a Second Chamber. To the Irish Constituent Assembly a Senate opposed to the democratic radicalism of the Constitution was unthinkable; one in agreement with it was necessarily experimental.

Nomination by the Executive being discarded the two methods of direct and indirect election were tried in turn. Direct election had greater attractions. It was more demo-

---

[1] Bryce, op. cit., vol. ii, p. 437.

cratic. By a higher age limit, by a panel put forward by the Legislature, and by a national constituency it avoided becoming a reproduction of the Dáil. Continuity was secured by a longer term, while its powers were not sufficient for it to compete with the Dáil. It escaped therefore from the dilemma propounded by Siéyès, who is said to have asked: "Of what use will a Second Chamber be? If it agrees with the representative House it will be superfluous, if it disagrees, mischievous." Direct election, however, proving unsatisfactory, indirect election by the Legislature was adopted. If it minimized the difficulties, it also diminished the virtues of direct election. It has not appeared satisfactory. None the less it remains the only possible system of indirect election. Election by local colleges is generally agreed to be a harmful method. Functional representation has not as yet been put forward in a practical form. Such are the difficulties confronting the composition of the Irish Second Chamber, and it is impossible not to believe that there is a fundamental reason for their existence. It is perhaps due to the over-ambitious aims of the Constituent Assembly. It was felt that the Senate should be composed, not of party nominees, but of distinguished and experienced men. Yet the powers of the Senate were so small that able men might well hesitate before appearing as candidates. After all it is hardly reasonable to expect these men to content themselves with revising work. The proposed personnel of the Senate would lead one to expect wide powers; the powers would lead one to expect an undistinguished but capable personnel.

CHAPTER VI

THE LEGISLATURE

DISTRUST of the Legislature is a feature of post-War political practice. It is a distrust based, in some cases, on a deteriorating parliamentary personnel, in others on a belief that the Legislature of the nineteenth century is unsuited to deal with the problems of the twentieth. Its more obvious expression is to be seen in the diminution of the powers of the Legislature. The resultant decline in prestige is emphasized by an extreme democratic theory, founded on the teaching of Rousseau, which maintains that the authority of the people should not, and cannot, be delegated to representatives.[1] When democracy was first triumphant the Executive was regarded as the great menace to popular liberty. So it was that in the Constitutions of the French Revolution (particularly those of 1791 and 1793) the Executive was overbalanced by the Legislature. In the course of time the incompetence of such a governmental system was realized. "I could imagine nothing more terrible," Mirabeau had declared in the Constituent Assembly, "than a sovereign authority made up of 600 persons." Experience has vindicated his opinion. The Executive has been duly strengthened. The distrust of the Legislature has had two important results. It has placed either more power in the hands of the people, or it has increased the power of the Executive. Both results, indeed, point to more than a mistrust in the Legislature. They point to a lack of faith in Representative Government itself.

[1] It was Siéyès' contribution to modern political thought that he refuted this doctrine and held up Representative Government as the ideal form of government. Cf. T. H. Clapham, *The Abbé Siéyès*.

The Legislature

ITS STRUCTURE AND COMPETENCE

The Irish Constituent Assembly was not carried along by the current of Continental political theory. On the contrary it ran counter to it, in that it aimed at elevating the status of the Legislature. The authority of the latter, it is true, was carefully defined in a written Constitution, and, moreover, was infringed by the right of the people to decide by Referendum, and their proposed[1] right to legislate by the Initiative. None the less when one surveys the reasons for this limitation of power, it is evident that the object differs from that of Continental constitutionalists. It is made in the interests, not of the sovereign people, not of the community as a whole, but to safeguard the rights and interests of the individual. From this point of view therefore the Referendum in Ireland has little in common with the Referendum in Germany or Estonia. In the one it is introduced in the interests of democratic individualism, in the others of an organic community. The declaratory Articles aim at securing individual rights from infringement by the State. A history of rule from above made it essential that the individual Irish citizen should feel in a peculiar manner that the new Government was the Government of the people. So it was that when the proposals for the Initiative were not given practical effect, and when the Referendum (for ordinary legislation) was abolished, the spirit of the Constitution was not fundamentally changed. For they were introduced as a negative safeguard rather than as a positive organ of the Legislature.

The Irish Constitution originally divided the legislative power between the Oireachtas and the people expressing their will through the Referendum or the (proposed) Initiative. These legislative powers have since been withdrawn from the people by constitutional amendment.[2] The legislative power is now vested exclusively in the Oireachtas. The latter consists

---

[1] Not definitely prescribed by Constitution. Cf. Art. 48.
[2] Amendment, No. 10 Act.

of the Crown and two Houses known respectively as Dáil and Seanad Eireann. "The sole and exclusive power of making laws for the peace, order, and good government of the Irish Free State is vested in the Oireachtas."[1] The constitutional form of the Legislature was not intended to acquire reality. The conception of the King in Parliament is not merely opposed to the spirit of the Constitution; it is opposed also to the national ideals which led to the formation of the Irish Free State. Its practical effect is therefore negligible.

The competence of the Legislature is, in certain spheres, restricted. It is limited in the first place by the existence of a written Constitution. Secondly, there are specific constitutional clauses prohibiting all legislation, which endows any religion or which discriminates in any way between citizens on account of their religious beliefs,[2] and *ex post facto* legislation.[3] Unless, therefore, and until, the articles embodying these limitations are repealed the legislative power does not extend to such matters.

No discretionary power is left to the Representative of the Crown in his legislative capacity. It is provided, for example, that the Oireachtas shall hold at least one session every year.[4] Though formally summoned and dissolved by the Governor-General, the date of the reassembly and of the conclusion of each session of the Oireachtas is fixed by Dáil Eireann. Whilst the exclusion of the discretionary authority of the Crown is to be expected, it is interesting to notice how power is concentrated in the hands of the Dáil. There is a proviso inserted, to the effect that the sessions of the Senate shall not be concluded without its consent,[5] but notwithstanding this restriction the Lower House is invested with a formal measure of direct control in these matters which is greater than that enjoyed by the House of Commons or the French Chamber

---

[1] Art. 12.   [2] Art. 8.
[3] Art. 43. This prohibition was thought, quite wrongly as we believe, to invalidate the Land Act of 1926, See pp. 322–323
[4] Art. 24.   [5] Art. 24.

of Deputies. In Great Britain the decision lies essentially with the Cabinet; in France the date of reassembly is fixed by the Constitution.[1]

The Oireachtas has the exclusive right to regulate the raising and maintaining of the armed forces of the Saorstat,[2] and every force is subject to its control. This control, more usually placed in the hands of the Executive, is in the Free State given to the Legislature in order to limit the authority of the Executive Council. This article embodies those provisions of the Bill of Rights which declare "that the raising or keeping a Standing Army within the kingdom in time of Peace, unless it be with consent of Parliament, is against law."[3] In the devolved Constitutions of the Dominions such a power was not granted to Parliament. The control of the Army by the Oireachtas produces, as the calculated effect of positive law, the conditions which in Great Britain are the result of a series of constitutional conventions, checks, and balances. The elevation of the status of the Legislature at the expense of that of the Executive is further emphasized in the right of declaring war. "Save in the case of actual invasion the Free State shall not be committed to active participation in any war without the assent of the Oireachtas."[4] This provision is intended to meet two eventualities. The first arises from the association of the Saorstat with the British Commonwealth of Nations. The second is to prevent the Irish Government from taking any but defensive military measures without the consent of the Oireachtas.

In respect of inter-Commonwealth relations this clause is exceptional. It does not appear in any of the other Dominion Constitutions. Its purpose was to eliminate the possibility of the Free State becoming involved in a war, by reason of its membership of the British Commonwealth of Nations. The position, in the event of such a war, would be one of peculiar difficulty owing to the right of the British Government under

[1] Constitutional Law of July 16th, Art. 1.   [2] Art. 45.
[3] 1 Will. and Mary, Sess. 2, 1689.   [4] Art. 49.

the Treaty[1] to the use of such harbour and other facilities as it required for purposes of defence. Would the decision really lie in the hands of the Oireachtas? After all the use of such facilities by the British forces would in all probability expose the Free State to attack by the enemy forces. Then, no doubt, the Executive Council could take what measures they desired, for the country would be involved in a war of defence.

In respect of its internal application the required consent of the Oireachtas is an interesting solution of one of the most difficult problems of modern democracy. The conduct of foreign affairs by the Legislature is impossible. The Executive must have a discretionary authority. In Great Britain, declarations of war, like other executive acts, are subject to Parliamentary control. No Government would decide on war, unless it were assured of the support of a majority of the Members of Parliament. None the less the power to declare war is a Royal Prerogative and the ministry has the exclusive right to advise its use. The solution is not entirely satisfactory, for the ministry may direct foreign policy so as to make war inevitable. Lord Bryce wrote[2] that "the adjustment of relations between Executive and Legislature in the conduct of foreign affairs has been in many free countries, one of the most difficult and insoluble problems of practical politics." In England the ministry must, in the exercise of its power, be sure of being able to carry their majority with them. In the United States there is dual control. The plan does not work smoothly.[3] The Constitution assumes the President and the Senate will maintain friendly relations. It does not provide for a conflict à outrance between them. The solution adopted by the Irish Constituent Assembly does not, in reality, seriously diminish the control of the Executive. The Legislature is neither capable, nor in a position, to conduct relations with other Powers save through its ministers. The latter are responsible and responsibility means power. Further, in its conduct of foreign

---

[1] Art. 7, The Treaty.   [2] *Modern Democracies*, vol. ii, p. 80.
[3] Bryce, op. cit., vol. ii, p. 81.

The Legislature

affairs the ministry could bring about a situation in which the Legislature had no option but to declare war. The required consent of the Oireachtas is, however, a check on the policy of the Executive. It must be certain of its majority.

The statement that "the sole and exclusive power of making laws for the peace, order, and good government of the Irish Free State is vested in the Oireachtas"[1] has no precedent in the Dominions Constitutions. It is directed against the supposed power of the British Parliament to super-legislate over the Dominions Parliament. The words "sole and exclusive" were inserted with this intention and were suggested by Professor Berriedale Keith.[2] The words seem to conflict with the later introduction of the Initiative and Referendum. Super-legislation by the British Parliament (against which the clause is directed), is expressly claimed in the Irish Free State Constitution Act, which maintains the right of the British Parliament "to make laws affecting the Irish Free State in any case where, in accordance with constitutional practice, that Parliament would make laws affecting other self-governing dominions."[3] This power of the British Parliament did not affect the internal affairs of the Dominions. It had, however, a certain reality until the passage of the Statute of Westminster in 1931, in respect of the limitation imposed on the extra-territorial legislation of the Dominions. That Statute declared that "the Parliament of a Dominion has full power to make laws having extra-territorial operation."[4] It was more generally provided that no Act of the Imperial Parliament shall extend to a Dominion as part of the law of that Dominion, unless it is expressly declared in the Act that that Dominion has requested and consented to its enactment.[5] Legislation on matters of common concern is dependent on the sanction of the Dominions Parliament.

[1] Art. 12.
[2] *The Times*, June 9, 1922.
[3] Sec. 4, I.F.S Constitution Act, 1922.
[4] Sec. 3, Statute of Westminster, 1931.
[5] Sec. 4, Statute of Westminster, 1931.

THE CROWN

In the Oireachtas the structure of the British monarchical system is maintained. The inclusion of the Crown in the Legislature is purely formal. The Constitution divests it of any reality of power. The Oireachtas, it is declared, shall be summoned and dissolved by the Representative of the Crown[1] in the name of the King. It is added, however,[2] that Dáil Eireann shall fix the dates of the reassembly and the conclusion of the session. Moreover, the representative of the Crown is allowed no latitude in regard to the dissolution of the Dáil.[3] While he must signify the Royal assent to any Bill before it can have the force of law, yet he may no longer withhold that assent or reserve the Bill for the signification of the King's pleasure. These powers, though not legally abolished till 1934,[4] were by constitutional convention virtually abrogated throughout the whole existence of the Free State. Their significance in respect of the position of the representative of the Crown will be more conveniently discussed in connection with the Executive power. Here it is sufficient to remark that their abolition nullifies the remaining legislative function of the Governor-General, namely, the affixing of his signature to Bills.[5] Two copies of each law are to be made, one in English and one in Irish. The copy signed by the Governor-General is regarded as authoritative, in case of conflict between the two. It is enrolled for record by the Registrar of the Supreme Court. In practice all legislation has so far been passed in English.

SEANAD EIREANN

A logical application of extreme democratic theory found no favour with the Irish Constituent Assembly. Though perhaps

---

[1] Art. 24.   [2] Art. 24.   [3] Art. 53.
[4] Art. 41. The Constitution (Amendment No. 21) Act deleted that part of Art. 41 providing for exercise of such powers.
[5] Art. 42.

The Legislature 93

more in accord with Republican tradition, a uni-cameral Legislature did not secure the support of any large body of opinion. While the form of government could not be settled till the Unionist minority were assured of the existence of a conservative Senate, yet it is easy to exaggerate the effect of this insistence. The creation of a Second Chamber commanded almost universal agreement; the method of its composition was the subject of prolonged controversy. The purpose of the Senate was to act as a revising chamber. It was feared, not that the progressive aspirations of the people would fail to secure expression, but that the popularly elected Chamber would, under the impulse of the moment, or by some chance majority, pass ill-considered measures. This danger, it was thought, was increased by the introduction of Proportional Representation. The most probable result, it was felt, of this electoral system was the creation of many parties, and a consequent tendency towards group government. And group government implied unstable government. The fact that the French Cabinets are so frequently overthrown either by chance votes, or by a snap division, gave a certain reality to the fear. There seemed to be danger of irresponsible action were a uni-cameral system adopted. Moreover, the object of the Senate was not that it should act merely as a "cooling" chamber. It was intended further that it should act as a revising body. Modern legislation tends to be at times haphazard. The atmosphere of the Lower House does not favour calm deliberation. It was felt therefore that second consideration by a more stable, a more conservative body was necessary before a proposal became law.

The difficulties to be surmounted in order to secure a suitable personnel for the Senate have been related. Whatever method of composition was adopted, the Irish constitutionalists did not intend, by an over-strict adherence to democratic theory, to allow the Senate to become the rival of the Dáil. The tendency of the amendments, indeed, has been to diminish the democratic authority of the Upper Chamber. The authority lost by a less direct contact with the sovereign people would, it was hoped, be counterbalanced by the respect engendered by a distinguished and intellectual personnel.

In the Irish Free State the powers of the Senate are less, not merely in fact but also in law, than those of the Dáil. This marks a definite break from the practice of the Dominions Constitutions. In them, except in financial legislation, there is no formal acknowledgment of the ultimate supremacy of the Lower House. On the other hand a tendency common to the new European Constitutions is the diminution of the powers and competence of the Upper House. This formal acceptance of a constitutional reality is part of that "rationalization of power"[1] which is so notable a feature of modern constitutional practice.

Seanad Eireann is composed of sixty members. One-third of the members retire every three years, the whole chamber being thus renewed every nine years. The members of the Senate are paid.[2] Its legislative powers approximate to those of the House of Lords, as defined in the Parliament Act of 1911. Except in regard to Money Bills, the Senate has equal powers with the Dáil in the initiation of legislation.[3] In respect of Money Bills Dáil Eireann has "legislative authority exclusive of Seanad Eireann."[4] In respect of Bills, not being Money Bills, initiated in and passed by the Dáil, the Senate has a full power of amendment.[5] But it is not in a position to withstand the will of the Dáil. It can delay legislation, it cannot veto it.[6] In the Constitution, however, as promulgated by the Constituent Assembly, the Senate possessed the right of demanding a Referendum on a legislative proposal. Any Bill passed (or deemed to have been passed) by both Houses might be suspended for a period of ninety days on the written demand of two-fifths of the members of the Dáil, or of a majority of the members of the Senate. Such a demand had to be

---

[1] Mirkine-Guetzevitch, *Les Constitutions de L'Europe Nouvelle*, p. 25. [2] Art. 23, £360 and travelling facilities.
[3] Art. 39.   [4] Art. 35.   [5] Art. 38.   [6] Art. 38.

The Legislature

presented to the President of the Executive Council not later than seven days from the passage of the Bill. Such a Bill could then be submitted to a Referendum, if demanded, before the expiration of the ninety days, either by a resolution of the Senate assented to by three-fifths of its members, or by a petition signed by one-twentieth of the registered voters. The power of invoking the Referendum did not apply to Money Bills or Bills declared urgent by both Houses.[1] This power of a devolutive veto given to the Senate was exceedingly interesting. As there is no Executive veto, the appeal to the people was intended no doubt to provide an alternative means of checking the Dáil, should it pass legislation not desired by the electorate. The device might have proved of considerable constitutional service. It depended, however, to a peculiar extent on the spirit in which it was to be invoked. Its merit lay in the fact that it could secure, not only the verdict of popular opinion on an important or controversial legislative proposal, but also it guaranteed the position of the Senate against unwarranted control by the Dáil. The devolutive veto was not intended for constant appeal. In actual fact it was a power never invoked by the Senate. Later it was deleted by constitutional amendment.[2] This was probably wise, for, owing to the position occupied by the Senate in public opinion, it was a power at all times dangerous for it to exercise. The amendment had the effect of intensifying the functional inferiority of the Senate.

It now remains to examine the powers of the Senate in respect of ordinary and of Money Bills. In the former the Senate has full powers of initiation and amendment. In practice only a small number of Bills are originally proposed in the Senate. It is provided that the amendments of the Senate to a Bill sent up by the Dáil shall be reconsidered by the Dáil. Should the Senatorial amendments prove unacceptable, it was originally provided that the Bill as passed by the Dáil should be considered passed by both Houses not later than

[1] Art. 47. [2] Amendment No. 10 Act.

two hundred and seventy days after it had been first sent to the Senate.[1] The Senate could thus hold up a Bill for nine months. This period was, however, subsequently amended.[2] Under the new provisions the period of delay, which the Senate may enforce, is extended to twenty months. A longer period may be secured only by agreement between the two Houses. The period of twenty months may moreover be lessened by an intervening dissolution of the Dáil. In which event the Bill, if accepted once more by the Dáil, is considered passed within sixty days of its reassembly.[3] The effect of this provision is to secure a formal and definite superiority in legislative power to the Dáil. This superiority is emphasized in financial legislation. That the popularly elected House should have control of financial legislation tends to become a dogma of modern political practice. None the less in this respect the powers of the Senate are more considerable than those of the House of Lords, as modified in the Parliament Act of 1911. In the matter of Money Bills the Dáil has authority exclusive of the Senate.[4] The Bills, however, are sent to the Senate for its recommendations, which must be made within a period of twenty-one days. These recommendations may be accepted or rejected, wholly or in part.[5] The rôle of the Senate in respect of financial legislation is therefore purely advisory.

The difficulty that has been raised owing to the lack of an adequate definition of a Money Bill[6] has been met by a system of checks, in which the authority of the Speaker is subject to appeal. It is the duty of the Speaker to certify Money Bills as such. In that the precedent of the Parliament Act of 1911 is followed. It was felt, however, that his decision should be subject to review. It may therefore be challenged by reference to a Committee of Privileges. Such reference may be demanded within a limited time, (a) by two-fifths of the members of

---

[1] Art. 38.   [2] Art. 38, Amd. No. 13 Act.
[3] Art. 38a.   [4] Art. 35.   [5] Art. 38.
[6] Cf. similar proposal contained in Report of Lord Bryce's Conference on the Reform of the Second Chamber, 1918 [cd. 9038].

either House who address a notice in writing to the Chairman of the House of which they are members, or (*b*) by a majority of the members of the Senate voting at a sitting at which not less than thirty are present. In the event of such a demand the Bill is referred to a Committee of Privileges composed of not more than three members of each House, and a chairman who shall be the senior judge of the Supreme Court able and willing to act. The chairman is entitled to vote only in the event of an equality of votes.[1] By this means the legislative powers of the Senate are adequately safeguarded.

The amended powers of the Senate preclude the possibility of a prolonged controversy between the two Houses. The prospect of such a conflict has indeed always been remote. Once the devolutive veto of the Senate was abolished it had become almost impossible. There was consequently no real need for elaborate machinery by which the differences could be settled. In the Constitution, as promulgated in 1922, the Senate was given the power of convening by resolution a joint sitting of the members of both Houses for the purpose of debating, but not voting upon, the proposals for amendments to a Bill other than a Money Bill.[2] This provision was subsequently deleted.[3] The extensive revision of the powers of the Second Chamber which took place in 1928–1929 was caused neither by mistrust nor by conflict. The failure of direct popular election was in part responsible, but to a greater extent the revision was due to the abolition of the Referendum.[4] The power of the Senate to invoke the verdict of the people was thereby destroyed. But the Senate gained more than it lost. "The compensation which is offered in respect of that particular right which is being delivered up," declared the President in the debate in the Dáil,[5] "is that the Senate can hold up a Bill for eighteen or at most twenty months as against nine."

[1] Art. 35, Amendment No. 12 Act.
[2] Art. 38.
[3] Amendment No. 13.
[4] Amendment No. 10 Act.
[5] *Dáil Debates*, vol. 24, col. 968.

The extent to which the Senate has used its powers is worthy of attention. The following figures show that the initiation of Bills in the Senate is very rare.

	Number of Bills initiated in Senate	Number of Bills initiated in Dáil
1928	2	51
1930	3	53
1932	none	45
1933	2	66

It is evident indeed that it is in the sphere of revision that we must look for the primary function of the Senate. The following figures show the number of amendments inserted by the Senate.

Years
1927—269 all agreed to by the Dáil, except 1
1928— 67 all agreed to by the Dáil, except 8
1929— 58 all agreed to by the Dáil, except 2
1930— 80 all agreed to by the Dáil
1931— 87 all agreed to by the Dáil, except 2
1932— 94 all agreed to by the Dáil, except 8
1933—178 all agreed to by the Dáil, except 18

Subsequent to 1931 a considerably larger proportion of Senate amendments have been rejected, owing to the small Fianna Fail representation in the Upper Chamber. In general it would appear from these figures that the Senate, till 1932 at any rate,[1] has in no way attempted to deflect or hinder the popular will as expressed by the elected representative of the people. As a revising Chamber its functions have been performed to the satisfaction of all parties; but the manner of its composition renders it liable to be opposed to the Government of the day. The period of twenty months, during which the Senate may hold up legislation, appears excessive. It is

---

[1] E.g., its refusal to pass the Oath Bill unamended, after a General Election has endorsed the action of the Dáil, is open to criticism.

The Legislature

long enough to enable the Senate to stultify a governmental programme. The period of three months, allowed in the Bill introduced by the Fianna Fail Government in 1933, might have provided a possible solution had it not subsequently been decided to abolish the Senate.

In the modern parliamentary state the ministry must enjoy the confidence of the elected assembly. Joint responsibility, though common to many of the older Constitutions, is not now regarded as practicable. The definite functional inferiority of the Irish Senate would in any event give it little or no control over the Executive Council. It is none the less definitely stated that the Executive Council shall be responsible to Dáil Eireann.[1] Moreover, ministers who form the Executive Council must, with one exception,[2] be members of the Dáil. The Irish Senate has no extra-legislative functions. Unlike the Senate of the United States it performs no executive acts. Unlike the House of Lords it discharges no judicial functions.

Senators are elected for nine years, but not all are elected at once. Every three years the term of one-third of the Senators expires. This practice of partial election was applied to the American Senate in the eighteenth century and was adopted by France under the Constitution of the Third Republic. The practice tends to preserve continuity, but at the same time makes the Senate less responsive to public opinion. The indirect system of election emphasizes this irresponsiveness. A Senator nearing the close of his nine-year term may be more than nine years from the voters; for at the time of election the members of the electoral body (the Dáil and Senate) may have been nearing the end of their respective terms of office. The Senate therefore represents old ideas. Its small numbers and its personnel secure a conservative outlook and a deliberative calm. It would scarcely be true to claim that opinions in the Senate are less extreme. The Right is more fully represented than in the Dáil. None the less the atmosphere of discussion

[1] Art. 51.
[2] Art. 52, Amd. No. 15 Act.

is less acrimonious. Party ties are less rigid. But since the adoption[1] of the new system of election the divisions in the Senate have been hardening. After the Triennial election in 1931 the membership of the various parties was as follows:

Government (Fianna Fail)	12
Cumann na nGaedheal	23
Labour	6
Farmers	2
Independents[2]	16

These figures show how the system of election creates a majority in the Senate liable to be opposed to the Government of the day.

The Senate was intended to provide full representation to the Unionist minority as well as to act as a legislative chamber. It was hoped that in the course of time the former of its *raisons d'être* would disappear. The Senate would then have two functions to fulfil. It was to hold up legislation upon which the mandate of the people was uncertain. It was (secondly) to revise legislation which was inadequately drafted. For these purposes its powers are sufficient. It has a real power of delay. If it cannot enforce its will, it can at least secure ministerial attention to its objections.[3] Outside of its legislative functions, its powers are negligible. Though ministers may speak in either House the proposal of and debate on measures of importance takes place, with rare exceptions, in the Lower House. The inferiority of the Senate in status is emphasized by the fact that the speech of the Governor-General at the opening of the session, on the only occasion on which it was delivered, was delivered in the Dáil. It is evident that the nature of ministerial responsibility in the Irish Free State determines the status of the Upper House. Had the system of extern ministries proved successful it is very probable that the real influence of the Senate would have been considerably

---

[1] In 1928.
[2] Eleven of these form a cohesive group, the other five attached to no group.
[3] Cf. Debate on Oath Bill.

increased. The fact that the two most successful Second Chambers of modern democracy are to be found in countries where the parliamentary system has not been introduced, is significant.[1] They are the American Senate and the Swiss Ständerat (Council of States). The American Senate possesses more influence than the House of Representatives and attracts a higher level of political talent. The fact that it represents State interests and that its small personnel leads to greater efficiency has obscured the fundamental cause of its influence, namely, that such executive functions as are entrusted to Congress belong exclusively to the Senate. In Switzerland the functions of both Chambers are identical. The Executive is responsible to neither. Such control as does exist is divided equally between them. In both these cases the Constitution is federal. It has therefore been supposed that a Senate formed on a federal basis is alone successful. In reality, however, the absence of a Cabinet government is responsible. When there is no ministry responsible to the Lower Chamber it loses its preponderance. The comparative strength of the French Senate is due to the relative weakness of the French Cabinet. It is therefore to be presumed that had the Cabinet system been modified in Ireland as was intended by the infusion of non-parliamentary ministers on the Swiss model, the influence of the Senate would have been more considerable. It is the dependence of the Executive Council on the Dáil that seals the impotence of the Senate. It cannot act as an organ of control. It must justify its existence by improving the legislation of the Dáil, and by initiating Bills which, important in themselves, are likely to be overlooked by the Lower House. And all the while the Senate must rely on attaining its object by finesse rather than by force. Among the various political parties there is agreement that the powers of the Senate should not, at most, exceed those necessary for a purely revising chamber. While the Fianna Fail Party is hostile to the Chamber as at present constituted, it has not yet crystallized

[1] Cf. Headlam-Morley, op. cit. p 164, note.

its own alternative proposals. It has however introduced two Bills, the one reducing to three months the period of Senatorial delay, the other abolishing the Senate itself. A uni-cameral Legislature has some attractions in a country in which political questions arouse continuous interest, and in which election results are consequently an accurate guide to public opinion. A less radical solution would be provided by a Second Chamber on the Norwegian pattern,[1] in which the Houses are elected at the same time, thus securing in both the predominance of the same political parties. Such a system of election would serve to emphasize the purely revising function of the Upper House.

DÁIL EIREANN

The Dáil is composed of one hundred and fifty-three deputies, elected by universal suffrage. It is proposed to reduce this number, which is subject to decennial revision, to one hundred and thirty-six;[2] it being provided in the Constitution that the total number of members shall be fixed at not less than one member for each thirty thousand of the population, or at more than one for each twenty thousand. University representation, whose abolition is now contemplated, did not rest upon a numerical basis. Each University—there are two—which was in existence at the date of the coming into operation of the Constitution, was entitled to elect three representatives.[3] There was a certain, but not very marked, hostility to University representation. The term of the Dáil was originally four years,[4] but by amendment[5] it was extended to six years or such shorter period as may be fixed by legislation. At a General Election the polls are held on the same day throughout the country, and that day is fixed at a date not later than thirty days after

---

[1] This system attracted considerable attention in 1921–22.
[2] Electoral (Revision of Constituencies) Bill, 1934.
[3] Art. 27 and Constitution (Amd. No. 23) Bill, 1934.
[4] Art. 28.   [5] Amendment No. 4 Act.

The Legislature

the dissolution. The day of a General Election is no longer declared a public holiday.[1]

The Dáil constitutes the central organ of the legislative system. It provides motive force in the legislative machine. Its authority extends to two spheres—the legislative and the executive. In the former it is a creative force. As we have seen, all Bills (with insignificant exceptions) originate in the Dáil. The Senate is powerless to defeat measures upon which the Lower House is determined. There is no Executive veto. And now that the Referendum is abolished for ordinary legislation there remains no means by which a Bill passed by the Dáil and not conflicting with the Constitution may be finally rejected. In addition, till 1938 amendments to the Constitution may be passed in the same manner as ordinary legislation. The legislative power and the constituent power thus for the present coincide.

The Dáil is more amply endowed with means whereby the Executive may be controlled, than the majority of legislative chambers. In the first place the Executive Council is responsible only to the Dáil.[2] Secondly, all the members of the Council must, with one exception, be members of the Lower House.[3] Thirdly, the Dáil is granted the power to fix the opening and termination of its own sessions.[4] Finally, and most important, it is provided that the Oireachtas shall not be dissolved upon the advice of an Executive Council which has ceased to retain the support of a majority in Dáil Eireann.[5]

It was the intention of the Constituent Assembly to enhance the status of the Legislature. The most effective means of doing so appeared to be in augmenting the power and authority of the popularly elected Chamber. So it was that the powers granted to the Dáil were considerably in excess of those vested in the House of Commons. In any event the Lower House would have proved the preponderating influence in the Legislature. It was intended that it should prove the central

[1] Amendment No. 3 Act. [2] Art. 52.
[3] Art. 53.   [4] Art. 24.   [5] Art. 53.

force in the government of the country. This intention was never realized. The extent of the failure will be gauged in dealing with the Executive. The reasons for it will emerge from a consideration of the reality underlying the forms of parliamentary Procedure.

CHAPTER VII

THE PROCEDURE OF THE LEGISLATURE

THE importance of parliamentary Procedure is becoming more widely acknowledged, but there is yet no adequate realization of its significance in respect of the success or failure of parliamentary institutions. The attitude of political thought and of practical politics to representative government has, with the passage of time, undergone no inconsiderable change. In the nineteenth century the first principles of popular government were under investigation. Parliamentary government was engaged in a struggle for existence with the forces of absolutism. That struggle has now closed, and with its close there came to an end (what Redlich has termed)[1] the heroic age of Continental parliamentarianism. That the flood tide of popular government should ebb with some rapidity is not surprising. None the less, it is becoming increasingly evident that this decline was hastened because of the summary attention paid to Procedure. Defects in machinery were mistaken for defects in principle. The theory of representative government was, on occasion, discredited because of weaknesses which on closer inspection would have been found due to an incomplete or ill-contrived Procedure.

The recognition of the importance of parliamentary Procedure has led to the insertion of constitutional clauses which outline its framework. In this respect the Irish Constituent Assembly followed the practice of the Continental Constitutions. In so doing it is at variance with British and Dominion precedent. The general effect of this arrangement is to diminish the discretionary power of the Executive. Each House makes its own Rules and Standing Orders.[2] Its authority in this respect is limited only by certain provisions of the Constitution.

[1] *Procedure of the House of Commons*, vol. i, p. xxiii.
[2] Art. 20.

These provisions deal with important aspects of Procedure which, it was felt, required careful definition.

THE SPHERE OF PARLIAMENTARY PROCEDURE

The Irish Parliament meets in Dublin, but it is empowered by the Constitution[1] to hold its sessions in such other place as it may, from time to time, determine. The insertion of this proviso was no doubt intended to enable alternate sittings to be held in Dublin and Belfast, should Northern Ireland agree to enter the Free State. As in France[2] and in the United States, the Constitution provides that the Legislature must hold one session at least every year.[3] Unlike them, it does not fix a definite time for the meeting of Parliament.[4] Such a constitutional provision is both inconvenient and superfluous, whilst that requiring a session every year falls in a lesser measure under the same criticism. The necessity of voting the budget, indeed the very functioning of the parliamentary system, makes it certain that the Legislature will be active enough without a provision of this nature. It is in another direction that we must seek for the motive of the Constituent Assembly. The elastic British practice under which the session begins, without compulsion of law, whenever circumstances make it advisable, throws no inconsiderable measure of discretionary authority into the hands of the Executive. To the Irish Constituent Assembly this seemed undesirable as giving a real measure of control. In accordance with British and Dominion precedent, the convocation and dissolution of the Legislature is vested in the hands of the Representative of the Crown. Its exercise is expressly subjected to the will of Dáil Eireann.[5] The latter is entitled by the Constitution to determine the date both of the re-assembly of the Oireachtas and of the conclusion of the session of each House. The sittings of the Senate may not be concluded without its own consent.

[1] Art. 13. [2] Constitutional Law of July 16th, Art. 1.
[3] Art. 24. [4] In France second Tuesday in January. [5] Art. 24.

The Procedure of the Legislature

In theory the Oireachtas has therefore control over its own sessions. In practice this power has passed to the Executive Council, in whose hands rests the responsibility for a definite legislative programme. On the other hand the fact that the Oireachtas cannot be dissolved on the advice of an Executive Council which had ceased to retain the support of a majority in Dáil Eireann[1] imposes a definite limitation on Executive discretion. In the Free State Parliament the session extends over the life of the Dáil. The latter is not (as the House of Commons) prorogued annually. In view of the tendency both to diminish the authority of the Executive and to make the Legislature master of its own procedure, it is interesting to notice that when, in obedience to the Proclamation summoning a new Oireachtas, writs are issued, they are issued by the Clerk of the Dáil. In the United Kingdom they are issued by an officer of the Crown, the Clerk of the Crown and Hanaper.

The right of the Legislative Chambers to regulate their Procedure was further limited by the Constitution in respect of the Oath to be taken by members. The Constitution prescribed that the Oath embodied in the Treaty should be taken and subscribed by every member of the Oireachtas before taking his seat therein.[2] The Oath was taken in the following form.

"I . . . do solemnly swear true faith and allegiance to the Constitution of the Irish Free State as by law established, and that I will be faithful to H.M. King George V, his heirs and successors by law in virtue of the common citizenship of Ireland with Great Britain and her adherence to and membership of the group of nations forming the British Commonwealth of Nations."

The Oath was to be sworn before the Representative of the Crown or some person authorized by him.[3] It was, in fact, taken before the clerk of the respective Chamber in his office. This was a deviation from British Procedure, where the members are sworn in the House with the Speaker in the Chair.

[1] Art. 53.   [2] Constitution, Art. 17.   [3] Art. 17.

Under the terms of the Treaty the Oath was mandatory. But whereas the Treaty merely prescribed the obligation of members to take the Oath, the Constitution provided when and how it was to be taken.[1] The Oath has played a very considerable part in the political history of the Free State. From the point of view of the Procedure of the Oireachtas, it has been important in that the obligation to take it resulted in the abstention of the Republican Party from the Dáil. For almost five years (till August 1927) the opponents of the Treaty declined to take their seats. In August 1927, as a sequel to the assassination of the Vice-President of the Executive Council, an amending Act was passed which required parliamentary candidates prior to their nomination to swear a declaration of their readiness to take the Oath, if elected, and disqualified elected members who failed to do so within a specified period.[2] These provisions brought the issue to a head. The Fianna Fail Party, representing the bulk of the Opposition, decided to subscribe to the Oath rather than to face permanent exclusion. In this they were not followed by a small group of extreme Republicans.[3] The controversy between the parties in respect of the Oath remained unabated. It was responsible for an agreement between Fianna Fail, Labour, and the National League to form an administration, pledged to negotiate with the British Government with a view to securing the modification of the compulsory subscription to the Oath. This plan did not mature owing to the failure of a "no confidence" motion in August 1927—it was defeated by the Speaker's casting vote—and subsequently the General Election held in October resulted in the return of the Cosgrave Administration. In March 1932 the first legislative proposal introduced by the new Fianna Fail Administration was a Bill for the removal of the Oath. This Bill, being defeated in the Senate, did not take effect till 1933. Article 17 of the Constitution was thereby deleted. To do so it was necessary to repeal the repugnancy

[1] Art. 17.   [2] Electoral Amendment Act (No. 33 of 1927).
[3] Known as the Sinn Fein Party.

The Procedure of the Legislature

clause of the Constitution Act[1] which declared any amendment of the Constitution repugnant to the Treaty to be void. The restrictive clause to the same effect in Article 50 of the Constitution was also deleted. As a result members of the Oireachtas are now under no obligation to take an Oath or subscribe to any declaration whatsoever.

In two further respects the control of the Oireachtas is limited by the Constitution. The first is in respect of privilege, the second in respect of money resolutions. The privileges enjoyed by members of the Legislature will be considered later. Here it is sufficient to remark that a statement of parliamentary privilege in the Constitution[2] places it in a peculiar manner under the control of the Courts. The Constitution provides that the sitting of each House shall be public.[3] In cases of special emergency a private sitting may be held, but only with the assent of two-thirds of the members present. Not only is the traditional device of espial replaced, but also the power of the respective Houses is diminished by the demand for an artificial majority. In the House of Commons a simple majority suffices to exclude the public.[4] It is to be remarked here that the Constitution formally declares that all questions are to be settled by a simple majority vote.[5]

In respect of money resolutions the Constitution provides[6] that they must be proposed by a member of the Executive Council. By this proviso a great constitutional principle is embodied in positive law. In England it is a convention, in the Free State it is a law of the Constitution.

In general it may be said that the powers of the Oireachtas to regulate its own Procedure are both less extensive and more carefully defined than in the British Parliament. The diminution in authority is due mainly to the existence of a written

---

[1] No. 1 of 1922.   [2] Arts. 18, 19, 20, 22.
[3] Art. 25.   [4] Standing Order 90.
[5] Art. 22. Standing Order 17 requires unanimous vote for the suspension of the Standing Orders without previous notice. Is this a violation of Art. 22 of Constitution?   [6] Art. 37.

Constitution in which the necessity of definition involves a restrictive interpretation of discretionary power.

PRIVILEGE

In the Irish Free State parliamentary privilege is guaranteed by the Constitution. Such a guarantee precludes any possibility of an attempt by either or both Houses to exceed the privileges accorded to them. The definition of the scope of parliamentary privilege eliminates the latent and extensive powers still vested in the British Parliament. In all other respects the Constituent Assembly modelled the privileges of the Oireachtas on those enjoyed by members at Westminster. And privilege being assured by the Constitution, the Speaker does not, as in England, claim it from the Crown at the beginning of the new Parliament.

There are two aspects of parliamentary privilege, one as it affects the individual deputy, the other as it affects the Oireachtas as a whole. The individual deputy has two fundamental privileges, freedom of speech and freedom from arrest. The former privilege, guaranteed by the Constitution, assures that all utterances made by members of either House shall be exempt from judicial proceedings. A member remains accountable to the House for words spoken in debate. He is subject to disciplinary action by the House. The nature of this penalty is laid down in the Standing Orders. The Oireachtas does not possess, as the British Parliament still possesses, the right to expel a member.

At one period the right of freedom from arrest was of great importance in the development of the rights of Members of Parliament. It is no longer so. "Freedom from arrest is now no very important matter," wrote Professor Maitland,[1] "because this immunity does not extend to imprisonment on the charge of an indictable offence, and in 1869 imprisonment for debt was abolished." The Constitution of the Free State

[1] *Constitutional History of England*, p. 377.

provides that the member's immunity shall not extend to every indictable offence. It is excluded in cases of treason, felony, or breach of the peace.[1] The privilege is valid while the member is going to and returning from and while within the precincts of either House. In Great Britain the member is protected from arrest in civil cases for the duration and for a period of forty days before and after the session.[2] His privilege is therefore, in matter of time, more extensive than that of a member of the Oireachtas.

All official reports and publications of the Oireachtas, or of either House, as well as utterances in either House wherever published, are privileged.[3] The question of parliamentary publications and reports has been the subject of much controversy. The Irish Constitution by defining the position has done much to clarify it. In the question of reports and publications of Parliament the privilege seems to be extended more fully than in Great Britain. The enactment of the Parliamentary Papers Act in 1840 accorded the protection of law to all publications issued by order of Parliament. This privilege is extended to newspaper reports. It would not, however, cover a report of a debate which, though correctly reported, was published with malicious intent. The Irish Constitution, however, expressly protects all reports of the debates of the Oireachtas. The Minister for Home Affairs (Mr. Kevin O'Higgins), who was the minister in charge of the Constitution Bill, stated that this article "would not protect garbled or malicious accounts written by ordinary journalists of the proceedings of Parliament."[4] That the minister's interpretation of this article of the Constitution would be accepted by the courts, is open to question.

The Oireachtas, in that its privileges are defined by the Constitution, has less power in this respect than the Houses

---

[1] Constitution, Art. 18.
[2] Cf. Campion, *The Procedure of the House of Commons*, pp. 39–49.
[3] Constitution, Art. 19.
[4] *Dáil Debates*, vol. 1, col. 1087.

of Parliament. The privileges given, however, are of sufficient scope for the conduct of business and the maintenance of the legislative authority.

THE CHAIRMAN

In parliamentary Procedure the Dáil is peculiarly indebted to the practice of the House of Commons. It was from the model of the Speakership that the functions and duties of its Irish counterpart were derived. In the Free State, however, the force of political circumstances has changed the conception of the office. The remarkable authority wielded by the Speaker of the House of Commons is due, not to rules and powers, but to custom and a long tradition. His authority is based on his absolute and unvarying impartiality which is the main feature of his office, the law of its life.[1] This impartiality is in no way mistrusted because now, as in former times, the majority nominates one of its own number in the event of a vacancy. That this is so is due to two rules which have been strictly observed. In the first place a Speaker who does not wish to resign his office is regularly re-elected. Secondly, this re-election takes place whether or no the party which he represented is a minority in the new Parliament. Consequently the practice adopted in the election of a Speaker has a considerable bearing on the nature of the office. The Speaker of Dáil Eireann (an Ceann Comhairle) is elected immediately upon the assembly of the Chamber. On election he takes the Chair.[2] Since the enactment of the Constitution the mode of electing the Speaker has changed considerably. In 1922 Deputy Michael Hayes, a member of the Government Party, was elected unopposed. His name was proposed for election by the President, and was seconded by the leader of the then Opposition, the Labour Party. This practice was observed till

---

[1] Redlich, op. cit., vol. ii, p. 132.
[2] The Speaker of the House of Commons must first make his submission to the Crown.

1927. On the re-assembly of the Dáil, after the September election of that year, the motion to re-elect the outgoing Speaker was not seconded by the leader of the new Opposition, the Fianna Fail Party. That party thus showed a desire to break with the traditions associated with the election of a non-party Speaker. In 1927, however, the Speaker was elected unopposed. This was not the case at the assembly of the succeeding Dáil in 1932. The Fianna Fail Party, now the strongest in the Chamber, moved the election of one of its members as Speaker. Both the proposer and seconder were deputies of that party. The outgoing Speaker, Deputy Hayes, was also proposed. A division was challenged, and the representative of the new majority was elected.[1] Subsequent to the General Election in 1933, the Fianna Fail Speaker was proposed for re-election by a member of his own party, and seconded by the Leader of the Labour Party. The Cumann na nGaedheal Party did not oppose the motion.[2]

Till 1932 it may be said that the tradition of the House of Commons was accepted, in that till that year no formal opposition had been offered to the re-election of the outgoing Speaker. The actual division of the House on the election of the Speaker is an event of very great importance. As a division was not challenged in 1933, the position remains somewhat obscure; the more so, in that the Fianna Fail Party assigned no reason for their opposition in 1932. It seems, indeed, that while one party desires to maintain the traditions of the House of Commons, the other aims at converting the Speakership into a party office. If in accordance with this intention, the Speaker is to become a party nominee, if his election is to be made a test of party voting strength, then the character of the office will be transformed, its dignity will be diminished. Election by a party vote will bring in its train distrust of the impartiality of the Chair. The conception of a party Speaker was quite alien to the intention of Irish constitutionalists. The conventional guarantee of the impartiality of the Speaker of

[1] *Dáil Debates*, vol. 41, col. 19.   [2] Ibid., vol. 46, col. 17.

the House of Commons is given a legal sanction by the Irish Constitution. At a General Election in England no opposition has hitherto been offered to the Speaker by any other party in his constituency.[1] In the Free State the Constitution provides that the Speaker, unless declining re-election, shall be deemed automatically re-elected as a member of the constituency which he previously represented.[2]

The impartiality of the Speaker of the House of Commons has been gained upon two fields.[3] As regards his relations to the Crown, it is secured by the Act of Parliament which forbids his acceptance of any office of profit under the Crown and by the adoption of the idea, now a matter of principle, that after resigning the Chair he ought not to appear in the House either as a member of the Government or as a private member. The former precedent is accepted by the Dáil. No minister or Parliamentary Secretary may act as Chairman or Vice-Chairman.[4] The latter precedent has not been followed. When in March 1932 the Speaker of the Dáil, Deputy M. Hayes, was defeated on a party vote, he did not retire from parliamentary life, but played an active part in the business of the House. It seems, indeed, that, once re-election has been opposed on party grounds, there is little to be gained by continuing the precedent of the Speaker's retirement from public life.

Like the Speaker of the House of Commons the Chairman of the Dáil never takes part in debate either in the House or in Committee. He may not vote except in the event of an equality of votes, in which case he has and must exercise a casting vote.[5] In the House of Commons there are two principles which have guided Speakers in their decisions upon casting votes. These two principles, so far as one may judge from a very limited number of precedents, have been adopted by the Speakers of the Dáil. The two principles are, that the

[1] Redlich, vol. ii, p. 133.   [2] Art. 21 Amd. No. 2 Act, 1927.
[3] Redlich, vol. ii, p. vi.   [4] Standing Order 13.
[5] Constitution, Art. 21.

The Procedure of the Legislature 115

Speaker should give his vote, if possible, so as to avoid a final settlement of the question before the House, and secondly, when giving a vote upon the merits of the issue he does so freely according to his own convictions and the dictates of his conscience, first stating the grounds upon which he decides.[1] The material from which one may judge the manner in which the casting vote is to be exercised is very limited. It is, in fact, confined to three occasions. The first instance was in 1923. A motion had been introduced to compensate the potato-growers of North Louth for the loss of their crops.[2] An equal number of votes had been given for and against the motion. The Speaker gave his vote against the motion. He said "that a motion which calls for the expenditure of public funds for a particular purpose . . . ought to command a majority of votes in the Dáil independent of the Speaker's."[3] The second instance took place on August 16, 1927. It was of peculiar importance in that the fate of the Government was in the balance. The Opposition united in supporting a motion of censure. The voting resulted in a tie.[4] The Speaker gave his casting vote against the motion. He declared that the vote of the Chair should be given in such a way as to provide, if possible, that the House would have an opportunity of revising its decision. Moreover, the *status quo* should if possible be preserved. "In my judgement," the Speaker continued, "a motion of no confidence in any Executive Council should be affirmed by a majority of Deputies and not merely by the casting vote of the presiding officer of the House."[5] These decisions uphold the precedents laid down by the Speakers of the House of Commons.

[1] Redlich, vol. ii, part vi, chap. i.
[2] Rendered unsaleable by the scheduling of the district covered under the Black Scab in potatoes Order 1923.
[3] *Dáil Debates*, vol. 3, col. 1331.
[4] On this memorable occasion the Opposition had a majority of one if they had polled full strength. Alderman Jinks, National League member for Sligo, however, refrained from voting, and left the House.
[5] *Dáil Debates*, vol. 20, col. 1750.

It seems evident, surveying the limited material that is as yet available, that there is in the Dáil a division of opinion as to the nature of the Speaker's office. The Cumann na nGaedheal Party regarded the office as one whose essence is impartiality. They accept the British precedent. The Fianna Fail Party tends towards an acceptance of the French practice. It is probable that the latter view will triumph. It is to be noticed, in support of these opinions, that Cumann na nGaedheal has never opposed the re-election of the Speaker. In 1933, after the Speaker had been, in the previous year, elected on a party vote, no opposition was offered. Admittedly the former Speaker did not retire from political life, but no doubt it was felt that once the principle of an impartial office had been violated, it was unnecessary to fulfil the detail. A complete adoption of the French system is at this moment impossible, without a repeal of certain of the Standing Orders. The President of the French Chamber is selected as a suitable analogy, in that his position is midway between that of the Speaker of the House of Commons and that of the Speaker of the House of Representatives. His first duty is impartiality to all. By usage—and not by compulsion of the Constitution as in Ireland—he refrains from voting. But possessing all the privileges of an ordinary member he may at any time leave the Chair and engage in debate.[1] He remains in effect a politician. Moreover, the President of the French Chamber is elected on a party vote. In 1905 the election to the Presidency aroused party animosities to a fever heat. The candidacy and the subsequent election of Paul Doumer in place of the out-going President helped to force the Combes Ministry out of office.[1] The precedent of 1932, if it is followed, will result in a conception of office similar to that held in France. It is, moreover, instructive to notice that the Presidents of the French Chamber have almost all been leading politicians who have reached the presidency through the premiership, or the premiership

---

[1] Sait, *Government and Politics of France*, pp. 200-201.

through the presidency.¹ The former process is extremely improbable in Ireland, but so far as one can judge (there having been only two occupants of the Chair) the tendency is for prominent politicians to be proposed.² That being so it is unlikely that the British precedent of retiring from political life, on surrendering the office of Speaker, will be maintained. In general it appears that the party opposition to the outgoing Speaker in 1932 has established a precedent that it is difficult to destroy. It marks a turning-point in the nature of the office. A reversion to the British system is possible, but for reasons, which have been outlined, it seems that the current is flowing in the opposite direction. The nature of the functions and powers attached to the office, on the other hand, make it unlikely that a Speakership on American lines will emerge.

The short history of the Irish Speakership has shown nothing more plainly than that a careful definition of powers and functions cannot recreate an institution whose peculiar merits are the result of a long and memorable tradition. It is not the legal status of the office, but the attitude in which it is regarded that determines its nature. For these reasons a discussion on the powers of the Speakership has been postponed till now. For, after all, a mere summary of legal rights enables no estimate to be formed of the actual power of the office. The Irish Constituent Assembly accepted as their model the English Speakership. In this they were followed by the framers of the Standing Orders. In general, therefore, the status and functions of the Chairman of the Dáil conform to those of the Speaker. The ceremony and outward dignity of the latter has been discarded. There is no mace, no wig and gown. On the other hand the dignity of his position is enhanced by his precedence

---

[1] Sait, op. cit., pp. 203 seq. In England in 1801, Speaker Addington stepped straight from the Chair to the Premiership.
[2] Professor M. Hayes, the first Speaker, was Minister of Education in the Provisional Government, 1922. Mr. Fahy was a prominent member of his party before election.

over the Chairman of the Second Chamber. In one notable respect the duties of the Chairman of the Dáil are wider than those of the Speaker of the Commons. He presides over Committees of the Whole. This is simply a matter of convenience. The pressure of business being less, it is felt that the Chairman might undertake with advantage this addition to his functions. The powers in the hands of the English Speaker are both wide and discretionary. Their adoption in Ireland has in no sense led to grounds of complaint against the Speaker. If the election of the Speaker tends to become partisan, there has been no similar charge in respect of the execution of his duties. In that respect much is owed to the high conception of office consistently maintained by Deputy Hayes, the first Speaker. The duties of the Speaker in the Dáil are exercised partly in virtue of the practice of the Dáil, and partly under Standing Orders and the Constitution.[1] In virtue of practice he presides over the House, enforces the rules of debates, and decides questions of order. He calls members who wish to speak, proposes and puts the necessary questions, and announces the decisions of the House. He exercises a general censorship over notices and satisfies himself that any motion is in order, before he puts the question on it.[2] In virtue of powers exercised under the Standing Orders the Speaker may check irrelevance and repetition in debate, he may refuse dilatory motions, secure the avoidance of unnecessary divisions, and examine questions to be asked of ministers to assure himself of their compliance with the rules of the House.[3] He maintains order in debate. He may suspend deputies for disorderly conduct. Should this prove inadequate, he has power to "name" the offender with a view to his suspension by the Dáil for a longer period.[4] Closure can only be applied when the Speaker is in the Chair, and he has the power to refuse a motion of closure should he consider the question has not been adequately discussed

---

[1] Art. 24.
[2] Cf. Campion, *Procedure of the House of Commons*, pp. 50–56.
[3] Standing Order 30.   [4] This power has not been used.

The Procedure of the Legislature 119

or that the rights of a minority are thereby infringed.[1] He has, moreover, the same wide powers as the Speaker of the House of Commons to refuse amendments of an irrelevant or an obstructionist character. This discretionary authority is of great importance in the course of parliamentary business, and the evidence tends to show that the Speaker of the Dáil has used it more freely than the Speaker of the Commons. Only one form of closure is commonly used, namely, the simple closure, "That the Question be now put." The Chair has not the power to select amendments. Closure by compartments, known as the guillotine, can and has been applied under orders of the House made *ad hoc* in each instance. The failure to invest the Speaker with the power of selecting amendments, known as "the Kangaroo," is a regrettable lacuna in Irish Procedure. The Speaker, as in England, affixes his certificate to a Money Bill, but his decision may be challenged. If it is challenged it is referred to a Committee of Privileges.[2]

The position of the Vice-Chairman of the Dáil (an Leas Ceann Comhairle) differs in some respects from his British counterpart, the Chairman of Ways and Means. In the Dáil the Vice-Chairman is in every respect the understudy of the Chairman. He is elected by the House, he holds office for the whole term of the Dáil, in the absence of his superior he takes the Chair both in the House and in Committee. In the House of Commons, on the other hand, the Chairman of Ways and Means is the nominee of the Government, and while refraining from active politics during his term of office, he is unlikely to be re-appointed on a change of government.[3] In the Dáil a member of one of the smaller parties is frequently elected Vice-Chairman.

In the Dáil the authority of the Speaker to refuse dilatory motions and to reject amendments of an irrelevant or obstructionist character has been used more freely than in the House

---
[1] Standing Order 52.
[2] Constitution, Art. 35, Standing Orders 110-112.
[3] Cf. Campion, op. cit., p. 55.

of Commons, and thereby the progress of business has been much facilitated. It has been suggested in evidence before an English Select Committee[1] that a strict enforcement of the rules against irrelevance and repetition by the Speaker would save an invaluable amount of parliamentary time. Such proposals are difficult to put into effect in the House of Commons, on account of the practice established by traditional usage. The Speaker in the Dáil is more fortunate in that he is bound by no such precise tradition in the exercise of his authority.

PROCEDURE ON BILLS

The Procedure on Bills differs in only one respect—and that a purely formal one—from the practice of the House of Commons. In the Dáil consideration of a Bill on Report is made a definite stage. The first stage corresponds to the British First Reading; the second stage to the British Second Reading. The third stage is the Committee Stage. The fourth corresponds to the British consideration on Report, and the fifth to the British Third Reading. The forms and formulae of opposition are the same as in the House of Commons. A Bill, having been passed by the Dáil, is sent up to the Senate. In cases of disagreement between the Dáil and the Senate on amendments to Bills, an exchange of views is carried by means of Conferences, composed of members of both Houses. It is felt that Conferences afford a greater opportunity for compromise than do "Messages" embodying reasons, which is the British practice.

In the Dáil Bills are almost invariably retained in Committee of the Whole. This practice, whilst securing greater publicity, does not secure such careful examination of the details as would a small Committee. The debate on the Second Reading must be confined to the general principle of the Bill.[2] In Committee amendments must not conflict with the principle of the

---

[1] Lord R. Cecil, Committee on Procedure, 1914.
[2] Standing Order 83.

Bill as read a second time.¹ The debate in Committee is therefore confined to a discussion on detail. In the House of Commons Bills unamended in Committee are automatically read a third time. This practice has not been accepted by the Dáil.

The Procedure and practice followed in dealing with private Bills is of interest. Such Bills are to be distinguished from private members' Bills. The latter are public Bills introduced by members in their personal capacity. The former are Bills affecting particular interests. The Procedure by private Bill enables companies or corporations to promote Bills for powers to undertake enterprises in the interests of the public. These Bills frequently deal with such matters as the construction of railways, tramways, or harbours. In the majority of cases land must be compulsorily acquired or the rights and property of persons may be otherwise interfered with. Such difficulties can be surmounted, and such privileges obtained, only by invoking the supreme authority of the Oireachtas. The Bills are examined by semi-judicial Committees. What is of importance to notice here, however, is that such Bills are now rarely brought before the Dáil.² The system of Provisional Order Confirmation Bills gives statutory force to orders granted (under powers conferred by Statute) by Departments of State. These orders make provision for undertakings of public and general utility. This method is more rapid and less costly than Procedure by private Bill. It was recommended by Sir Courtenay Ilbert to the Select Committee on Procedure in 1914. "I should like," he said, "to see the amount of Private Business reduced: the tendency has been to reduce the amount of time occupied by private Bills very much under the system of Provisional Order Bills and Departmental orders. I should like to see that carried further."³ While the practice diminishes the control of the Legislature, it is evident that such matters are more competently and more cheaply dispatched by an executive authority.

[1] Standing Order 89. [2] The procedure was extremely expensive.
[3] *Select Committee on House of Commons Procedure*, 1914, p. 181.

LEGISLATIVE COMMITTEES

In the work of the Dáil the Committees exercise an influence which is less than originally was intended. The effective leadership of the Executive Council prevents any devolution of legislative control. The Council invested with a popular mandate, responsible for the fulfilment of a legislative programme, has no desire to see its Bills either mutilated or distorted out of their original shape in Special or Standing Committee. The embarrassment to the Cabinet, which the Committee system in France has caused, is a sufficient warning of the inconvenience of divided responsibility.

A Committee of the Whole Dáil is constituted for the discharge of certain stages in Bills or of certain types of business. Among deputies it is popular and is used whenever possible. It allows of greater freedom of discussion than is possible in a formal meeting of the House. From the point of view of the ministers, it is convenient in that it enables them to guide their legislative proposals, with the support of the Government majority. Moreover, in Committee of the Whole, publicity is assured to the debates, whilst Standing Committees become lost to view. Increasing pressure of business might lead to a development of the Standing Committee system, but at the moment this does not seem probable.

A Committe of the Whole is constituted for the third or Committee Stage of Bills. Almost invariably Bills are retained in the House in contradistinction to the English practice of sending upstairs, to the Standing Committees, all Bills, except those of major importance. The only Bills which must, under the Standing Orders, be committed to Special Committee are Bills introduced by private deputies. The debate in the Committee of the Whole is peculiarly suited (and intended) for the discussion of detail. The debate is less formal than in the House itself. Motions or amendments need not be seconded; a deputy may speak more than once on the same question.[1]

[1] Standing Order 62.

The Dáil automatically goes into Committee of the Whole when business on the order paper for consideration in that Committee is reached. This eliminates the formal resolution required by the Procedure of the House of Commons. The Speaker of the Dáil presides over Committee of the Whole. The British practice of moving the Speaker out of the Chair, on going into Committee of Supply, would consequently be meaningless. The quorum in Committee is the same as that of the House itself. In either case a count may be demanded at any time. There is no interval, as between 8.15 and 9.15 p.m. in the House of Commons, during which counts are not permitted.

The Dáil sits as a Committee for other purposes than the debate on the third stage of Bills. It is in this form that it considers both amendments made by the Seanad to Bills received from the Dáil and Bills received from Select or Joint Committees which have been empowered to take evidence. Resolutions dealing with supply for the Public Services and the imposition of taxation must be introduced in a Committee of the Whole, which is termed the Committee of Finance. In a Committee of the Whole the Executive retains its voting strength and the ministers are in a position to guide their own legislative proposals. A Committee system—and it has not found favour with the Dáil—involves a definite control over a Bill by a Committee on which the Government supporters may not be in a majority. There are, it is true, certain permanent Committees appointed by the Dáil, but they are in no position to modify the legislative programme of the Executive Council. The Dáil does less through permanent Committees than does the House of Commons. This is in large measure due to the lighter pressure of business, and to the smaller membership.

The smaller Committees are designated Select, Joint, and Special Committees. Select Committees are appointed by the Dáil to consider and, if so permitted, to take evidence upon any Bill or matter, and to report its opinion for the information and assistance of Dáil.¹ When inquiry into a proposed subject is desired it is usual to set up a Select Committee. Such a Committee is frequently armed with the power to "send for persons, papers, and records."² Joint Committees are appointed when the Senate and the Dáil are at the same time interested in a Bill or other matter, and agree to investigate it in common. It is provided that if the Bill be a Public Bill the deputy in charge shall be one of the deputies appointed by the Dáil to sit on the Joint Committee. The purpose of the Select and Joint Committees is to investigate into certain matters and report to the Dáil. The Special Committees on the other hand constitute a definite stage in the passage of a Bill. They correspond to the Standing Committees of the House of Commons. To them only a small number of Bills are referred. The Dáil may fix the date upon which the Committee shall report.³ Under the Standing Orders all Bills introduced by private deputies must be referred to a Special Committee.⁴

The nature of the Committees is best examined in the light of parliamentary practice. At the beginning of every session a Committee of Selection is appointed,⁵ who, unless it is otherwise ordered, nominate the members to serve on Select or Special Committees.⁶ This Committee of Selection consists of eleven deputies. It is constituted so as to be impartially representative of the Dáil. It has the power to discharge members from Committees for non-attendance or at their own request.⁷ Committees of all kinds may be appointed for a specified period or permanently. The Special Committees are appointed to deal with a particular Bill, and, though constituting a stage in legislation, they do not sit throughout the session. In this respect they differ from the Standing Committees in the House of Commons. The principal permanent Committees of the Dáil are:

---

[1] Standing Order 65. [2] Ibid., 66. [3] Ibid., 67.
[4] Ibid., 79. [5] By Proportional Representation.
[6] Standing Order 70. [7] Ibid.

The Committee on Procedure and Privileges.
The Select Committee on Public Accounts.
The Joint Committee on Standing Orders (Private Business).
The Selection Committee.
The Joint Library Committee.
The Restaurant Committee.

It will be seen at once that the nature and purpose of these Committees preclude any possibility of a Committee system on the French model. There is no question here of Committees to which all Bills are automatically referred. The Committees are constituted to deal with matters of parliamentary convenience. They do not deal with matters likely to arouse controversy. Matters of moment and partisan importance are dealt with on the floor of the House. The purpose of the permanent Standing Committees is illustrated by their titles. The Select Committee on Public Accounts is of importance. It reports to the House on the Appropriation Accounts, which show the expenditure of the voted monies. This expenditure is audited by the Comptroller and Auditor-General. He furnishes a report to the Dáil. Both this report and the Accounts are sent to the Select Committee. The Committee can then summon the Accounting Officers to defend their administration in view of the queries of the Comptroller and Auditor-General. The personnel of the Committee is selected annually. Ministers can take no part in its work. In accordance with the Standing Orders a member of the Opposition is selected as Chairman.[1] The nature of this Committee, which possesses no inconsiderable powers, merits attention, in that it shows how the Committee system is permitted in no way to interfere with the legislative control of the Executive Council. The powers given to the Opposition are intended to secure that the expenditure of public monies is in accordance with the financial resolu-

[1] Standing Order 109.

tions passed by the Dáil. It is a matter of accounts; it is not a matter of policy. The Committee of Public Accounts under the Standing Orders may "suggest alterations and improvements in the form of Estimates submitted to the Dáil."[1] This power, limited though it is, is illusory. In financial matters the Executive insists on undivided responsibility.

The practice of the Dáil in retaining all matters of importance to be discussed in the House is illustrated by an examination of the Committees, not of a permanent character, which sat during any one year. In 1931 (for example) Committees were appointed to deal with the following subjects: The Moneylender's Bill, 1929; the Revision of Private Bill Standing Orders; a Bill to extend the benefits of the Hospital Sweepstakes to a certain nursing organization; a Bill to extend the benefits of the Sweepstakes to a particular hospital in Cork city.[2] From this list of subjects allotted to Committees it will be seen that the rôle played by them in the work of the Dáil is of considerably less significance than that which they fill at Westminster.

THE PARLIAMENTARY TIME-TABLE

Throughout the whole period of the session private members —unless indeed the Government move to take all the time— have one and a half hours on Wednesdays and two hours on Friday. A minister may move without notice that ministerial business shall not be interrupted if at the time fixed for taking private deputies' business it is still under consideration.[3] After notice a minister may move that Government business shall take the time allocated to private deputies for a specified period. Definite provision is also made in the Standing Orders for extended sittings over a specified period.[4] In the House of Commons the suspension of the 11 o'clock rule has to be

---

[1] Standing Order 109.
[2] Quoted in Flynn, *Irish Free State Parliamentary Guide*, p. 116.
[3] Standing Order 78.   [4] Ibid. 20.

moved daily. The Dáil, by surrendering greater power to ministers, eliminates this inconvenience. Power is given to the Chair,[1] if an order has been made for an extended sitting, to suspend the sitting for a period not exceeding two hours. This break affords relaxation to a minister in charge of a complicated measure.

A deviation from British practice was made in the provision that the termination of the session was not to be destructive of Bills which had not reached their final stage.[2] This provision has been interpreted as extending to a dissolution as well. It has not been much used. It is, however, a definite advantage from the point of view of the private deputy. At Westminster numerous private members' Bills get through certain stages and are then "slaughtered" by the termination of the session. Under the Standing Orders of the Dáil a lapsed Bill can be restored to the Order paper and reconsidered at that stage which it has reached in the preceding session. The following figures enable one to form an estimate of its value:

Year	Number of Government Bills carried over to Following Year	Number of Private Deputies' Bills carried over to Following Year	Total
1930	8	4	12
1931	9	2	11
1932	9	3	12

The right to control its own time rests ultimately with the House. In effect this right is exercised by the Government of the day. The allocation of parliamentary time is in the hands of the Executive. The President determines the order in which ministerial business shall be taken.[3] Under the Standing Orders private members are entitled to three and a half hours a week throughout the whole period the Dáil is in session. Such a period is not, perhaps, inadequate. It is, however, not infrequently claimed by the Government. This may be done by

[1] Standing Order 21.   [2] Ibid. 99.   [3] Ibid. 22.

a simple motion. The Government's share of parliamentary time is liable to be extended by virtue of certain privileges. It may from time to time obtain from the House precedence for some particular proposal, even to the extent of securing the whole time of the House for some Bill or other measure. Then the simple closure, which is generally applied, is a severe limitation on non-official members. Moreover, the Government (and this is a more extensive privilege than is enjoyed by the British Cabinet) may enlarge their opportunities by moving the suspension of the 9 o'clock rule over an extended period. A bare majority suffices for the adoption of these measures.

The Executive Council enjoys a great preponderance in arranging and controlling the time of the Dáil. In no respect was the adoption of British Procedure of greater importance. For the Procedure of the House of Commons is the Procedure of the majority. It is the Procedure of the Cabinet. The Government is endowed with a far-reaching, almost complete power of disposition over the time of the House and the organization and arrangement of its work. This concentration of power was built up under a two-party system. It is the logical outcome of majority government. It would be impracticable, or would at any rate require modification, under a group system of government. This preponderance of the Cabinet is partly the outcome of the obstructionist policy pursued by the Irish members at Westminster. It is probable, however, that these tactics only intensified a tendency that was already becoming apparent. The complicated business of modern legislation requires both unity of direction and unity of control. The Executive must give a lead in legislation.

The importance of the Irish obstructionist tactics at Westminster lies in the fact that they made evident a problem of whose existence men were but dimly aware. Obstruction is the natural method of opposition by a party which does not accept the basis on which the Government is founded. As such it can in no sense be claimed that it was invented by the Irish members at Westminster. Its object was to prevent parliamentary government from being carried out. In a former age it was felt to merit a poetic description. "All that could be done," wrote Ludlow,[1] in the time of the Commonwealth, "was only to lengthen out their debates and to hang on to the wheels of the chariot that they might not be able to drive so furiously." Such a menace to parliamentary debate could be met in only one way: by the concentration of power in the hands of the Government. This is precisely what happened. The House of Commons became "an organ of the State with the capacity and duty of providing for the speedy and well-timed despatch of certain State business."[2] A realization of this change of character alone enables one to understand the power of the Executive Council over the business of the Dáil. The adoption, with only slight alterations, of the House of Commons Procedure has done much to establish in Ireland an Executive which is not only more powerful than intended by the Constitution, but also overshadows and controls the Legislature.

In modern times it is evident that the ministry must allocate the time of Parliament. This does not in itself in any way bring the Legislature to a state of impotence. In the Irish Free State, however, both the history of the last ten years and the personnel of the Dáil has tended to exaggerate this leadership of the ministry. In times of difficulty and crisis a wide discretionary power is placed in the hands of the Executive. We shall consider the nature of this power later. Here it is sufficient to remark that national difficulties emphasize the position of the party leaders, tighten party discipline, and thereby place the private deputy more under the control of the front benches. It is not only by the course of events that the control of the Executive Council has been created. The Standing Orders place more power in the hands of the Executive than do those of the House of Commons. In the first place the time allocated to private deputies may be taken for ministerial business, not merely for a day but

[1] *Memoirs*, ii.   [2] Redlich, op. cit., vol. iii, p. 22.

for a specified period. Secondly, and more important, all Government Bills are in practice kept in Committee of the Whole. In a Standing Committee Government control is, to a certain extent, relaxed. In Committee of the Whole the Executive relies on its majority. There is almost no chance of any amendment being carried against the ministry, unless, indeed, it has no working majority. When it is remembered that only details are discussed in Committee, it is evident that there is a peculiarly unfortunate temptation for the ministry to use the majority rather than attempt to debate. Thirdly, it is to be noticed that while a closure is required in almost every legislative assembly, the form used in Ireland, namely, the simple closure "that the question be now put," is peculiarly unfavourable to the minority. Under the Standing Orders[1] it is possible, and there have been cases of closure by compartment, known as the guillotine. But its use is rare, and under the simple closure the debate tends to be robbed of all reality. It is to be regretted that the Chair has not been given the power of selecting amendments to be debated. This power, known as the "Kangaroo," permits debate on amendments or clauses of importance or interest. It is allowed that the Opposition should have the preference in determining these clauses. It is possible, though difficult, to imagine that a partisan use might be made of the Kangaroo closure which would be disastrous. That would, however, imply a partisan or a very weak Speaker.[2] The preponderance of the Government in the time of the Dáil is intensified as the session proceeds. A legislative programme, it is felt, must be put through. As a result wholesale closure is used on Bills which have not gone through all their stages at the end of the session.

From the point of view of the private deputy it must be said that under the Standing Orders his opportunities are adequate. One and a half hours on Wednesday and two hours on Friday are allocated to private deputies' business. There

---

[1] Standing Order 78.
[2] *Select Committee Report on Procedure*, 1914, p. 45.

is no demand for greater facilities. From the standpoint of the departments of State, private member legislation is, generally speaking, mistrusted. It tends, and must inevitably tend, to be ill-conceived and badly drafted. The complexity of modern legislation destroys the value of private members' Bills. The number of such Bills as compared with the number of Government Bills initiated and carried during the years 1928–33 is as follows:

Year	Number of Government Bills Introduced[1]	Number of Government Bills which became Acts	Number of Bills Introduced by Private Deputies[1]	Number of such Bills which became Acts
1928	45	36	6	1
1929	49	36	13	4
1930	42	33	11	2
1931	61	52	8	3
1932	49	34	7	—
1933	73	53	5	—

Ministerial legislation is drafted by the State departments, who have at their disposal information and statistics not available to the private deputy.

The extensive control over the time of the Dáil exercised by the Executive Council is in part the result and in part the cause of the tightening of party discipline. For while the party vote enables the Government to wield its power, the control of legislation by the Executive places the deputy, if he is not to be powerless, in the hands of the party, and it is not the constituencies, but rather the party machine which tightens the bonds of discipline. Prospective candidates of the larger parties are required to sign a document guaranteeing their obedience to the party whip. The ministry can rely on their votes. The temptation is therefore to legislate, not after debate, but by a solid vote supported by the closure. On the other hand it is not to be forgotten that Irish members have always proved themselves to be masters of the forms of Pro-

[1] Inclusive of Bills carried over each year.

cedure. Their tactics of obstruction at Westminster is a tribute to this ingenuity. It is not therefore improbable that a Procedure more favourable to the minority would be used for purposes other than those of legitimate debate. Cross voting among the large parties has been rare. They are well organized. In the smaller parties it has not been infrequent.[1] It is usually punished by expulsion from the party. The Procedure of the Dáil, emphasizing as it does the control of the Government, is part of a general tendency in parliamentary institutions. Power tends to pass from the elected to the electors. The dependence of the Executive is not on Parliament but on universal suffrage.

The time-table of the Dáil is drawn up by the Executive. It initiates almost all important legislation. It does not dominate debate. The private deputy has a far greater chance of making himself heard than has his counterpart at Westminster. Full-dress debates are rare. There is more informality, even on important occasions, than in the House of Commons. Long speeches are comparatively infrequent. Members of the respective front benches do not usurp all the time at the disposal of the chamber. As a result the private deputy speaks frequently. The full complement of deputies, amounting as it does to only one hundred and fifty-three, permits in any event of a larger measure of time for the speeches of each individual member than would be possible in a House of over six hundred.

FINANCIAL PROCEDURE

The most important legislative activity of the Dáil is in the field of finance. The power of the purse, the control over the granting of supply, must be regarded as a fundamental attribute of modern assemblies. It was mainly through this power that the English Parliament gained its ascendency over the Executive. On the other hand the most important Standing Order in

[1] Deputies Morrissey and Anthony, members of the Labour Party, voted against the instructions of the Party Whip on Constitution Amendment (No. 17) Bill, and were subsequently expelled from the party.

The Procedure of the Legislature

English Procedure declared that the introduction of financial proposals is the prerogative of the Executive. This proviso, essential both to unity of financial control and to the whole conception of ministerial responsibility, is embodied in the Irish Constitution.[1] Money, it is stated, shall not be appropriated by vote, resolution, or law unless recommended by the Executive Council. While this article secures ministerial responsibility, it does not preclude the introduction of legislative proposals involving public expenditure by private members. It does demand that a Financial Resolution giving effect to the proposal must originate with the Executive Council.[2]

The Financial Resolutions (they are not termed the budget) must be introduced each year before April 1st. The resolutions deal with two aspects of finance—the raising and the spending of money, revenue, and supply. The distinction maintained in the House of Commons between Committee of Supply and Committee of Ways and Means is not retained. In the Dáil all financial business is taken in a Committee of the Whole, termed the Committee of Finance. With this exception the financial Procedure of the House of Commons has been adopted. There are some minor points of difference. The Speaker is not moved out of the Chair in Committee of Finance. Moreover, as the Constitution[3] provides that the salary of a minister cannot be reduced during his term of office, the British expedient of moving a reduction of a minister's salary by £100 for the purpose of an attack on his policy cannot be followed. In its place it is permissible under the Standing Orders to refer an Estimate back for reconsideration, upon which a general debate on policy can take place. As in England it has been found necessary to impose

[1] Art. 37. As amended by Constitution (Amendment No. 20) Act.
[2] Led to the resignation of the Cosgrave administration on March 27, 1930. The Dáil passed Second Reading of an Old Age Pensions Bill after the Government had indicated their opposition to the financial expenditure involved.   [3] Art. 59.

a limit on the period for the discussion of the Estimates. This period extends from fourteen days after the presentation of the Estimates (which must be presented by April 1st) until, usually, the middle of July. The period in the House of Commons is confined to twenty sitting days, with a possible extension of three days.

In respect of Money Bills the Senate has wider powers than the House of Lords. The Speaker affixes his certificate to a Money Bill. It may be challenged within seven days.[1] It has not been challenged yet. Whilst the Senate has no power of amendment in regard to Money Bills, it has the power of recommendation. Such recommendations may be accepted or rejected by the Dáil. The recommendations of the Senate have not proved of great value as is shown by the following statistics:

Year	Number of Recommendations to Money Bills proposed by the Senate	Number accepted by Dáil
1927	—	—
1928	1	1
1929	4	3
1930	—	—
1931	—	—
1932	24	12
1933	5	5

The annual debates on the Financial Resolutions are protracted. The first stage is usually a general debate in which questions of a broad nature are raised, such as the possibility of realizing economies or reforms. It is followed by a scrutiny of individual items, with criticism, and amendment. A ministry with a stable majority is unlikely to be compelled to change its proposals in any way. It is rare for even an individual item to be radically amended. In Committee of the Whole a party vote will carry the Financial Resolutions, and the debates are

[1] At first it was within three days.

The Procedure of the Legislature 135

terminated by a free use of the closure. The private deputy is in no position to decide on the merits of a proposed economy. He votes as he is directed by the Party Whips. An amendment carried against the Government is regarded as a vote of censure. It is not surprising that the debates show no real grasp of the financial measures proposed. They are debates on policy. The publicity no doubt has an indirect effect both on the ministers and the departments. But that does not make the control of the Dáil a reality. Questions of finance are crowded out by questions of policy. The ministry brings forward its proposals, but very few of the items are carefully debated from a financial standpoint. Moreover, a large part of the Estimates are passed under the closure.

The Legislature in the Irish Free State has no adequate control over national finance. This is in part due, as we have suggested, to the control of the Executive, to the discipline of the party. It is also due to the inadequacy of the machinery for legislative control. The action of the Ministry of Finance is undoubtedly invaluable. But the Ministry of Finance is a part of the Executive. It is not a substitute for the control of the Dáil. The Committee of the Whole on Finance, even apart from other objections, is too large and unwieldy to secure careful financial supervision. A minute examination is not possible, witnesses and experts cannot be called. While the Committee of Finance secures publicity and provides the occasion for a full-dress debate on policy, it cannot both by its nature and practice carry out a searching examination of the financial proposals of the Executive. The Comptroller and Auditor-General is, it is true, an officer of the House. His duty is, however, the scrutiny of accounts, not the scrutiny of proposed expenditure. The functions of the Committee on Public Accounts are of the same nature. It examines and reports to the Dáil on the appropriated accounts which show the expenditure of the voted monies. Its reports are usually presented two years after the monies have been voted. In consequence the report does not receive the attention it deserves.

It is regrettable that the Dáil has not appointed a Select Committee of Estimates. Such a Committee, suggesting economies, but not increased expenditure, would attract the notice of deputies to the purely financial aspect of the Estimates. The Committee would in no sense deal with policy, but purely with the financial proposals. It would bring the attention of deputies to the manner in which and in respect of what items the Estimates proposed increased expenditure. The responsibility of the minister would not be thereby impaired.

It must not be supposed that the Executive is financially irresponsible. It is true that its financial proposals receive no adequate scrutiny in the Dáil. But modern financial legislation does not originate *in vacuo*. It is discussed, and in all probability comes before the electorate prior to being voted in the Dáil. Moreover, outside the chamber pressure may be exerted by deputies on their party leaders, should they consider certain proposals objectionable. In broad outline the financial proposals of the Government receive considerable attention in the country. These outlines provide planks in the party platform at a General Election. But in matters of detail the Estimates do not receive adequate scrutiny. It is in the Dáil or in Select Committee that this criticism should be applied.

CHAPTER VIII

THE REFERENDUM AND THE INITIATIVE

IN the framework of the Free State Constitution provision is made for the direct action of the people in legislation. This insertion is common to a large majority of the post-War Constitutions. It was widely held that Rousseau was guilty of no exaggeration when he declared that "the English people believes that it is free; it is grossly mistaken. It is free only whilst it elects Members of Parliament; as soon as they are elected it is once more a slave, it is nothing."[1] This attitude, combining with the prevalent mistrust of the Legislature, produced in most of the new Constitutions a highly complex mechanism of direct legislation by the people. A mere enumeration of the Constitutions in which provisions of such a nature are to be found is in itself an acknowledgement of the extent of the needs which called them into being. In Austria, in Germany, in Czechoslovakia, in Lithuania, in Latvia, in Estonia, in Greece, as well as in the Free State, the people may exercise a continuous control on the Legislature by means of Initiative or Referendum. The mechanism of direct legislation in the Free State owes a not inconsiderable debt to the elaborate designs evolved by Continental constitutionalists. Its spirit, however, is more in sympathy with that of the older democratic States.[2] In modern Europe direct legislation is regarded as the necessary postulate of democracy; it is almost universally accepted as a logical corollary to the theory of popular sovereignty. It is by means of such machinery that the final expression of the people's will, of the *volonté générale*, can be ascertained. But in the Free State the trend

[1] Rousseau, *Du Contrat Social*, livre iii, chap. xv.
[2] Kohn is of a contrary opinion, believing that the Constituent Assembly found its model, not in the older, but in the new European Constitutions. Cf. Kohn, op. cit., pp. 238 seq.

of democratic thought was decisively individualist. It involved no acceptance of an organic view of the State. This attitude is reflected in the purpose for which direct legislation was inserted in the Constitution. It was intended to provide, not a representation of the people's will, but rather a safeguard for individual rights. Its aim was, in this respect, negative rather than positive. That is the broad distinction in spirit between the Referendum and Initiative as established in the Free State Constitution and in the new Continental States. In the former it is outside the legislative structure; in the latter it was introduced as an organic part of the Legislature. In both it may be said that direct legislation by the people has scarcely fulfilled the hopes of its supporters. In the Free State this disappointment has led to subsequent constitutional amendment which has abolished the Initiative and Referendum; and from Poland, Yugoslavia, and Czechoslovakia direct action by the people in legislation has almost entirely disappeared.

In the Constituent Assembly, no careful consideration was devoted to the principle of popular legislation. The years which followed the Peace of Versailles witnessed the heyday of the supremacy of democratic theory. So universal was the acceptance of the more doctrinaire of the guarantees of popular sovereignty that their insertion tended to become automatic. Moreover, as we have suggested, the proposal was regarded from the individualist standpoint. It was considered as a guarantee to the individual against the exercise of unwarranted powers by the State. As a result it commended itself to an assembly composed almost entirely of men who had actively resisted a government imposed from above. The history of the Irish nation made it, to a peculiar extent, desirable to associate the people in the work of government. A tradition of opposition to government is not destroyed within a day. It lingers on after the injustice which called it into being has been rectified. The minister in charge of the Constitution Bill declared that "personal actual contact between the people and the laws by which they are governed is advisable in a country ... where the traditional attitude of the people is to be against the law and against the government."¹ This consideration was no small recommendation for the acceptance of the Initiative and Referendum. It was further suggested that direct legislation by the people would prove a stimulus to their "political thought and political education";² a view which had received support from Lord Bryce, who considered it "unequalled as an instrument of practical instruction in politics."³

The use of the Referendum was mandatory only in cases of constitutional amendment.⁴ On all ordinary legislation it was optional. An appeal to the people had to be preceded by the demand of a prescribed number of the members of the Legislature or of qualified voters. In ordinary legislation a Bill passed by the Oireachtas was to be submitted to a Referendum upon the fulfilment of the following conditions. The Bill was to be suspended for ninety days on the written demand of two-fifths of the members of Dáil Eireann or of a majority of the members of the Senate. Such a demand was to be presented to the President of the Executive Council not later than seven days after its passage by the Legislature.⁵ The President was invested with no discretionary power. A request presented by either two-fifths of the Dáil or of the majority of the Senate was mandatory. The suspension being secured a Bill might now be submitted to a Referendum only if demanded before the expiration of the ninety days, either by a resolution of the Senate assented to by three-fifths of its members, or by a petition signed by not less than one-twentieth of the registered voters.⁶ In the Referendum to be held, upon fulfilment of these demands, a majority of the votes recorded was to decide. Money Bills or such Bills as were declared by both Houses to be necessary for the immediate preservation of the public peace, health, or safety were excluded from these

¹ *Dáil Debates*, vol. 1, col. 1220.
² Ibid., col. 1221.
³ Lord Bryce, op. cit., vol. ii, p. 477.
⁴ Art. 50.
⁵ Art. 47.
⁶ Ibid.

provisions.[1] They could not be submitted to a Referendum. In the early years of the Free State no inconsiderable use was made of this declaration, and in consequence the proposed legislation could not be suspended.

The means by which the Referendum might be invoked is of interest in respect of the powers wielded by the Upper House. By the vote of a majority of its members the Senate might secure the temporary suspension of a Bill passed by the Dáil. Consequent upon this temporary suspension, it might by the vote of three-fifths of its members invoke the Referendum. The onus of invoking the sanction of the people by Referendum lay with the Senate. In this manner democratic theory was enabled to survive unscathed. For the check on the action of the representatives of the people was supplied by the intervention of the people themselves. Should the Senate fail to appeal to the decision of a Referendum, the appeal might be made on the demand of a prescribed number of qualified voters. In actual fact this "devolutive veto" was never exercised by the Senate. It was a dangerous power for the Upper House to use. The rather elaborate process by which a Referendum might be invoked served to divide responsibility. Furthermore, it made it unlikely that an appeal to the people would take place save in very exceptional circumstances. The Referendum, if it be optional, requires as a preliminary a delay in the promulgation of legislation. In the older democratic Constitutions this presented no difficulty. In Switzerland, for example, every law when passed takes ninety days before coming into effect. The conditions of modern legislation make such a delay undesirable. Hence the Free State Constitution provides a means whereby a temporary suspension may be effected previous to deciding upon the submission of a Bill to a popular vote.

The Constituent Assembly displayed considerable reluctance in regard to the introduction of the Initiative. The Referendum is after all negative. The Initiative is a means whereby the

[1] Art. 47.

electorate may exercise a positive influence in the legislative work of government. From the point of view of the national legislature the purpose of the Referendum, as President Lowell has remarked,[1] is to correct its sins of commission, that of the Initiative to remedy its sins of omission. Practical experience of the working of the Initiative has not, however, engendered any confidence in its inherent merits. Moreover, from the standpoint of the Constituent Assembly, with its emphasis on individualist democracy, the Initiative was not likely to receive a great measure of support. Some check, it was felt, might be needed to curb the rashness of the Dáil; but that did not imply a need for the association of the people in the actual work of legislation. As a consequence we find that whilst the right of appeal to a Referendum is mandatory under the Constitution, the insertion of the Initiative in the Constitution is optional. The Oireachtas might provide for the Initiation by the people of proposals for laws or constitutional amendments, but should they fail to do so (as actually happened) within two years, its introduction might be effected through the medium of a popular Initiative.[2] On the petition of not less than seventy-five thousand voters, of whom not more than fifteen thousand are registered in one constituency, the Oireachtas must either make such provision or submit the question to the people for decision by Referendum. It was further provided in the Constitution[2] that should the Initiative be created in accordance with the above conditions, that (*a*) proposals might be initiated on a petition of fifty thousand voters on the register, (*b*) if the Legislature rejects a proposal thus initiated it shall be submitted to a Referendum. If the Legislature accepted a proposal thus initiated, it would be subject to the provisions governing ordinary legislation. It is to be conjectured from the nature of these provisions that the Constituent Assembly was unwilling to sanction an immediate insertion of the Initiative in the machinery of the Constitution. This reluctance did not, however, lead the Assembly to define

[1] Cf. Lowell, *Public Opinion and Popular Government.*   [2] Art. 48.

with care the extent of its subsequent operation. The proposals, indeed, suggest a far-reaching adoption of extra-parliamentary legislation, in that the proportion of the electorate who might initiate legislation is undeniably small. It was on this account subjected to a pertinent criticism in the Constituent Assembly.[1] It is a further and notable example of a widespread desire that the right of minorities should be fully safeguarded.

The history of the Initiative and Referendum in the Free State was too brief to enable one to form an opinion of their merits. In 1928 they were both deleted from the Constitution.[2] During the six years which had elapsed since the promulgation of the Constitution, the Initiative had not been introduced, and only one attempt had been made by a minority in the Dáil to effect the suspension of legislation with view to an appeal to the Referendum.[3] The support of the required number of voters could not be enlisted. In 1924 a Cabinet Sub-Committee was set up to consider necessary amendments to the Constitution. This Committee reported in favour of the abolition of both Initiative and Referendum. The Government did not act at once upon its recommendations. In the meantime the Fianna Fail Party organized a campaign, whose intention was to enforce the creation of the means through which the Initiative was to be exercised. The ultimate objective was to abolish the Oath by means of extra-parliamentary legislation. In the country the aims of the Fianna Fail Party received a considerable measure of support. It resulted in the presentation of a petition, signed by ninety-six thousand[4] electors, to the Dáil in May 1928. The first difficulty arose in that no provision had been made in the Standing Orders as to how such petitions should be presented. It was on that account decided that consideration of the petition should be postponed until the Oireachtas had decided the

[1] *Dáil Debates*, vol. I, cols. 1220 seq.
[2] Constitution (Amendment No. 10) Act (No. 8 of 1928).
[3] In respect of the Electoral (Amendment No. 2) Act, 1927.
[4] Seventy-five thousand was the number required by the Constitution, Art. 48.

procedure to be adopted. Before any conclusion had been reached the Government introduced a Bill to delete those articles[1] of the Constitution which provided for the direct action of the people in legislation. The ministry had published their intention of proposing such legislation at an earlier date. On the other hand the Opposition maintained that the Government proposals were *ultra vires* in that a petition, having been presented in accordance with the terms of the Constitution, the Oireachtas "must either make such provisions (for the Initiative) or submit the question to the people for decision in accordance with the ordinary regulations governing the Referendum."[2] The introduction of the Bill gave rise to one of the most bitter and prolonged debates which the Dáil has experienced. The conflict was centred fundamentally, not on the abstract merits of the direct action of the people in legislation, but rather on the Treaty issue. It is to be noticed that the leaders of the Opposition were not altogether enthusiastic for a wide use of the Initiative in ordinary legislation. The case in respect of constitutional amendment was held to rest on a different basis. "The body of law as a whole," said Mr. de Valera, "is a large matter. The Constitution generally is a comparatively small document which can be digested and understood by the average person."[3] The Government, on the other hand, claimed that the Initiative was likely to be used in order to nullify a vital part of an international settlement. Its introduction would impose upon a Government, commanding a majority in the Dáil, the onus of carrying out a policy to which they were directly opposed. The Bill was passed through both Houses by a frequent use of the guillotine. It was still possible for the minority to demand a Referendum under the provisions of Article 50.[4] Once more

[1] Arts. 47 and 48 were deleted *in toto*, consequential amendments were made in Arts. 14 and 50.   [2] Art. 48.
[3] *Dáil Debates*, vol. 24, col. 214.
[4] Which allowed Art 47 to apply to constitutional amendments until the expiration of the eight years during which they might pass as ordinary legislation.

they were forestalled. The Government secured the support a majority in both Houses, in declaring the Bill to be "necessary for the immediate preservation of the public peace and safety." By this proviso an appeal to the Referendum was prevented.

It is apparent that the high-handed action of the Government may in part be excused by the position in which they were placed. There can be no question but that Article 48 was badly drafted. It aimed at compelling the Legislature to legislate on the demand of a small proportion of the electorate. On the other hand the circumstances lend but little justification for the prevention of an appeal to the Referendum. To the outside world, at any rate, the danger likely to have arisen from a possible suspension of the Bill was not very obvious. The Government, it is now widely admitted,[1] were right in their opposition to the direct action of the people in legislation. They were wrong in the manner in which they acted. The effect of the constitutional amendment was to destroy the optional Referendum on all legislation other than constitutional amendment. The Initiative can no longer be provided for by way of ordinary legislation. The constitutional Referendum, though suspended till 1938, remains a part of the Constitution.

The manner in which the Referendum and Initiative were destroyed was unfortunate. It provides a forcible example of an unwarranted exercise of voting strength by the majority in the Dáil. It is an action which lends justification to the claim that a check should be imposed upon the impulses of the popularly elected Chamber. It was such a check that the Referendum was intended to provide. On the other hand, while the manner of its abolition may have cast a halo around the virtues of the direct action of the people in legislation, yet the conditions of Irish political life lead one to suppose that no significant rôle was open for it to fill. The supremacy

[1] The then Opposition (now the Government) no longer support it. It is regarded as too cumbersome.

of the larger parties reduced its importance; Proportional Representation would tend to render its decisions redundant. It is not easy to suppose that the decision of the Referendum would have differed fundamentally from that of the Dáil. The elector votes for a certain deputy. That deputy and his party stand for a definite political programme. In that programme all the important questions of the day are considered. The Referendum puts before the elector one concrete question. If that question is of fundamental importance it will have appeared on the party programme. In that event it is reasonable to expect that the elector is solidly behind his deputy. If the question is not fundamental it is unlikely to be submitted to a Referendum. The elaborate machinery by which the decision of the people is invoked would not permit of the posing of issues of secondary importance. In effect, with the existing electoral system, with the supremacy of the large parties and the clear-cut issues between these parties, it may be said that the elections following the dissolution of the Dáil are in the nature of a Referendum. In voting for the deputy the elector decides the concrete political questions of the day. The Initiative, resting on a different basis from the Referendum, would in practice increase the power of the parties. Moreover, its proposed insertion in the Irish Constitution was somewhat in the nature of a paradox. That Constitution emphasized the need for technical, non-partisan legislation. To facilitate such legislation it embarked on the creation of an experimental Executive. But those very ends, which the extern ministries were designed to achieve, would have been rendered impracticable by any extensive use of the Initiative. It appears impossible that direct legislation by the people would be forthcoming except under the leadership of the political parties. Moreover, in any event, legislation by the people is certainly not likely to pay attention to the technical needs of administration. Experience in Switzerland and the United States has shown that, customarily, popular legislation is badly drafted. It is also incapable of amendment. Popular action in legislation was never an essential feature of the structure of the Free State Constitution. Its abolition, whilst detracting from the democratic appearance of the Government, has to no appreciable extent diminished the measure of popular control.

CHAPTER IX

THE EXECUTIVE

THE structure of the Executive provides the most original feature of the Irish Constitution. In it there is an attempt to combine the "responsibility" of the Cabinet system with that continuity of policy and permanence of personnel secured by a non-parliamentary Executive. That the system evolved has not survived is due, not to its defects, but to the political events of the early years of the Irish Free State. It remains one of the most interesting experiments of post-War constitutional thought. If it was not an entirely satisfactory solution, it had none the less the great merit of realizing a difficulty only too frequently ignored. The Cabinet system, with its insistence on collective responsibility, cannot use the services of men of specialized knowledge or technique. The Constituent Committee for this reason favoured the creation of extern ministries. The holders of the Executive offices were to be individually appointed and to be individually responsible to the Dáil. These proposals were subsequently modified to an extent which divested them of their constitutional significance. The evolution of a Cabinet system along orthodox lines has not detracted from the power of the Executive in constitutional reality. The Executive Council provides the motive force in the political life of the Free State. Government is to a remarkable extent the government of the Executive. We have seen how the Council controls the Dáil. Later we shall examine its control of the administration.

THE CROWN

The structure of the Executive is that of a constitutional monarchy. Its essence is that of a Republic. This divergence between the form and the substance of constitutional machinery was necessitated by the Free State's acceptance of Dominion status. The monarchical element was divested of the reality of power, not, as in Canada, by convention, but by explicit statement in the Constitution.

The framework of the modern Cabinet system involves the existence of a supreme and permanent symbol of authority in whose name Executive functions are performed. Such an embodiment of Executive power may be divested of all functions, except those of a purely formal nature. None the less its existence is expedient, in that it emphasizes the continuity of the legal order through all the vicissitudes of political life. The holder of such an office, be he President or King, is invested with a greater or less degree of discretionary authority. In the Irish Free State that discretionary authority is so far as is possible entirely eliminated. The Constituent Assembly was compelled to design the Executive in accordance with the formal framework of the British Dominions. In the latter the Governor-General "holds in all respects the same position in relation to the administration of public affairs in the Dominion as is held by H.M. the King in Great Britain."[1] No reader of Walter Bagehot will fail to remember how deeply a constitutional monarch may influence the course of public events by knowledge and a wide experience. In the Dominions it is rarely that a Governor-General can attain to a position of equal power. In the Irish Free State it is rendered impossible.

Before considering the Executive functions of the Governor-General attention must be directed to the method of appointment. Since the creation of the Free State the position of the Representative of the Crown has been modified. The tendency is towards the abolition in form as well as in fact of all the powers of the Governor-General. In the Anglo-Irish Treaty it was provided, "that the Representative of the Crown in Ireland shall be appointed in a like manner as the Governor-General of Canada, and in accordance with the practice ob-

[1] Inter-Imperial Relations Committee of the Imperial Conference, 1926.

The Executive

served in the making of such appointments."[1] The position of the Governor-General was one of much controversy. It required further definition. This was given in a letter from the Prime Minister to the Chairman of the Irish Peace Delegation. In it Article 3 of the Treaty was interpreted as meaning "that the Government of the Irish Free State will be consulted so as to ensure a selection acceptable to the Irish Government, before any recommendation is made to His Majesty."[2] This statement of the existing practice makes it clear that, while the assent of the Dominion Government must be obtained, the initiative in selection remained with the British Cabinet. The Free State claimed that the initiative should lie with the Dominion Government. Professor Keith regards this view as untenable in respect of Dominion practice. "The rather comic insistence laid by the Irish Government on the occasion of the swearing in of the second Governor-General of the Free State, when it was stated that he had been selected by the Free State Government for appointment must therefore," he declares, "be reduced to its true value."[3] Yet the persons appointed to be Governors-General of the Free State make it quite plain that the Executive Council played a more than negative rôle in their appointment. Moreover, the Irish point of view received substantial ratification in 1930. At the Imperial Conference assembled in that year the change in the position of the Governor-General was formally recognized. In respect of the mode of appointment six rules were laid down; the import of which is that the appointment is made by the King on the advice of the Dominion Cabinet. The King acts on the advice of his responsible ministers, and on such an occasion "the ministers who tender and are responsible for such advice are His Majesty's ministers in the Dominion concerned."[4] Moreover, the Governments of the Dominions communicate

[1] The Treaty, Art. 3.
[2] *Treaty Debate*, p. 21, read by Mr. A. Griffith.
[3] Professor Keith, *Government of the British Dominions*, p. 250.
[4] Report of Proceedings of Imperial Conference, 1930. Cmd. 2202.

directly with the Crown. The British Cabinet no longer need act as an intermediary. In accordance with the new practice the instrument containing the Governor-General's appointment in 1932 was issued not by the Dominions office, but by the Secretary of the Executive Council in the Free State.[1] The official communiqué expressly stated that the Governor-General was appointed on the advice tendered to the Crown by the President of the Executive Council.

The Executive Council of the Irish Free State had always claimed those rights in respect of the appointment of the Governor-General which were subsequently sanctioned by the Imperial Conference. It had, since the creation of the Free State, been realized that in this respect its peculiar position and history required a treatment not sanctioned by Dominion practice. Whilst the negotiations, which led to the appointment of the various Governors-General, have not been made public, it does seem that the British Cabinet made no attempt to force their nominees on the Executive Council. It has been stated that on a recent occasion, when a list of candidates was submitted to the Canadian Government by the British Secretary of State, the Canadian Government rejected the whole list and put forward a nomination of its own, which was accepted.[2] Such a procedure would have led at any time to a grave friction in the case of the Free State. The two Governors-General who were appointed before 1930 were both distinguished national figures. The second was actually a distinguished civil servant. He was High Commissioner for the Free State in London at the time of his appointment. This implies that the Executive Council exerted an initiative in the making of the appointment, a practice that was exceptional before 1930. Subsequent to the Imperial Conference in that year, an Australian was, for the first time, appointed to be Governor-General of the Commonwealth. In 1932 the third Governor-

---

[1] *Iris Oifigiúil*, November 29, 1932.
[2] Professor Noel Baker, *The Present Juridical Status of the British Dominions in International Law*, p. 233.

The Executive

General of the Free State was appointed, on the advice of the first Fianna Fail administration. The hostility of this Government to the office led, as a matter of policy, to the appointment of a quite undistinguished Irishman. In effect the office is now one whose continued existence is a matter of party politics.

In the debate in the Constituent Assembly it was proposed to change the title "Governor-General." The title was defended on the grounds that "it has a known signification with known functions and known limitations."[1] These reasons emphasize the evolutionary as opposed to the static character of the office. The emphasis was more pronounced when the question of appointment was raised. It was suggested that, instead of reference to Canadian practice, an express provision should be inserted to the effect that the Representative of the Crown should be appointed "with the assent of the Executive Council."[2] The amendment was resisted on the ground that the definition would hamper future development. Should Canada attain to the position of electing her own Governor-General, the Free State under the original clause would share the fruit of this advance. The adoption of the amendment, it was claimed, would stereotype a position which is capable of development elsewhere. The amendment was rejected and subsequent events have justified the attitude of the Provisional Government. The position in respect of the powers and appointment of the Governor-General was successively strengthened at the Imperial Conferences held in 1926 and in 1930.

As in the mode of appointment, so also in the nature of the powers of the Representative of the Crown, the Irish Free State has played no inconsiderable part in securing a modification of the older practice. The restrictions on the discretionary power of the Representative of the Crown are imposed in the Constitution, and receive subsequent modifications in the reports of the Imperial Conference. We have

---

[1] *Dáil Debates*, vol. 1, col. 1626.
[2] Amendment by Mr. Gavan Duffy, *Dáil Debates*, vol. 1, col. 1785.

already dealt with the position and powers of the Crown in the Legislature. In the Executive the same tendencies are evident. The exercise of the Governor-General's Executive power was confined within the limits of the practice and constitutional usage of the Dominion of Canada. Moreover, each individual function was subjected to a restrictive proviso which rendered it purely formal. These powers may be considered under two principal headings. First, we have the position of the Governor-General as titular head of the National Executive, and secondly, his position in respect of inter-Commonwealth relations.

In internal affairs the powers and duties fulfilled by the head of a State, governed under the Cabinet system, are threefold; namely, when a ministry is appointed, during its continuance, and when it ends. In the Free State Constitution the Governor-General is empowered to appoint an Executive Council "to aid and advise in the government of the Irish Free State."[1] He cannot, however, exercise any choice. The President of the Executive Council is elected by the Dáil and the other ministers are nominated by the President. No discretionary power whatsoever is given to the Head of the State in the formation of the ministry. This practice was dictated, not by constitutional expediency, but by the nature of the office of the Representative of the British Crown. In the last century Walter Bagehot, with quiet irony, disposed of the idea that the House of Commons should "appoint the premier, quite simply, just as the shareholders of a railway choose a director."[2] Yet that is the actual proceeding in the Dáil. No disadvantages have so far become apparent. The result is, however, to throw more power into the hands of the Executive Council. The lack of any discretionary power vested in the Head of the State, in certain circumstances, might lead to uncertainty and encourage intrigues within the Chamber. Such circumstances are unlikely to arise unless and until a group system evolves. The present predominance of two large parties,

[1] Art. 51. [2] *The English Constitution*, p. 62.

both possessing leaders neither of whose positions is contested by the rank and file of their respective parties, would in any event have left no scope for the exercise of discretionary authority by the Representative of the Crown. Should Proportional Representation lead eventually to a multiplicity of parties, then a choice by the Head of the State (assuming that the office of Governor-General is radically transformed or replaced) would clarify the situation. In France, where such a position frequently arises, the President of the Republic exercises a discretionary choice. He must choose a man who has the confidence of the majority of the Chamber. A majority may frequently be formed by several different combinations among the various groups, so that the President is not always limited to one particular politician.[1] Such a choice is not entrusted to the Governor-General. As yet the lack of it has had, so far as can be seen, no influence on the course of political events. In the Dáil the majority makes the ministry. In the French Chamber the ministry makes the majority. Should some form of group government emerge in Ireland, than a choice by the Head of the State would possess advantages over a direct vote in the Dáil.

During the continuance of the ministry the Governor-General has no authority either in advising or in influencing the Executive Council. His office represents the formal embodiment of Executive power. It represents nothing more. It has been noticed that at the opening of the Dáil the Governor-General's speech is no longer delivered. Whilst legislation is promulgated in his name, the legislative practice of the Free State has emphasized the narrow limit of his authority. The "Governor-General in Council" is a phrase which has never appeared on the Irish Statute Book. There are certain, but very few, statutes which give statutory powers to the Governor-General. In every such case the constitutional practice is explicitly stated.[2] Thus it is to "the Governor-General acting

[1] Cf. Sait, *Government and Politics of France*, pp. 50-52.
[2] E.g. Finance Act, 1927, section 4.

on the advice of the Executive Council" (or some similar expression) that such powers are given.

The most remarkable restrictions on the discretionary authority of the Governor-General is to be found in the exercise of the power of dissolution. In the Dominions the Representative of the Crown enjoys the same status in relation to the administration of public affairs as is enjoyed by the King in Great Britain. Though this position has not been defined in constitutional law, the extent of the authority it confers is to be gathered from a series of precedents. In the Free State no vestige of such discretionary authority is left in the hands of the Governor-General. The President of the Executive Council may advise a dissolution only when he retains the support of the majority in Dáil Eireann.[1] A defeated ministry may not advise a dissolution. In respect of the position of the Governor-General this proviso denies to him any discretionary power. He must accept the advice of a President who retains the support of a majority in the Dáil; he cannot accept the advice of one who has lost it. In fact, this denies to a ministry the right to appeal to the country against the Legislature in which they are defeated.

In respect of the external character of the office of Governor-General the tendency in the Free State has been to emphasize its national as opposed to its Commonwealth aspect. In accordance with the constitutional practice of the Dominions the Governor-General is the Representative of the Crown in the Free State. The Executive Council has reduced to a mere formality any significance in this rôle as the official intermediary between the Crown and the Dominion. The position of the Governor-General as the King's representative in the Dominions was defined by the Imperial Conference in 1926. It was declared, that "it is an essential consequence of the equality of status existing among members of the British Commonwealth of Nations, that the Governor-General of a Dominion is the Representative of the Crown holding in all essential respects

---

[1] Art. 53.

The Executive

the same position in relation to the administration of public affairs in the Dominion, as is held by His Majesty the King in Great Britain, and that he is not the representative or agent of His Majesty's Government in Great Britain or of any Department of that Government."[1] This statement covers the actual position held by the Governor-General of the Free State in his relation to the Crown. The persons nominated emphasized the national character of the office. In another respect, however, this statement of the Imperial Conference cannot with accuracy be applied to the position in the Free State. The Governor-General of the Free State does not "hold in all essential respects the same position in relation to the administration of public affairs . . . as is held by H.M. the King in Great Britain." He possesses no discretionary Executive authority. That still remains an essential feature in the part played by the Crown in Great Britain.

The continued existence of the office of Governor-General has become one of the more prominent political questions of the day. Neither limitation of function nor nationalization of the character of the office has enabled it to avoid the hostility of the Republican parties. Had the Constituent Assembly not been confined within the formal framework of the Dominions Constitution, it would, no doubt, have vested a larger measure of discretionary power in the Head of the State. As it is, the latter, being the Representative of a Crown whose status is viewed with hostility by Irish Republicans, is deprived of constitutional powers which such an officer of State might with advantage exercise. It is inconceivable (should the office survive) that any administration will increase the Executive authority of the Representative of the Crown. The tendency is towards a diminution of power, and every such diminution increases the authority of the President of the Executive Council. In effect he combines the powers and privileges of two offices. He is both President and Prime Minister.

[1] Summary of Proceedings, p. 16. Cmd. 2768.

THE EXPERIMENT OF THE "EXTERN" MINISTRIES

The Cabinet system has been seen to best advantage when working under the two-party system. The alternating predominance of each of the parties, combined with a suppression of the initiative of the private member, were consequences which the Constituent Committee had no desire to see reproduced in Irish political life. The principle of non-parliamentary ministries was introduced to eliminate the evils of the Cabinet system. We shall see later to what extent this object might have been achieved. Here it is sufficient to remark on one miscalculation involved. The Constituent Assembly contemplated an emergence of the group system as a consequence, partly of the character of Irish political life, but more largely because of the electoral system. The division of opinion on the Treaty issue falsified these hopes. The continued existence of a form of non-parliamentary Executive would thereby in any event have been jeopardized. The actual form of this Executive aroused considerable interest. It did not conform to any type, but rather represented an amalgam of the Swiss and English systems. The Swiss Executive was the inspiration for the creation of the extern ministries. Its influence was reinforced by a hostility to the rigidity of the Cabinet system.[1]

The Draft Constitution[2] of June 1922 remodelled not merely the framework, but also the fundamental requirements of the

[1] The origin of the extern ministries is not entirely clear. Kohn implies that it was derived directly from the "technical" ministers in the Republican Constitution adopted by the Revolutionary Dáil of 1919. In the Cabinet then established there was appointed in addition to the "Cabinet" ministers a Director of Trade who was not to be a member of the Cabinet. The post was created solely because of administrative and military convenience. It appears inaccurate to suggest that it exerted any direct influence on the proposals of the Draft Constitution. These proposals were the response of the Constituent Committee to certain defects in the Cabinet system, and so far as can be ascertained owed nothing to the precedent established in 1919. See, however, Kohn, p. 273.

[2] Draft Constitution, Arts. 50–59.

The Executive

Cabinet system. The proposals were subjected to a lengthy and somewhat haphazard criticism in the Dáil, and emerged in the Constitution so amended as to destroy both the balance of the system and its original purpose. Under the proposals put forward in the Draft Constitution an Executive Council, responsible to the Dáil, is to consist of not more than twelve Ministers.[1] Of these twelve ministers four at least must be members of the Dáil. The remaining eight are to be chosen from all citizens who are eligible for membership of the Dáil, but they shall not during their term of office be members of either House.[2] If they are members at the time of appointment they must vacate their seats. In normal circumstances it was proposed therefore that there should be four ministers, who are members of the Legislatures, and eight non-parliamentary ministers. These provisions were not rigid; upon occasion a particular minister or ministers, not exceeding three, of the non-parliamentary group, might be members of either House if so determined by the House on a motion moved by the President.

The parliamentary ministers held a position similar to that held by the Cabinet ministers in England. The President is appointed on the nomination of the Dáil. The remaining three are to be appointed by the Dáil on the nomination of the President. The latter, in effect, selects his colleagues. These ministers are to be bound by the traditional conventions of the parliamentary system. They must be members of the Dáil; they are collectively responsible; they must resign should the support of the majority in the Dáil be withdrawn. It was provided that the more important political offices were to be in their hands. The four parliamentary ministers are to include[3] the President of the Council and the Vice-President. They were to have complete control over all matters relating to foreign affairs.[4] It was suggested, moreover, by the minister in charge of the Bill, that the four parliamentary ministers

---

[1] Draft Constitution, Art. 50.
[2] Ibid.
[3] Ibid., Art. 51.
[4] Ibid., Art. 54.

should include the Minister for Defence and the Minister for Home Affairs. The President and Vice-President, he suggested, should also hold portfolios, namely, the Ministries for External Affairs and for Finance.[1] The parliamentary ministers would thereby have under their control and be responsible for all matters relating to External Affairs, National Defence, and Finance.

The status and functions of the non-parliamentary ministers rested on a quite different basis. During their term of office they were not to be members of either House. Acceptance of office involved the vacation of a seat held in the Legislature. Extra-parliamentary status was mandatory.[2] In exceptional circumstances, however, it was allowed that on the motion of the President the Dáil might permit a number of ministers, not exceeding three, to be members of the Legislature. The non-parliamentary ministers were to be nominated, not by the President, but by a special Committee of the Dáil. The method of composing this Committee, a matter of considerable importance, was not decided, but it was to be chosen so as to be fairly representative of the Dáil.[3] The Committee was to nominate each minister for a particular ministry. The nominations were to be submitted to the Dáil individually for acceptance. The ministers were to be chosen "with due regard to their suitability for office, and should as far as possible be generally representative of the Irish Free State as a whole rather than of groups or of parties."[4] The nature of these ministerial offices was clarified by the provision that, should arrangements for functional or vocational councils be made, such ministers may be members of and be nominated on the advice of the councils.[5] Though the councils never materialized, yet the proposal shows the drastic nature of the suggestions put forward. Not merely would the control of the Legislature be diminished, but a very extensive administrative decentralization would appear to be involved. Each of these

[1] *Dáil Debates*, vol. 1, col. 1254.   [2] Draft Constitution, Art. 52.
[3] Ibid.   [4] Ibid.   [5] Ibid., Art. 53.

non-parliamentary ministers would possess all the privileges enjoyed by members of the Dáil except the right to vote.[1] They were entitled to speak. They might be required to attend the Dáil to answer questions in respect of their official duties. They would hold office for the whole term of the Dáil. They would not resign on the parliamentary defeat of the President and his colleagues. At the same time they were to act collectively as an Executive with the parliamentary ministers. Moreover, they were to be individually responsible to the Dáil for their respective ministries. During their term of office such a minister was to be irremovable, unless a report were presented by a parliamentary Committee declaring that he had been guilty of malfeasance in office, incompetence, and unsatisfactory performance of his duties, or failure "to carry out the lawfully expressed will of the Oireachtas."[2] It was intended that the non-parliamentary ministers should hold internal ministries of a technical as opposed to a political character.[3] The minister in charge of the Constitution Bill suggested the following ministries—Education, Justice, Post Office, Trade and Commerce, Local Government, Public Health, Agriculture, Labour, Fine Arts.

Such was the broad outline of the proposals put forward in the final Draft Constitution. They deserve examination from two points of view. In the first place the object of this structure of the Executive was to eliminate certain evils deemed inseparable from the Cabinet system. In the second its more positive purpose was to establish, in the more technical departments of internal administration, ministers appointed on the ground of special knowledge or ability. At a period when capacity and technique were essential in order to reconstruct the basis of the new State, it was felt that ministers appointed on political grounds would not prove equal to the task. Moreover, in order to build on a sound foundation, it was considered essential to secure a permanence of policy and a certain con-

---

[1] Draft Constitution, Art. 55.   [2] Ibid., Art. 53.
[3] *Dáil Debates*, vol. 1, col. 1255.

tinuity of personnel. In these circumstances it is not surprising that the Swiss Constitution attracted no inconsiderable attention. The Federal Council—the Swiss Executive—provided a solution to the problem confronting the Constituent Committee. It has three outstanding virtues. It is non-partisan. It enables administrative talent to be retained in the service of the nation. It secures continuity of policy.[1] Moreover, it coincided with Irish political speculation which regarded with disfavour the supremacy of large parties. The proposals were experimental. The acuteness of the administrative problem was their *raison d'être*. Not merely had a new political entity come into being, but also it would be many years before a well-trained and efficient civil service could be organized. Peculiar needs, it was felt, required exceptional remedies.

Before dealing with the technical devolution involved in the creation of the non-parliamentary ministries, the nature of the defects in the Cabinet system, which it was hoped by these means to eliminate, must be indicated. The framework of the British Cabinet system rests upon four principal foundations.[2] The first is the doctrine of collective responsibility. Each minister supervises the work of a particular department, and for that department he is individually answerable. But at the same time all ministers are jointly responsible for all the larger measures of policy. The second basis of the system is that the Cabinet is answerable immediately to the majority of the House of Commons and ultimately to the electorate. Thirdly, the Cabinet is, except under uncommon and peculiar circumstances, selected exclusively from one party. Finally, the Prime Minister is the keystone of the Cabinet arch. He chooses his colleagues and assigns to them their respective offices. Such are the fundamental conventions of the Cabinet system. Even a brief mention suffices to show the extent of the innovation proposed in the Draft Constitution. Each and every one of the main planks of the system were

[1] Bryce, *Modern Democracies*, vol. i, pp. 397–399.
[2] Morley, *Walpole*, chap. 7.

The Executive

to be remodelled in a manner which affected the whole balance of the Executive power. It was felt the framework of the Cabinet involved a rigid party system with whose evils the Constituent Assembly was so unfavourably impressed. That framework was to be fundamentally reconstituted. "The intention of the whole scheme" (of non-parliamentary ministers), said the minister[1] in charge of the Bill, "is to forestall the party system of government. The party system as in England depends for its effective working on two great parties." The defects of the English Cabinet system were subjected to a careful analysis. The Cabinet has control of the time of the House. The private member has no adequate power of initiation. He has not an independent vote. He has little effective influence in determining policy or shaping legislation. He has no freedom of thought, still less freedom of decision. Ministers are appointed for political services. No adequate consideration is paid to special ability or technical knowledge. Choice of ministers is not merely confined to the Legislature; it is confined to the largest party within the Legislature. Even on what may be termed technical or administrative measures, voting is very rarely on the merits of the proposal. It is made a party question. In the establishment of a new order, where progressive and constructive legislation was of first importance, such a practice would be disastrous. Continuity of policy was impossible under the two-party system. The swing of the pendulum replaced extreme conservatism by extreme radicalism. These evils, the minister maintained,[2] would be intensified by the introduction of Proportional Representation. A multiplicity of parties, arising from that electoral system, would lead to ministerial instability. Frequent changes in the Executive would prejudice the successful application of a constructive policy.

Such, in brief, is an analysis of the defects which the new proposals were intended to remove. The underlying principle on which this hope was based, was that it was possible to

[1] K. O'Higgins, *Dáil Debates*, vol. 1, col. 1256.
[2] *Dáil Debates*, vol. 1, col. 1257.

separate the technical from the political problems of government. Switzerland is the only democracy which has found a means of keeping its administrators practically out of party politics.[1] But the Executive in that country is contrived on more simple lines than those suggested in the Draft Constitution. It was the dualism of the proposed Executive that gave the most valid ground for criticism. It seems probable that by the appointment of non-parliamentary ministers certain of the defects of the Cabinet system would have been diminished, if not destroyed. A guarantee that some attention would be paid to administrative ability was assured by the proviso that such ministers should not be members of the Legislature during their term of office. While arousing very considerable criticism, their exclusion was justified on political, if not on historical grounds. Ministers, while remaining members of the Legislature, could not fail to become involved in the controversies of party warfare. On the other hand it took no account of Executive practice in Switzerland, where members of the Federal Council are permitted to be chosen from outside the Legislature, but who in actual practice are almost invariably selected from the members of either House.[2] The extra-parliamentary ministers, moreover, were to enjoy privileges and powers which would not permit of their subordination to the parliamentary Executive. They were to enjoy the authority of Cabinet status. They would be in a position to influence Cabinet decisions. They would not be collectively responsible. They would retain office independently of party support. They would therefore introduce measures of an administrative nature which could be examined on their inherent merits. The defeat of such a measure would not lead to resignation. Matters of technical importance would be given the attention they deserve, and would not be subjected to the narrowing influence of party politics. Consequently, private members would exercise a greater influence on legislation, and would vote in accordance

[1] Bryce, op. cit., vol. i, p. 394.
[2] R. C. Brooks, *Government and Politics of Switzerland*, p. 108.

with their individual judgment. Finally, and most important of all, the administration of the country would be in the hands of men selected, not for political services, but on account of technical qualifications. These men would hold office long enough to enable a constructive programme to be set in motion; they would not hold office long enough for their methods and policy to become "groovy" or departmental. They would be divorced from political associations; they would not be in a position to govern independently of public opinion.

The testing point in the proposals put forward in the Draft Constitution lay in the relations to be established between the parliamentary and the non-parliamentary Executive. This question may be regarded in its two aspects. Firstly, would a conflict arise between the two branches of the Executive? Secondly, would Executive responsibility be diminished?

The position of the parliamentary ministers was, it will be remembered, governed by the traditional practice of the Cabinet system. In their hands, it was provided, complete control over external affairs should rest.[1] This control was necessitated by the position of the Free State in respect of its membership of the British Commonwealth of Nations. It is because of that all-important and controversial issue that the practice of modern parliamentary countries is set aside. In Great Britain, in France, and in the United States foreign policy is to some extent secluded from the violence of party strife. In France there is, in spite of changing ministries, a pronounced tendency for the Minister for Foreign Affairs to retain his position in successive Cabinets. In Great Britain also the tendency is to withdraw foreign affairs so far as is possible from party debate. It was also suggested that in addition to external affairs the parliamentary ministers should have control over Finance, Defence, and probably Home Affairs.[2] They were collectively responsible to the Dáil and had to resign on an adverse vote. Responsibility means power.

[1] Draft, Art. 54.   [2] *Dáil Debates*, vol. 1, col. 1254.

On that ground it was maintained that the parliamentary ministers would form an inner Cabinet, and would thereby direct the whole administration. Moreover, the control of finance gave them a very real measure of authority over their non-parliamentary colleagues. On the other hand, in ordinary circumstances the "extern" ministers would number eight. They would therefore compose a considerable majority in the Cabinet. They would enjoy a definite term of office, untroubled by adverse parliamentary votes. Thus the co-existence of two types of ministers, holding office by different authority and under different conventions, would sooner or later have led to tension. The control of finance would no doubt have proved the decisive factor. Moreover, there was a probability that the Dáil would be hostile to ministers who were not deputies and who governed by a "bureaucratic" policy.

Similar considerations arise in defining the nature of Executive responsibility. On this question criticism in the Constituent Assembly was directed against the difficulty in fixing responsibility. The extern ministers were individually responsible. Were they responsible for the financial resolutions affecting their departments, or was the Minister of Finance and his parliamentary colleagues who introduced them? If the latter, then that gave them a real control over the policy of extern departments. Then, again, it was possible that the extern ministers would be made responsible to the Dáil by the invocation of the clause, providing for their removal on the ground of failure "to carry out the lawfully expressed will of Parliament."[1] This weapon might be used to secure that responsibility to the majority in the Legislature which it was intended to avoid. There can be but little doubt the proposed Executive might be subjected to considerable misuse. It contained the seeds of many possible conflicts. In it, in President Wilson's phrase, "Responsibility was spread thin."

The basic principle underlying the proposal is the existence of a dividing line between the political and administrative

[1] Draft, Art. 53.

The Executive

duties of government. The reality of that division is a question which does not permit of a categorical reply. It is a matter of emphasis rather than of fact. The Swiss Executive is a refutation of the claim that administration cannot be carried out independent of political motive force. It does appear, however, that the Provisional Government drew the dividing line too much in favour of the administrative point of view. An examination of the ministries, mentioned as suitable for administration by the non-parliamentary ministers,[1] makes it evident that they cannot all be placed in the same category. In departments such as the Post Office, Fine Arts, Justice, and possibly Public Health, the emphasis is on the administrative work. But surely in Education, in Labour, in Agriculture, the emphasis is on the policy to be pursued. It is on issues which concern these departments that elections are fought. This is a criticism of detail, but it is a detail which might require the remodelling of the whole scheme. For is it not too much to expect the electorate and the elected to allow departments, on whose policy an election has been decided, to be controlled by an administrative personnel? None the less the sponsors of the principle of non-parliamentary ministries have received no little justification from the progress of government in other countries. It has been increasingly felt that the needs of modern administration are not answered when departments are in the control of ministers appointed for political services. It is as a direct result of this practice that the administrative departments of State have acquired an immense accession of power. "Despite the fact," writes Dr. Robson,[2] "that Parliament places annually upon the Statute Book an ever-increasing burden of legislative efforts, it is nevertheles true to say that the centre of gravity in English government has shifted from legislation to administration in the past half-century, and the hegemony of the Executive, whether we like it or not, is an accomplished fact."

It was suggested that the institution of non-parliamentary

[1] See p. 159.   [2] *Justice and Administrative Law*, p. 33.

ministers was opposed to democratic theory.[1] In this claim there was substantial justification. The ministers were not elected by the people. They enjoyed security of tenure during the life of the Dáil, nor were they directly amenable to its will. They could be removed only for malfeasance in office, incompetence, or failure to carry out the will of Parliament.[2] It may be maintained, however, that the danger lay in another direction. Such provisions are susceptible of a wide interpretation, and it was possible that the ministers would be removed by the majority on no adequate grounds at all. In aspiring to make the Chamber a deliberative assembly, the framers of the Draft Constitution had to guard against the tyranny of the majority. It was suggested that this end would be more simply achieved by the insertion of a constitutional provision to the effect that an adverse vote on a departmental measure should be divested of the character of an adverse vote on the Government as a whole.[3] Such a proposal seems, however, to be quite impracticable.

THE FAILURE OF THE EXPERIMENT

The proposals presented in the Draft Constitution were a courageous experimental attempt to solve a peculiarly difficult problem. The same cannot be said for the articles dealing with the Executive which emerged in the Constitution. In the Draft the extern ministries presented a striking innovation. Subsequent modifications have deprived the idea of its creative force, and since then the history of these proposals has become nothing but a long and rather dreary epilogue. The Constituent Assembly approved the principle of the Executive proposals. A Committee was appointed to revise and inquire

[1] *Dáil Debates*, vol. 1, col. 1322.
[2] Ibid., K. O'Higgins, col. 1316.
[3] It was proposed by Lord R. Cecil in 1914 Committee on Procedure, and regarded as impossible on the ground that there could be no agreement or acknowledgement by Party leaders that a defeat in legislation did not matter.

The Executive

into the details. The Committee report led to a renewed debate on the principle. On this occasion the previous vote was reversed. The principle was rejected. Ultimately the recommendations of the Committee were moved as individual amendments to the articles in the Draft Constitution.

In the Constitution the vitality of the scheme disappeared. Apart from modifications in the status and authority of the extern ministers, the appointment of such ministers was no longer mandatory. It was permissive. Moreover, they were no longer to be members of the Executive Council. They were, in fact, specifically excluded.[1] Membership of the Dáil was not to be incompatible with the tenure of an extern ministry. The number of such ministers was not fixed. It was not provided (as it had been in the Draft) that such ministers were to compose a majority on the Executive Council. The position of the Executive Council, now composed only of parliamentary ministers, was correspondingly strengthened. Its members were to number not more than seven, and not less than five,[2] in a total of not more than twelve ministers. The parliamentary ministers might thus form a majority. It was formally provided that the Executive Council should include the President, the Vice-President, and the Minister for Finance.[3] Of more importance was the provision that the Executive Council should prepare the Estimates for each financial year.[4] In effect this deprived the extern ministers of adequate control over the affairs of their departments. It amounted to a re-assertion of collective Executive responsibility. Administration was subordinated to policy.

The framework of the Executive, as it emerged in the Constitution, was the result of a compromise. It suffered the fate that commonly awaits half-measures. It paved the way

---

[1] Art. 52. [2] Art. 51.
[3] Art. 52. The Minister of Finance was not specifically mentioned in the Draft. [4] Art. 54.

for the emergence of a powerful Cabinet system. This orientation of Executive power was facilitated by the method in which the extern ministers were appointed. They were to be nominated by a Committee impartially representative of, and elected by, the Dáil. On such a Committee the majority could select their party nominees, and in turn the Government majority in the House would secure their election. The ministers remained individually responsible and enjoyed security of tenure throughout the whole length of the Dáil. Both their power and their significance had, however, disappeared. Except in the mode of their appointment, the position of the extern ministers had become similar to that of the so-termed "technical" ministers who are appointed from outside the Legislature in Continental Cabinets. In France the Ministers of War and Marine are frequently professional men having no connection with politics. It is maintained that these two departments occupy a peculiar position because they are technical services.[1] In the Free State, on the contrary, all of the "extern ministers" appointed were politicians.

The weakness of the ultimate Executive proposals of the Constituent Assembly is shown by the history of their brief existence. In the first Dáil assembled, after the enactment of the Constitution, three extern ministers were appointed. The departments for which they were responsible were those of Agriculture, Postal Services, and Fisheries. In the following Dáil the number was increased by the addition of an extern minister for the department of Local Government. The procedure adopted in the selection of these ministers is of interest. The President, on election by the Dáil, nominates his colleagues on the Executive Council. The Dáil approves these nominations. Then the President, if he so desires, submits a list of ministries whose heads shall not be members of the Executive Council. A Committee is thereupon elected by the Dáil, voting on principles of Proportional Represen-

[1] Sait, op. cit., p. 70.

tation. This Committee recommends persons to be nominated to these ministries. Should a nomination of the Committee be rejected by the Dáil, the Committee continues to recommend names till one is found to be acceptable. No person may be nominated except by the Committee. This machinery places no obstacle in the way of party election. In effect all the extern ministers have been the nominees of the Executive Council. They have all been members of the Dáil. The Government majority in the Chamber secured their election. They have all been active politicians. In such circumstances the Government controlled every department of State. The continued existence of the "extern ministries" served no useful purpose. The complexity of the system was confusing. Since ministers were not appointed for technical ability, the most striking feature of the innovation disappeared. It was therefore a matter of no surprise that the experiment of extern ministers was virtually abolished by amendment in 1927.[1] Under the Constitutional Amendment Act passed that year it was allowed that the Executive Council might comprise the total number of ministers authorized by the Constitution. The President had the power to decide whether or no he would suggest the appointment of any external ministers. None have been proposed since 1927. It is unlikely that in the future a President will weaken the authority of the Executive Council by the appointment of ministers individually responsible to the Dáil. In the debate on the amendment the minister in charge declared its object was to give more latitude and discretionary authority to the President than was allowed under the Constitution. He added[2] that "our experience of the working of the extern minister idea has led us to think that it is not as valuable a constitutional idea as we once thought it would be."

In the Free State the Executive is now established on the broad principles of the Cabinet system. Its evolution was

[1] Constitution Amendment Act, No. 5 (No. 13 of 1927).
[2] 1926, *Dáil Debates*, vol. 17, cols. 417–420.

facilitated by the course of events. A division of opinion on the Treaty issue prevented the growth of a multiplicity of parties. The ministries have been remarkable, not for instability, but for stability. Long periods of office have so far been the rule. In such conditions the non-political ministries had but little chance of surviving. At elections political questions have provided the issue between the parties. Should public attention become focussed on economic and administrative questions, the atmosphere would prove more favourable to non-parliamentary ministries. Because of their failure to survive, it has been somewhat hastily assumed that the extern ministries were called into being to solve a non-existent problem. That the assumption is unjustified is shown by an examination of the proceedings of the Dáil. Voting is almost invariably on party lines. The Chamber is not a deliberative assembly. The fears entertained by the proposers of the non-parliamentary ministries have been realized, and the significance of the issue is illustrated by the manner in which the present system has redressed the balance; namely, by the withdrawal of administrative measures from the competence of the Legislature. Such measures require examination on their technical merits. They are unlikely to receive it in the Dáil. In its place they are dealt with by the trained departmental civil servants under the wide powers and discretionary authority which the Executive enjoys. The formal solution, by means of non-parliamentary ministers, having proved impracticable, it has been replaced by an informal growth of departmental control. We shall examine this development later. Here it is sufficient to remark that in both cases it has been found necessary to withdraw administrative and technical governmental questions from an active control by the Legislature. This is, no doubt, an inevitable result of the increasing complexity of modern government. But it is to be observed that it is opposed to democratic theory. The extern ministers were undemocratic, in that they were not elected by the people and in that they enjoyed security of tenure during the life of the Dáil. Control of technical legislation by the departments is also undemocratic, in that the civil servants are not directly responsible to the people. In both cases the Legislature does exercise a measure of indirect control. In both cases we see what has been termed "democracy at one remove."

CHAPTER X

THE MINISTERS. THEIR POLITICAL RÔLE

The evolution of the Executive in the Free State on the broad principles of the Cabinet system is now complete, in that no party sponsors an appointment to the extern ministries. The Executive Council fills the rôle of the British Cabinet. It is the centre of gravity in the parliamentary system. It is the agent which serves to co-ordinate the different organs of government. The ministers govern the country. In association with the permanent Civil Service, they superintend the administration. Increasing centralization augments their authority. The advance of State Socialism enlarges the field of governmental action under their control. The interests of the individual are affected at countless points. Finally, in the Oireachtas, the ministers take the initiative in shaping all important legislative proposals. There, at the same time, they must defend and explain their administrative conduct. Their tenure of office is dependent upon the vote of the Dáil. Under the existing two-party system such tenure is secure. Only once[1] has a ministry been defeated during the life of the Dáil.

In the Constitution the position of the Executive Council is defined with precision. The manner of its appointment differs from that of the British Cabinet in that the President is not nominated by the Head of the State, but is directly elected by the Dáil. In turn he nominates his colleagues. Acceptance by the Dáil must precede their appointment. In practice, however, this provision has no effect, in that opposition to the nominees of the President would be regarded as a vote of "no confidence." The direct election of the President by the Chamber was designed to raise the status of the Legislature. In that respect it has proved ineffective. The election of the Executive does not, in reality, rest with the Legislature. It

[1] The Cumann na nGaedheal Administration in 1930.

rests with the people. In the Free State the issue at a General Election is: which party is to provide the ministry. The President is, in effect, appointed by the people and in turn he has not a free hand in the appointment of his colleagues. Popular opinion indicates the men in whom it wishes to entrust the government, and the President, whilst retaining a certain and in some cases decisive choice, is at the same time bound to follow a clearly expressed wish of the people or more particularly of the party of which he is the leader. Moreover, in the selection of his colleagues the President must think as much of their political strength as of their administrative efficiency. He must pay as much attention to the qualities they display in the Legislature as to their technical abilities.[1]

THE PRESIDENT

The President of the Executive Council fills a position corresponding to that of the Prime Minister in Great Britain. He is the apex of the governmental system. It is paradoxical that in the Free State, where the pre-eminence of the President is so striking, that in the Constitution his status is lowered to an extent which at first sight seems incompatible with the Cabinet system. The President is not given a free hand in selecting his colleagues. He must submit their names collectively for approval to the Dáil. His field of choice is limited. With one exception, all his Cabinet[2] colleagues must be chosen from the Dáil. The exception is in favour of the Senate. Not till 1932[3] did the President make use of this power. In addition, the number of his colleagues is limited. It may not exceed twelve or be less than five.[4] He must retire from office should he fail to retain the support of a majority in the Dáil.[5] He can

---

[1] The dependence on influence, as opposed to ability, is less marked in the Free State than (for example) in Great Britain, owing to the keenness of party politics and of party criticism.

[2] Excluding extern ministers.

[3] Senator Connolly, Minister for Posts and Telegraphs in the Fianna Fail Administration.   [4] Art. 51.   [5] Art. 51.

exercise no discretion. Finally, and perhaps most significant, the President does not possess any but a very limited authority in dissolving the Dáil. In the first place, the power to advise a dissolution rests with the Executive Council as a whole, and not, as in England, with the head of the ministry.[1] Secondly, the Constitution denies to a defeated ministry the right of advising a dissolution. The effect of these two provisos is to deprive the head of the Council of those powers which *par excellence* distinguish his position from that of his colleagues. In Great Britain the power of advising a dissolution is vested in the Prime Minister alone. Under a group government, or a ministry formed on the lines of the National Government in Great Britain in 1931, the denial of such a power to the President might well prove a deciding factor in the course of events. Again, the proviso that a ministry which no longer retains the confidence of the Dáil may not advise a dissolution serves to curtail the authority of the President by diminishing that of the Council as a whole. It is none the less real on that account. The President of a coalition council cannot use the threat of dissolution to keep his colleagues stable in their allegiance.

In spite of these limitations, there can be no doubt as to the remarkable extent of the President's authority. It is wider than that exercised by the Prime Minister in Great Britain. In accounting for this pre-eminence there is no need to belittle the significance of the constitutional limitations on the President's discretion. They are by no means inconsiderable. But the fundamental basis of the President's power does not lie within the demesne of positive law. It rests rather upon the twofold foundation of popular character and the history of the Free State. Irish political life tends to produce pre-eminent but rarely eminent men. The Irish people emphasize political leadership. They place a personality before a programme. A General Election tends to become a Presidential Election. It is the leader who makes the party and not the party which

[1] Art. 53—by implication.

makes the leader. This narrowing of the political issue elevates the status of the President. There can be little question but that this tendency has been reinforced by the events of the last decade or more. In the years immediately preceding the formation of the Free State, the Republican conception of a President held sway, and later this operated to enhance the popular opinion of the office of the President of the Executive Council. Then the emergence of the new State, the civil war, and subsequent political disturbances, and finally the economic war with Great Britain were events which called for leadership. Should the political issue become less clear-cut, it is probable that public attention would not be focussed in so striking a manner on the office and personality of the President. Meanwhile, the decline and gradual extinction of the Governor-General devolves yet further influence and power upon the head of the Executive Council.

THE FORM AND STATUS OF THE EXECUTIVE COUNCIL

The Constitution has created the office of Vice-President of the Council. The Vice-President customarily holds a ministerial portfolio, there being no department attached to that office. Its existence tends to diminish the predominance usually enjoyed by the Minister for Finance. The Vice-President enjoys a higher status but smaller powers than the latter. He "acts for all purposes in the place of the President, if the President shall die, resign, or be permanently incapacitated, until a new President of the Council shall have been elected."[1] From 1927 till the resignation of the Cumann na nGaedheal administration Mr. Blythe was both Vice-President and Minister for Finance. The practice of amalgamating the two offices has not been followed. There is a decided advantage in keeping them separate, in that the capacity and character of a Minister for Finance do not often go hand in hand with those required

[1] Art. 53.

for a successful, if temporary, tenure of Presidential office. It is to be noticed that the Constitution recognizes the importance of these offices in that it specifically provides that the President of the Council, the Vice-President, and the Minister of Finance shall be members of Dáil Eireann.[1] The position of the Executive Council is similar to that of the Cabinet in Great Britain. There remain only certain rather minor differences. In the first place, the names of the ministers must be collectively proposed to the Dáil[2] for assent. No constitutional importance attaches to this practice under the two-party system. Secondly, the maximum and minimum number of Cabinet ministers is fixed by the Constitution. It is therein provided that the Executive Council "shall consist of not more than twelve nor less than five ministers, appointed by the Representative of the Crown on the nomination of the President of the Executive Council."[3] Recent practice has tended towards a small Council. The full complement of twelve ministers is not made up. In the Cumann na nGaedheal ministry of September 1927, the Executive Council was composed of nine ministers. The Fianna Fail Ministry, which succeeded it in 1932, was ten in number. Experience has suggested that a Council of this size is satisfactory, in that a smaller Council would tend to become autocratic, a larger to become inefficient. A third difference from the Cabinet system lies in the possibility of the appointment of extern ministers. Such ministers are not appointed by the Dáil unless the President proposes a list of ministries the heads of which shall not be members of the Executive Council. None have been proposed in the three last ministries. The practice of appointing comparatively small Councils necessitates a certain reliance on the under-secretaries. When a minister holds two portfolios, it is

---

[1] Art. 52 as amended.
[2] It was suggested by Mr. de Valera that the names should be submitted individually. Speaker ruled that the practice of submitting the names *en bloc* must be adhered to. *Dáil Debates*, vol. 21, col. 68.
[3] Art. 51.

The Ministers. Their Political Rôle

evident that in the Dáil and in the departments he requires assistance. It has become customary to appoint the Chief Party Whip parliamentary secretary to the President. In respect of the other ministries the Minister for Finance is assisted by a parliamentary secretary, who supervises a part of the business of that ministry. In recent ministries, members of the Executive Council have not infrequently held two portfolios. In President Cosgrave's fourth administration, formed in September 1927, Mr. Blythe was Vice-President of the Council, Minister for Finance, and Minister for Posts and Telegraphs. There served under him two parliamentary secretaries, one for Finance and one for Posts and Telegraphs. In the same ministry, Mr. McGilligan was Minister for External Affairs and for Industry and Commerce. There was a parliamentary secretary for Industry and Commerce. The same practice was followed in the subsequent Fianna Fail Administration. The Cumann na nGaedheal Council was composed of nine ministers and six parliamentary secretaries; the Fianna Fail Council of March 1932 of ten ministers and three parliamentary secretaries. In certain cases it has been the practice to appoint as secretaries persons whose services to the party are felt to merit recognition but who do not possess the qualifications needful for ministerial office.

The existence of the Cabinet, so long ingeniously disguised in English law, is expressly recognized in the Irish Free State Constitution. Not only does the Constitution make the ministers collectively[1] responsible, but also they must resign "should they cease to retain the support of the majority in Dáil Eireann."[2] The proceedings of the Council are secret, minutes are kept. The department of the President of the Council is responsible for, and has control of, the official publications of the Executive Council. These are published in the *Iris Oifigiúil*. There is a secretary and an assistant secretary to the Council. The Executive Council is responsible only to Dáil Eireann. They are collectively responsible for the general policy of the Govern-

---

[1] Art. 54 and Art. 51.   [2] Art. 53.

ment and individually for their personal acts. So long as the direction of affairs meets with parliamentary approval they remain in office. While dependent upon the vote of the Dáil, they are in no sense subservient to the Legislature. There can be no question but that the Executive assumes the rôle of leadership in the government of the country. The Council is responsible, therefore it is powerful. The extent to which the individual minister controls his department varies with the policy and personnel of the administration. In general, it seems that there is a tendency for a freer control in the Free State than in Great Britain. This is due partly to the authority of the Council as a whole in the Legislature, but more largely to the wide administrative powers vested in the departments. A constant possibility of defeat in the Dáil would no doubt weaken the independence of the ministers, but since 1922 the Executive Council has been defeated only once during the life of the Dáil. Its comparative security of tenure has enhanced its power and prestige.

In considering the Procedure of the Dáil we have noticed the extent of ministerial power. In the initiation of legislation the Executive Council enjoys what is almost a monopoly. It has a complete control over financial resolutions. It draws up the parliamentary time-table. It has means at its disposal whereby it may secure the vote upon any measure within a reasonably short time. It is, moreover, unhampered by any Committee system. There is no competition, as in France, between the *rapporteur* of a powerful Committee and the minister. There is not even a Standing Committee system as in England. More important still, the Executive Council has so far enjoyed the support of a secure majority in the Dáil. Proportional Representation has not displayed its customary characteristics. A group system of government has not evolved. The division of opinion on the Treaty issue has paved the way for majority government. Several small parties, it is true, have emerged. They have not infrequently held the balance of power. But to suppose that their existence weakens the position of the Council is a view that is merely superficial. On the all-important issue of the Treaty Settlement the smaller parties have at each election given a decisive answer. Either they support the Treaty or oppose it.[1] Either in consequence they support a pro-Treaty Government or oppose it. As a result the position of the Executive in the Dáil is secure. On the only occasion on which the Council has yet been defeated it was made apparent that so long as the Treaty issue remains predominant the alignment of parties is such that in each Dáil only one ministry is possible. There is no alternative. On March 27, 1930, the Second Reading of a Private Member's Bill to amend the existing law in regard to Old Age Pensions was carried, though opposed by the Government, by 66 votes to 64. On the following day President Cosgrave and his colleagues resigned. On the reassembly of the Dáil in April the first business considered was the election of a President. The leader of the Opposition, Mr. de Valera, was proposed. The motion was rejected by 93 votes to 54. The leader of the Labour Party was proposed, but was defeated by 78 votes to 13. Finally, Mr. Cosgrave was proposed for re-election and the motion was carried by 80 votes to 65. It is to be noticed that the Labour Party (then supporting the Treaty Settlement) voted against the election of a Fianna Fail President. Some years earlier, in 1927, there was an attempt to form an administration on a broad basis of Treaty revision. In this manner the support of Labour and the National League was added to that of Fianna Fail. A vote of "no confidence" was proposed in President Cosgrave's administration on August 16, 1927. It was moved by the leader of the Labour Party. On a division the voting was even—71 for and 71 against the motion. The Chairman gave his casting vote against the motion, which was thereupon lost. This was the only important attempt to form a

[1] The Labour Party, once pro-Treaty, are now in alliance with an anti-Treaty Government. Their change of opinion does not affect this statement in that in each successive Dáil their attitude is decisively defined.

180 The Government of the Irish Free State

ministry dependent on group support.[1] In the General Election which followed the membership of the smaller parties was considerably reduced.[2] This diminution in their numbers destroyed the material from which a coalition or group ministry might have been formed. As a result the Free State has always been governed by a party ministry. At the same time not one party[3] had a clear majority over all other parties in the Dáil before 1933. In that year the Fianna Fail Party (including the Speaker) secured 77 seats in a House whose total membership is 153.

The framers of the Irish Constitution aimed at enhancing the status of the Legislature in comparison with that of the Executive. Two means were adopted to secure that end. In the first place the conventions of the Cabinet system were reinforced by the sanction of positive law. The Constitution defines the authority of the President; it declares that resignation must follow the loss of support in the Dáil; that ministers are collectively responsible, and that they are responsible only to the popularly elected Chamber. In the second place, the powers of the Executive were diminished whilst those of the Legislature were increased. We have suggested the principal differences in the position of the individual ministers in the Free State and in Great Britain. We must now examine the variation in the powers accorded to the Executive in its relations with the Legislature in the two countries. In three cases the Executive Council is deprived of powers wielded by the Cabinet. The Constitution allows to the Oireachtas the right of fixing the date of the opening and conclusion of its session.[4] In Great Britain this right is in the hands of the Cabinet. The distinction is in effect merely one of verbiage, but it does show the trend of thought which influenced the Constituent Assembly.

---

[1] It would be inaccurate to term it a Coalition Ministry in that it was understood that Fianna Fail were not going to take seats in the new Government.

[2] Labour Representation dropped from 22 to 13, National League from 8 to 2, Farmers from 11 to 6.

[3] Till 1927 Fianna Fail did not take their seats. [4] Art. 24.

The Ministers. Their Political Rôle

A second limitation on the control of the Executive is to be found in the legislative control of foreign policy. In dealing with the Legislature, the nature and extent of this power has been considered. Here it is sufficient to remark on its constitutional import. The Free State cannot, except in the case of actual invasion, be committed to active participation in any war without the explicit assent of the Oireachtas.[1] The significance of this constitutional innovation is measured by a comparison with the practice in Great Britain. There the power of declaring war is part of the Royal Prerogative and the Cabinet enjoys the exclusive right of advising the Crown on its exercise. No Cabinet, it is true, would advise a declaration of war unless it were certain of the support of Parliament. At the same time the Cabinet may, by their conduct of foreign affairs, make war inevitable. Parliament has, after all, only a negative control. The Dáil has a positive control.

THE POWER OF DISSOLUTION

The third and more direct limitation of the authority of the Executive in its relation to the Legislature is to be found in the constitutional provision[2] which denies to a defeated ministry the power to advise a dissolution. The dissolving power is one of the key positions governing the relations between Executive and Legislature. In Great Britain an unrestricted use of the prerogative of dissolution has been maintained. Under the two-party system such a power was neither unjust nor unnecessary. It is not, however, so easily justifiable in the case of coalition ministries or government by groups. The framers of the Irish Constitution anticipated, at any rate, a tendency toward the group system. In that event a review of the nature and history of the dissolving power in France was of no inconsiderable significance. The French Chamber may be dissolved by the President with the consent of Senate.[3] Contrary to the

---

[1] Art. 49. [2] Art. 53.
[3] Constitutional Law of February 25th, Art. 5.

practice in England and the Dominions, where dissolution very frequently intervenes before the end of the mandate, the life of the Chamber has only once been interrupted in that fashion.[1] On that one occasion its use by the monarchists permanently discredited a device which Yves Guyot[2] considered "indispensable to constitute parliamentary majorities." Moreover a Cabinet in France is formed, not because it represents a majority, but because it creates one. It is in that sense less democratic than the Executive Council, for the character of the latter is determined by the people. But in attempting to avoid the evils of majority government, the Constituent Assembly did not blind itself to the faults of the French system. The new State, it was felt, required above all things stable and orderly government. The French Cabinet system is notorious for its instability; the English for its rigidity and its suppression of the Legislature. As a result of these considerations the all-important question of the dissolving power was decided in a manner which, it was hoped, would eliminate the evils of both. The ministry with a majority had a full power of dissolution; the ministry which was defeated had no power of any kind. In part, this provision was suggested by a desire to limit the discretion of the Governor-General. In that respect it has been entirely successful.

One of the most difficult tasks confronting the democratic constitutionalist of to-day is a decision on the question of the nature and extent of the power of dissolution. In accordance with modern democratic theory the right of dissolving the Representative Assembly may be regarded from three points of view.[3] If the Assembly no longer enjoys the confidence of the electors, the people either directly or through the President may cause a dissolution; if a conflict arises between ministry and Assembly the ministry before resigning have a right of appeal to the people; if the majority in the Assembly con-

---

[1] Cf. Sait, *Government and Politics of France*, p. 171.
[2] *Contemporary Review*, vol. xcvii, p. 147.
[3] Cf. Headlam-Morley, op. cit., chap. xii.

The Ministers. Their Political Rôle

siders that the existing Assembly is not fitted to fulfil its functions the Assembly may dissolve itself. In each of the post-War Constitutions provision is made for one or other of these forms of dissolution.[1] It has been found impossible to define clearly the circumstances and events which require a dissolution. The power carries with it a certain measure of discretionary authority. In the Free State this authority is vested exclusively in the hands of the Executive Council.[2] Neither the electors nor the head of the State may cause a dissolution. In the case of a contest between the Executive and Legislature the former may only dissolve whilst retaining the support of a majority in the latter. The most important application of the right of dissolution is that in which a defeated ministry may appeal to the people against a majority in the Assembly. The position of the English Cabinet is undoubtedly strengthened by the right of the Prime Minister to advise a dissolution on the defeat of the Government. Members are always afraid of the risk and expenditure involved in an election. The denial of this right to the Executive Council was intended to diminish this authority over the Assembly. It did not imply a fundamental break with the British system. But it did involve a very substantial modification.

Professor Keith[3] has analysed dissolutions in Great Britain during the last century. "Dissolutions since 1829," he writes, "have eight times out of twenty-seven been due to the approaching expiry of Parliament. Two were under the old rule that the demise of the Crown terminates Parliament, four were occasioned by disputes between the two Houses. One was the outcome of the desire of a King for a change of ministry. The remaining twelve were deliberate efforts by the Cabinet to secure from the electorate a more amenable Commons." Material for such an analysis in the Free State does not exist. A comparison of the practice since 1923[4] may serve, however, to indicate the tendencies at work. The Dáil has been dissolved

[1] Cf. Headlam-Morley, op. cit., chap. xii.   [2] Art. 28.
[3] *British Constitutional Law*, p. 49.
[4] August 1923 was the first election under the new Constitution.

four times, twice because of the approaching expiry of its term of office and twice because of a deliberate effort by the Council to secure a more amenable assembly. It will be seen at once from the foregoing comparison that the Irish practice does not deprive the Executive of its initiative in dissolution. So long as it retains its majority, it is the master of the life of the Dáil. Broadly speaking, a Government which retains the support of a majority advises a dissolution either because it requires a specific mandate from the people for the initiation of new legislation or of a new policy; or because its majority is small and unreliable; or because it considers the moment opportune for its own party interests. The two occasions on which a ministry has dissolved the Dáil were necessary because of an unreliable majority. In August 1927 the Cumann na nGaedheal Council dissolved the Dáil after it had been in existence for two months. The dissolution followed the "no confidence" motion of August 16th. The Government was saved only by the casting vote of the Speaker. Two by-elections[1] held on August 24th resulted in favour of the Government, and no doubt determined the President to dissolve the Chamber. The second occasion was on January 2, 1933. The dissolution was advised by the Fianna Fail ministry. The ministry was dependent on the votes of the Labour Party for a majority in the Dáil. Moreover, it was felt a decisive opinion on the party's programme, more particularly on the "economic war" with Great Britain, should be secured. On both occasions the dissolution of the Dáil resulted in the return of the ministry with an increased support. On both occasions an appeal to the country was justified by the position of the parties in the Dáil. This fact should not, however, blind us to the possibilities of misuse which the power of dissolution in the Free State provides. For purely party purposes an Executive Council might advise a dissolution in a moment of popular excitement in order to renew a mandate which in normal circumstances

---

[1] One of them caused by the assassination of Kevin O'Higgins, the Vice-President of the Council.

the electorate would be unlikely to support. This danger is reduced in the Free State by the remarkable insight of the people into the motives which prompt political action. As a people they are peculiarly difficult to "stampede." Besides, under Proportional Representation, a "snap" election is unlikely to be successful. A comparatively small turnover of votes will not, as in Great Britain, secure a quite disproportionate number of seats.

The phrasing of the Constitution does not leave the intention of its framers in respect of the exercise of the dissolving power quite apparent. It is not certain[1] whether or no an explicit vote of consent is required from the Dáil prior to a dissolution. The more recent (and presumably final) interpretation is that such a vote is not required. This issue is one of some practical importance. If an explicit vote of consent from the Dáil is not required then the discretion of the Executive Council is considerably augmented. Not till 1933 has any one party secured a majority in the Dáil. In consequence, the Government of the day frequently depends upon the support of allied groups. Such groups, whilst giving loyal support to the ministerial programme, might in certain circumstances decline to assent to a dissolution. In this respect a direct vote of the Dáil would hamper the discretion of the Executive. The history of the interpretation of this issue is instructive. The first Dáil subsequent to the promulgation of the Constitution was dissolved in August 1923. At a sitting of the Dáil, President Cosgrave moved "that the present session of the Oireachtas, and of each House thereof, do conclude at the termination of the sittings of the two Houses on this 9th day of August 1923. Provided that the session of Seanad Eireann shall not be concluded without its own consent."[2] The date of reassembly was pro-

---

[1] See Arts. 24 and 53.
[2] The position of the Labour Party in 1932 is a case in point. The Fianna Fail ministry depended for a majority on their support. At the same time Labour might well be opposed to an election which was not likely to improve their position.

posed and the motion agreed to.[1] The same procedure was observed prior to the dissolution of the succeeding Dáil in May 1927.[2] On August 16th in the same year (when a "no confidence" motion in the Government was defeated by the Speaker's casting vote) the Dáil adjourned to October 11th. On August 25th, however, the Dáil was dissolved by Proclamation. An election was held and the new Dáil assembled on the date October 11th—to which the old one had been adjourned. By this astute procedure the President kept within the terms of Article 24, which declared that "the Dáil shall fix the date of reassembly of the Oireachtas." It is of interest to notice that B. O'Brien[3] (writing in 1928-29) considered that "when neither House is actually in session, an Executive Council which has not been defeated in the Dáil can advise a dissolution without the consent of both Houses, but no Executive Council can cause the Oireachtas to be dissolved without its own explicit consent so long as both Houses happen to be actually in session." This statement[4] of the position subsequent to the dissolution of August 1927 has since been considerably modified. It so happened, however, that both in 1932 and 1933 the Dáil was dissolved by Proclamation while not in session. No vote of consent was sought on either occasion. The Proclamation[5] read as follows:

"Whereas by the Constitution of the Irish Free State, it is provided, that the Oireachtas shall be summoned and dissolved by the Governor-General of the Irish Free State in the name of the King and that Dáil Eireann may not at any time be dissolved except on the advice of the Executive Council; provided that the Oireachtas shall not be dissolved on the advice of an Executive Council which has ceased to retain the support of a majority in Dáil Eireann.

[1] *Dáil Debates*, vol. 3, col. 4604.   [2] Ibid., vol. 19, col. 2620.
[3] *The Irish Constitution*, pp. 82-83.
[4] It is extremely doubtful whether it was the accepted opinion even at the time it was written.   [5] Jan. 3, 1933, published in *Iris Oifigiúil*.

"And Whereas the Executive Council of the Irish Free State has advised that it is expedient to hold a General Election for Dáil Eireann and that for this purpose the Oireachtas should be dissolved.

"And Whereas the Executive Council retains the support of a majority in Dáil Eireann.

"Now therefore . . ."

The now accepted position in respect of a dissolution is this—that a Council which retains the support of a majority in the Dáil may advise a dissolution whether during a session or during an adjournment without an explicit vote from the Dáil. It is necessary to stress the scope of this new interpretation of the Constitution. In the first place it gives to the Executive Council the advantages of a surprise dissolution. Their intention need not be communicated to the Dáil. In the second place it destroys the power of the small groups, on whose alliance a ministry in the Free State frequently depends, from preventing a dissolution. It is one thing, after all, to support the legislative programme of the ministry, it is quite another to assent to a dissolution which may have drastic effects on the strength of the small allied groups. Moreover, an Executive Council, certain of defeat, could advise a dissolution before the issue arose.

It is the Convention of the Irish Constitution that the Council retains the support of a majority in the Dáil so long as it has not been defeated on an issue of major importance. If there is any doubt as to whether the ministry has that support, the Opposition, as in August 1927, can introduce a vote of "no confidence." In both the larger parties the opinion is held that the restrictive clause in the right of dissolution is in general beneficial, though its constitutional import has not, as yet, been fully tested.

Proportional Representation does not tend to create large majorities. The resultant narrowness of the ministerial majority has drawn attention to the fact that a situation might arise in which no party would enjoy a majority in the Dáil and that therefore that Chamber could not be dissolved. It is to be noted, however, that as an explicit vote of consent is no longer required from the Dáil prior to a dissolution, such a situation is less likely to arise than under the old practice. In the second place it is suggested destructive tactics of such a kind would be terminated by calling into play a certain undefined residuum of constitutional power existent in every parliamentary system.

The history of the relations between Executive and Legislature throws no light upon the constitutional import of the restrictive clause in the right of dissolution granted to the ministry. For the one occasion on which the Executive was defeated in the Dáil the vote did not imply a vote of "no confidence" in the Government. The Executive Council resigned and was re-elected. An appeal to the country would, even if possible, have been quite unnecessary. As a result, the position is that no case has arisen in which Executive is deprived of a power which, under the English system, it would certainly exercise. We are left, therefore, with the ironic reflection that the most important innovation in the Free State Constitution has proved of no significance whatsoever. But there can be no doubt that there remains an important rôle for it to fill.

MINISTERIAL AUTHORITY

The provisions of the Constitution were designed to elevate the status of the Legislature in relation to the Executive. Whilst the modifications of the Cabinet system introduced to achieve this end were of undoubted importance, they have yet failed in their object. For the paradox that we noticed in the position of the President is repeated in that of his colleagues. A formal limitation in their powers has not checked the extent of their authority. The Executive Council controls the Procedure of the Dáil, it enjoys a remarkable security of tenure, it wields a wide discretionary authority in administration. The ultimate reason for its present position is to be found in the will of the people expressed through their representatives. The people wish to be governed. They desire strong government. For this end the deputies are willing to sacrifice a certain measure of their independence. It cannot be emphasized too strongly that the Dáil is not jealous of the extensive powers of the Executive. It is continually urging greater authority, a wider discretion, upon the Executive Council and upon individual ministers. After all, both Executive and Legislature are means by which the government of a country is to be carried out. There can be no absolute separation of their respective functions. If the former becomes too predominant the remedy lies in the hands of the Legislature. It is for the Oireachtas to see that its own control is not impaired.

CHAPTER XI

THE MINISTERS. THEIR ADMINISTRATIVE RÔLE

THE ministers are more than parliamentary leaders. They are responsible for the executive departments, and through these departments they control the administration of the country. In the Oireachtas their power is very considerable. It is yet more notably displayed in their executive capacity. As heads of the Departments they enjoy a range of power which is continually widened by the growth of State activities. Their authority is further augmented in that they govern a unitary State. All matters, both of local and national concern, are subject to the will of the Oireachtas.[1] The State is highly centralized. The field of local autonomy tends to become somewhat restricted, and even where the local authorities are competent to act they yet remain in many directions under the supervision and control of the central government. It must, at the same time, be remembered that a centralization of government in no way implies a concentration of administrative power. There remains in the hands of the agents of the central government a very considerable initiative and discretion. The comparatively recent establishment of the Free State is the most powerful factor militating against excessive supervision and departmental "red tape." It is not a permanent factor, and it is probably only a matter of time before the citizens of the Free State have cause to cry out against the hydra-headed monster of accumulated regulations.

DISTRIBUTION OF THE FUNCTIONS OF GOVERNMENT

As long ago as 1861, John Stuart Mill wrote: "It is equally true, though only of late and slowly beginning to be acknow-

[1] A different position from that proposed in the Government of Ireland Act, 1920.

ledged, that a numerous assembly is as little fitted for the direct business of legislation as for that of administration."[1] It is a view to which modern conditions lend no inconsiderable justification. In the Free State as elsewhere the practice of parliamentary institutions has undergone a striking change, in that the primary initiative in legislation has been transferred from the legislative assembly to the Council. The Oireachtas is not in a position to maintain a continuous and coherent policy in the direction of legislation. Its purpose is to ventilate grievance and to discuss the broad outline of measures. It tends to legislate by principles and not by details. While this practice is held by many[2] to be unsound, it seems none the less inevitable. So long, indeed, as due attention is paid to the wishes of the Legislature, it cannot be supposed to be unhealthy. But in any event, whether approved or condemned, there can be no question but that in the Free State the stream is flowing in that direction. Moreover, it is flowing with an ever-increasing volume. The tendency is to be noticed in most countries where representative government survives. Its cause is succintly outlined in the following passage from the Macmillan Report[3]: "The most distinctive indication of the change of outlook of the government of this country in recent years has been its growing preoccupation, irrespective of party, with the management of the life of the people. A study of the Statute Book will show how profoundly the conception of the function of government has altered. Parliament finds itself increasingly engaged in legislation which has for its conscious aim the regulation of the day-to-day affairs of the community and now intervenes in matters formerly thought to be entirely outside its scope." The new orientation is the result of changes in political, social, and economic ideas. In

---

[1] *Representative Government*, chap. 5.
[2] E.g. Evidence of Lord Robert Cecil, Select Committee on Procedure, 1914.
[3] *Report of the Committee on Finance and Industry*, 1931, pp. 4-5. Cmd. 3897.

turn it has brought about a need for delegated legislation. The
Legislature is not in a position to work out coherently and
efficiently the details of large legislative changes. As a result
it has become customary to delegate minor legislative powers
to subordinate authorities and bodies. The ministers are the
principal repositories of such powers, but they are conferred
to a smaller extent upon local bodies and various institutions.

We have suggested that this development in the practice of
Representative Government is a healthy one. There is, however,
one condition upon which this viewpoint ultimately depends.
It is that the Cabinet and the ministers who compose it are
in a position to take full advantage of the new field in which
they exercise their discretionary authority. In this respect,
indeed, the Executive Council is peculiarly fortunate. In the
first place it has hitherto enjoyed comparative security of
tenure; in the second it governs a country primarily agricultural and whose internal administration is consequently a
matter of less complexity than that of most Western European
States. On the other hand, it is faced with one peculiar difficulty.
In Ireland there is no acceptance of what has been termed the
positive State. The people are intensely individualist. State
action is regarded as something coming from without. There
is no sense of a corporate body with a unity of interests. It
is, therefore, all the more remarkable that there is little or no
jealousy of the extension of ministerial powers. Outside of the
legal profession there is no general demand for their diminution. Within the Dáil, indeed, there is a not infrequent demand
for their extension. Deputies feel that the minister, with his
administrative experience, is in a better position to decide upon
matters of detail. This confidence in ministerial ability has
been engendered by the success of delegated legislation. It
possesses a coherence, a co-ordination, a flexibility which is
frequently lacking when the Oireachtas seeks to formulate
each item of a proposed measure. It makes for increased
administrative efficiency, but at the same time the extent to
which it is now employed is plainly an innovation on the

The Ministers. Their Administrative Rôle

classic form of parliamentary control. In consequence, the possibilities of its misuse merit the closest scrutiny.

From this increased dependence upon delegated legislation there has followed as a logical consequence the devolution of judicial functions upon administrative and quasi-administrative tribunals. From the decisions of these bodies there is frequently (as we shall see later) no appeal to the ordinary courts. Thus it is that in certain cases a ministerial department legislates, administers its own legislation, and decides on justiciable issues arising out of its administration.

THE EXTENT OF MINISTERIAL DISCRETION

We have suggested that the discretionary powers vested in the Free State ministers are exceptionally wide. The explanation is to be found in the large legislative output of the last ten years. The emergence of the Free State involved a comprehensive programme of reconstruction. It was largely to meet that need that the extern ministries were designed. Their failure led to an increasing dependence, in technical and administrative questions, on delegated legislation. The era of reconstruction was followed by the accession of the Fianna Fail Party to power. That party made a yet more extensive use of this means for putting its programme into practice.

The extent of ministerial power is difficult to classify in that it has been built up upon no clearly defined principles. It has not been developed in accordance with any logical system. There is no distinction drawn between the executive, legislative, and judicial functions which the ministers are empowered to perform. To deal with the problem upon the time-honoured principle of the division of powers would involve its restatement in terms which reduce its true complexity to a false simplicity. Medieval historians assert (with considerable frequency) that the early Plantagenet kings of England were intent upon the destruction of the feudal system. Were the analogy to hold good, the historian of the future will assert that the ministers of to-day are intent upon the destruction of *laissez-faire* individualism. It is obviously a very inaccurate view-point. They are intent upon better administration. The new discretionary power has been introduced because it is considered necessary to efficient government. The wiser course appears, therefore, to consider it as a whole and not purely from the point in which it interferes with accepted means of control.

DELEGATED LEGISLATION

While the system of delegated legislation has been built up, without plan or logic, there yet remains a general recognition that, in normal circumstances, there are certain limits within which the scope of such legislation should be confined. In other words, the normal type of delegated legislation has two distinguishing features:[1] one positive and the other negative. The positive characteristic is that the limits of the delegated power are defined so clearly by the Enabling Act as to be made plainly known to the Oireachtas, to the Executive, and to the public, and to be readily enforceable by the Judiciary. The negative characteristic is that delegated powers do not include power (*a*) to legislate on matters of principle or to impose taxation; (*b*) to amend Acts of Parliament, either the Act by which the powers are delegated or other Acts. Certain examples will illustrate the scope of these limitations. Under the Local Government Act,[2] 1925, the minister is empowered to make such regulations as he thinks fit as to the materials to be used in road construction, the erection of road signs, and the road signals to be used. He can, moreover, regulate the speed of any specified vehicle on any specified highway. Under the Road Transport Act of 1932 a wide discretionary power is vested in the minister. Unlicensed passenger road service is prohibited, but subject to certain provisions the minister "shall

[1] Cf. Report of Committee on Ministers' Powers, 1932. Cmd. 4060.
[2] Section 36.

have an absolute discretion to grant or refuse an application for a passenger licence." The provisions are that he shall not refuse a licence, except on certain specified grounds, to a person who carried on an existing service. In that event he may refuse only on the ground that, in his opinion, such service was not efficiently carried on; that it was not sufficient to meet the requirements of the public; that the organization and equipment at the disposal of the applicant were not such as to enable him to comply with the conditions which the minister considers should be inserted in a passenger licence, or that the minister is authorized by any other section of the Act to refuse such application. In the same way the minister, whenever he grants a passenger licence, may attach to it such conditions as he thinks proper. He may attach conditions in respect of the terminal points and route of such service, in respect of its frequency, its daily duration, the minimum number of vehicles to be kept available for its operation, the maintenance of a particular standard of fitness, cleanliness, and appearance of the vehicles used, the publication of time-tables, and the rates of wages and hours of duty of employees. Of the extent of these powers there can be no question, but they are of a type for which an administrative body is peculiarly fitted to deal. They are, broadly speaking, matters of legislative detail (with the exception of conditions which the minister may attach to wages and hours of duty of employees), and on that account could not be drafted satisfactorily by a large body. The powers of the minister to restrict or even prohibit the driving of any specified class of vehicle on any specified road (for example) are powers to which even the staunchest upholder of legislative control could scarcely object. On the other hand, in the granting of licences and in the conditions in which he may attach, the order of the minister is final and enforceable and is not subject to any review by the courts. To that extent, therefore, it is an infringement of judicial control in that the minister is empowered to perform judicial functions.

Sections of the Road Transport Bill have been quoted as

indicating the *normal* form of delegated legislation. It must be remembered that this description does not cover all the legislative powers conferred upon the minister in this particular Act. In that the minister may, by regulation,[1] prescribe a scale of maximum charges for the carriage of passengers and luggage, he is in effect empowered to legislate on a matter of policy, as opposed to a detail of administration. The same may be said of the provision[2] under which the minister in granting or refusing a licence shall have regard "to the extent to which vehicles used . . . are or will be manufactured in Saorstat Eireann, and also the extent to which such vehicles are or will be kept in repair by Saorstat Eireann labour." Now the emphasis with which the minister may or may not enforce this provision is of great importance. It is most decidedly a matter of policy which he, by regulation, is in a position to formulate. A mention of these two clauses in the Road Transport Bill is sufficient to show that in each individual Act the nature of the power delegated to the minister is incapable of being placed within a single category. What we have termed normal and exceptional forms of delegated authority are indiscriminately intermingled. With this reservation we may continue an examination of the normal form of such legislation.

Under the Intoxicating Liquor (General) Act, 1924,[3] the Minister for Justice may, by order, prescribe the sizes of the bottles in which any specified intoxicating liquor might be sold, and anyone who sold liquor in contravention of this provision was liable on summary conviction of a penalty not exceeding five pounds for the first offence, and not exceeding ten for any subsequent offence. The careful safeguarding of public rights and the clarity and precision with which the offence and the nature of the penalties are indicated make these provisions an excellent example of what may be termed the classic form of delegated legislation. A similar position is to be found in the Wireless Telegraphy Act of 1926, under which the minister may, by order, make regulations prescribing

[1] Section 23. [2] Section 21. [3] Section *a*.

the form of licences required, the period during which they are to continue in force, the terms on which they may be renewed, and the conditions to be observed by the holders. Under the Sea Fisheries Act of 1931 the Minister for Lands and Fisheries may, by order, prescribe any specified area as a district to which a specified part of the Act shall apply. He has a discretionary power in the granting of fish sales licences. Under the Agriculture Act, 1931, the minister[1] may, by order, make regulations in respect of the accounts of committees of agriculture and the audit of such accounts, and in respect of the procedure of committees of agriculture in connection with the business imposed upon them by the Act. Under the Dairy Produce Act, 1931, the minister (for Agriculture) may serve a notice in writing on a registered proprietor requiring him to keep such records as the minister shall specify of all butter manufactured, acquired, or disposed by him. Similar notices may be served on butter traders and warehousemen. If any person fails to keep the records required he shall be guilty of an offence, and liable on summary conviction to a fine not exceeding twenty pounds.

The powers which these Acts authorize the minister to exercise are of a detailed nature. It is true that in prescribing the conditions under which licences shall be issued he is exercising a legislative power, but in these cases the definition and limits of such power are sufficiently precise to provide a guarantee against misuse. The Oireachtas has outlined its policy and it leaves to the minister the duty of making such regulations as it has specifically authorized. Moreover, the legislative supremacy of the Oireachtas is customarily preserved by a proviso that such regulations must be laid before each House. The form of this reservation of authority varies considerably, but its intention is uniform. The general principle is illustrated in the section of the Dairy Produce Act, 1931, which provides[2] that: (1) "the Minister may, by order, make regulations in regard to any matter or thing referred to in this Act as pre-

---

[1] Section 40.   [2] Section 8.

scribed or as being or to be prescribed; (ii) every regulation made by the Minister under this Act shall be laid before each House of the Oireachtas as soon as may be after it is made, and if either House shall, within twenty-one days on which such House has sat after such regulation is laid before it, pass a resolution annulling such regulation, such regulation shall be annulled accordingly but without prejudice to the validity of anything previously done thereunder."

In reviewing the nature and extent of exceptional powers delegated by the Oireachtas it must be remembered that term "exceptional" indicates, not the frequency with which they are conferred, but the innovation in constitutional practice which this delegation implies. Such exceptional powers may be classified as follows:

(i) power to legislate on matters of principle or policy;
(ii) power to impose taxation;
(iii) powers to amend Acts of the Oireachtas, either the Act by which the powers are delegated, or other Acts;
(iv) powers conferring so wide a discretion that it is impossible to say what limit the Oireachtas did intend to impose.

(i) Legislation on matters of principle is, perhaps, the first duty of the Legislature. Supporters of the constitutional usages of parliamentary government may, in certain cases, regard legislation on details of an obscure or technical nature as a task which might with advantage be devolved on the departments; they could, under no circumstances, regard with equanimity the devolution of powers on matters of principle. None the less, such devolution is by no means unusual. It represents, unquestionably, a break with the time-honoured traditions of parliamentary practice and on that account it merits careful consideration. We have already had occasion to notice the powers conferred upon the minister in the Road Transport Bill, 1932, which involve a decision upon matters of principle. A better example is to be found in the School Attendance Act, 1926. Under this Act the parent or person

The Ministers. Their Administrative Rôle

having custody of a child between the ages of six and fourteen is obliged to send the child to one of the national or other suitable schools.[1] The minister may extend the application of the Act. He may,[2] by order, apply its provisions to children, or any class of children, who have attained the age of fourteen and have not attained the age of sixteen years. In other words, he may, by order, raise the school-leaving age from fourteen to sixteen.

A power of similar nature is vested in the Minister for Agriculture under the Livestock Breeding Act, 1925. The Act provides that no person may keep a bull without securing from the ministry a licence permitting him to do so. The minister shall not grant a licence in respect of any bull which appears to him calculated to beget inferior or defective progeny, or one that is diseased. He may also, by regulation made under the Act, declare that any particular breed or breeds of bull is or are unsuitable for any specified area. Before making such a regulation he must give consideration to the advice of a consultative council, but ultimately the decision rests in his hands. In a pastoral country the issue is one of great importance. When the minister by regulation reserves an area for a certain breed of cattle and declines to license bulls of other breeds within that area, he is unquestionably legislating upon a matter of primary importance. The technical consideration involved renders it an impossible subject for decision by the Legislature, but obviously the extent to which powers, now devolved upon the minister, are used, is a major issue of agricultural policy.

The Dairy Produce (Price Stabilization) Act, 1932, provides concluding examples of delegated legislation on matters of principle. Under section 22, "the Minister may from time to time by order . . . *prohibit* the importation of any particular class or classes of dairy produce." Under section 30 the minister may, subject to certain limitations, prescribe the general rate of bounty on creamery butter. Under section 47 "the Minister may from time to time, by order, fix in relation

[1] Sections 2 & 4. [2] Section 24.

to any class of butter the price beyond which butter of that class may not be sold wholesale by the manufacturer or producer thereof." The Act, as a whole, exemplifies the wide discretion now vested in the minister.

(ii) The power to impose or remit taxation is one not frequently devolved upon the departments. At the same time the practice is not unknown. The Finance (Customs Duties) (No. 3) Act, 1932, enacts a certain duty shall be levied on all wheat flour and wheat meal coming into the country. It is also provided that whenever the Minister for Finance, after consultation with the Minister for Industry and Commerce, is satisfied that wheat flour or wheat meal is not obtainable in sufficient quantities from manufacturers in Saorstat Eireann, and whenever he considers it desirable, the Revenue Commissioners may, by licence, authorize any persons to import, without payment of duty, such wheat meal or wheat flour as they think proper. The most striking illustration of this power is to be found in the Emergency Imposition of Duties Act, 1932. It is an Act "to authorize the Executive Council to impose, vary, and remove by order customs, duties, excise duties, and stamp duties." It vests complete control over these forms of indirect taxation in the hands of the Executive. It may impose new customs or rescind existing duties. Every order made by the Executive Council under the Act has statutory effect. If, however, after eight months of its being made, such order is not confirmed by the Oireachtas it shall cease to have statutory effect but without prejudice to the validity of anything previously done thereunder.

(iii) In certain cases the Executive is invested with powers to amend Acts of the Oireachtas, either the Act by which powers are delegated or other Acts. Such authority usually is devolved in cases where a vast mass of previous legislation has somewhat obscured the field. This is made evident in the provisions of various Land and Housing Acts. The Land Law (Commission) Act, 1923, provides[1] "that the Executive Council . .

[1] Section 11.

may from time to time make all such general and specific adaptations of or modifications in any Act or order to which this section[1] applies as, in the opinion of the Executive Council, are necessary to remove doubts or difficulties in regard to the application of such Act or order to the Irish Land Commission, or to the members thereof appointed under this Act or are *otherwise*[2] necessary to give effect to the provisions of this Act." In the Land Act of the same year it is laid down that "for the purpose of carrying this Act into effect the Executive Council, may, by order, make such adaptations of any enactment relative to Land Purchase in Ireland passed prior to the passing of this Act, as appear to them to be necessary or proper. . . ."[3] Similar powers are conferred by the Land Act, 1931.[4] In legislation on housing the same practice has been followed. The Housing Act, 1925, declares "that in so far as the provisions of any local Act or of any by-law . . . relating to the construction, laying-out, or drainage of new buildings or new streets are inconsistent with any regulations prescribed by the Minister under this section, those provisions shall not apply to any house to which this Act applies. . . ."[5] The same provision is inserted in the Housing Act (1929), the Housing (Gaeltacht) Act, 1929, and the Housing (Financial and Miscellaneous Provisions) Act, 1932. The Juries (Amendment) Act, 1924, gives somewhat wider power in permitting the Executive Council "by order to make such adaptation in the provisions of any Act, as may seem to them necessary to make those provisions conform with the provisions of this Act. . . ."[6] A further example is to be found in the Local Elections and Meetings (Postponement) Act, 1931, under which the minister may, by order, make such modifications of any statute as may, in his opinion, be necessary, to enable such statute to have effect in accordance with the provisions of the Act.[7]

---

[1] It applies to every Act of the United Kingdom still in force on December 6, 1922, and every act of the Oireachtas.
[2] The italics are mine.   [3] Section 74.   [4] Section 51.
[5] Section 11.   [6] Ibid.   [7] Section 14.

(iv) Finally, we come to consider Acts conferring upon the ministers powers so wide that it is not possible to indicate with any precision what limits upon their discretion the Oireachtas intended to impose. There are on the Statute Book several enactments of this kind which contain no limiting definition of powers, but leave everything to the minister's discretion. The Land Act, 1923, provides "if any difficulty arises in determining the land which by virtue of this Act is vested in the Land Commission or *otherwise for carrying this Act into effect*[1] the Executive Council may, by order, authorize the Land Commission to take all such steps and do all such things as may appear to them necessary or expedient for carrying this Act into effect, and any such order shall have effect as if enacted in this Act."[2] The position, though not so decisively stated, is similar in the Housing Act, 1925, wherein it is laid down[3] that the minister may provide all such rules and regulations as are in the Act referred to as being or to be prescribed, "and *such other regulations*[4] as may be required for carrying this Act into effect." A like provision is to be found in the Housing Act, 1933, where the minister is empowered to do any matter or thing which is necessary for carrying a part of that Act into effect.[5] The Creamery Act, 1928, lays down that "the Minister may, by order, make regulations, in relation to any matter arising under this Act and generally for the purpose of carrying this Act into effect."[6] The adaptation of Enactments Act, 1931, provides that, in respect of any Act passed by a Parliament sitting in Ireland at any time before the Union Act, 1800, the "Executive Council may, from time to time, by order, make all such general or specific adaptations of, or modifications in, any Irish Statute having the force of law in Saorstat Eireann as are, in the opinion of Executive Council, necessary in order to enable such statute to have full force and effect in Saorstat Eireann."[7]

[1] The Italics are mine.
[2] Section 75.
[3] Section 11.
[4] The italics are mine.
[5] Section 14.
[6] Section 17.
[7] Section 2.

The Ministers. Their Administrative Rôle

Not infrequently the Oireachtas leaves to the minister the power to decide the day on which a certain Act shall be enforced. The authority thus conferred is not altogether to be ignored. In certain cases it is a matter of the greatest importance. The School Attendance Act,[1] 1926, provided that "this Act shall come into operation such day as shall be fixed for the purpose by the Minister. . . ." The minister's discretion is more closely circumscribed in the Road Transport Act, 1932,[2] whereby he "may, by order, appoint a day not less than three months nor more than six months after the passing of this Act to be the appointed day for the purposes of this Act."

ARE THERE ADEQUATE SAFEGUARDS?

Even a brief survey makes it evident that in the Free State the extent of delegated legislation is very considerable. What safeguards have we against abuse or objectionable exercise of such authority? On the one hand, there is the jurisdiction of the Courts of Law, but they are in a position only to decide whether or no a minister has acted within the limits of his delegated power. On the other, the Oireachtas has provided certain safeguards against the danger of possible misuse. These are of two kinds:

(i) the stipulation in the delegating Act that the regulations made thereunder shall be laid before the Oireachtas;
(ii) a system of publicity.

(i) There is no general statute which requires regulations to be laid before the Oireachtas, but in a number of cases the delegating statute requires regulations to be so laid. Once again the requirement that the regulation should be laid is not reduced to a uniform type. In the first place, the regulation may be laid with no further instructions. The usual practice is, however, to insert a provision that, if within a specified period of time a resolution is passed by either House for annul-

---

[1] Section 27.   [2] Section 3.

ling the regulation, the regulation shall be annulled. The most usual formula runs as follows: "Every regulation made by the Minister under this Act shall be laid before each House of the Oireachtas as soon as may be after it is made, and if a resolution is passed by either House of the Oireachtas, within the next twenty-one days on which such House has sat, annulling such regulation, such regulation shall be annulled accordingly but without prejudice to the validity of anything previously done under such regulation."[1]

A further variation is to be found in the practice of laying . . . with provision that the regulation shall not operate (or shall not operate beyond a specific period) unless approved by resolution within that period. The Emergency Imposition of Duties Act, 1932, illustrates this procedure. It is therein enacted[2] that "every order made by the Executive Council under this section shall have statutory effect upon the making thereof and unless such order is confirmed by order of the Oireachtas within eight months after the making thereof . . . such order shall cease to have statutory effect at the expiration of such eight months, but without prejudice to the validity of anything previously done thereunder." Under certain statutes, moreover, the minister may make only provisional orders—that is, orders which do not take effect and have "no validity or force whatever unless and until confirmed by the Oireachtas." The Pier and Harbour Provisional Order Confirmation Act, 1932,[3] provides an example.

The control given to the Oireachtas under these provisions tends to be underestimated, in that it is very rarely exercised. It is very unusual indeed for a deputy to move the annulment of a ministerial regulation. At the same time the abuse of ministerial power could be called in question with comparative ease. It is unfortunate, however, that the procedure in respect of the laying of regulations is not standardized. Unnecessary variations lead to confusion. And, moreover, it is to be remem-

[1] E.g. Dairy Produce Act, 1931, Section 8.
[2] Section 1.
[3] No. 1 (Private) 1932.

bered that in certain important statutes no provisions of such a kind are made at all. In the Creamery Act, 1928, the minister may "by order, make regulations in relation to any matter arising under this Act, and generally for the purpose of carrying this Act into effect,[1] but while the discretion thus conferred is undeniably wide, no provision whatsoever is inserted requiring the laying of regulations before the Oireachtas. Were the procedure standardized such omissions would not occur.

(ii) Antecedent publicity is a safeguard of the highest value. This is particularly the case where it involves consultation with the interests most closely concerned. Orders and regulations must, in certain cases, be published in the *Iris Oifigiúil*. Under the Civil Service Regulation Act, 1933, it is provided that,[2] "all orders and regulations made under this Act by the Commissioner or by the Minister for Finance shall be published in the *Iris Oifigiúil* immediately after they are made." Under the Electricity Undertakings (Continuance of Charges) Act, 1924, the requirement in respect of publicity is of a somewhat different nature. It is therein enacted that "the Minister shall give public notice in such manner as he shall consider best adapted for informing persons likely to be affected by the order."

Special safeguards for antecedent publicity are sometimes contained in certain statutes. Such safeguards are of the very greatest importance and serve to illustrate the close and continuous co-operation between the ministries in the Free State and those whose interests are bound up with certain branches of the administration. A few examples of statutes which require a preliminary consultation, between the minister empowered to make regulations and certain consultative bodies, will suffice to explain the principle involved. Under the Land Acts, 1929 and 1931, it is provided that the "Land Commission may, after consultation with the President of the Incorporated Law Society of Ireland, make rules for carrying into effect the provisions of this Act. . . ." Under the Live-

[1] Section 17.   [2] Section 11.

stock Breeding Act, 1925,[1] the minister may, by regulation . . . declare that any particular breed or type of bull is unsuitable for a certain specified area, but he "shall not make, revoke, or vary any such regulation until he has consulted the consultative Council established under this Act in regard thereto. . . ." It is to be noticed that under the Agriculture Act, 1931, a consultative Council is established, which shall meet whenever summoned by the minister or on such other occasions as it shall itself determine. It is to consist of persons of experience and special knowledge who may give advice or assistance to the minister. While the minister usually retains full power of enforcing regulations under any specified Act, such consultative bodies impose a very real check on arbitrary action.

JUDICIAL FUNCTIONS OF THE EXECUTIVE

It is advisable to consider the extent of the judicial powers exercised by the ministers before passing a judgment on the status they have acquired. It has been noticed that the constructive and social legislation of the past decade has hastened the introduction of a new element in Representative Government. On the one hand, this development has led to an increase in the volume and extent of delegated legislation; on the other, it has resulted in the placing, by the Oireachtas, of an increasing number of judicial functions in the hands of the departments of State or under the jurisdiction of tribunals controlled, directly or indirectly, by the ministers of the Executive Council. From the point of view of our inquiry the vital feature in this arrangement is the fact that there is no regular appeal to the Courts of Law.

In dealing with the judicial functions exercised by the departments it is unnecessary to devote attention to the Public Safety Acts and other measures to meet emergencies. Such Acts represent, not the general tendency of constitutional practice,

[1] Section 5.

but the suppression of constitutional guarantees in times of crisis.

ADMINISTRATIVE TRIBUNALS

The Railway tribunal is an interesting example of a body whose functions lie midway between those of a Court of Law on the one hand and those of an administrative tribunal on the other. The tribunal, as established under the Railway Act of 1924, consists of a chairman and two ordinary members, appointed by the Governor-General on the advice of the Executive Council. Under the Railways (Amendment) Act, 1929, the Governor-General by order declared that no appointment of ordinary members should be made, and that the tribunal should consist of a chairman alone. The latter must be either a practising barrister of twelve years' standing or a judge. The tribunal exercises the functions formerly vested in the Railway and Canal Commission. It has such powers, rights, and privileges as are vested in the High Court for enforcing the attendance of witnesses, punishing persons for refusal to give evidence or for contempt, and for the enforcement of their orders. It has the power and jurisdiction to hear and determine all matters, whether of law or fact, which are duly brought before it under the Act. There is an appeal from the Railway tribunal to the Supreme Court on questions of law. It is only on questions of fact that the tribunal's decision is final.[1] The existence of this right of appeal distinguishes the tribunal from what may be termed administrative tribunals. The vital feature of any system of administrative law is that there is no appeal to the regular Courts of Law.

In striking contrast to the somewhat indeterminate position of the Railway tribunal stand the more recently established bodies performing functions of a similar character. The Prices Commission,[2] established in 1932, with the object of controlling

---

[1] Railways Act, 1924, Section 22.
[2] Control of Prices Act, 1932. See also the powers of the Tariff Commission and the Film Censorship Board.

commodity prices, provides a good illustration. The Commission is appointed by the minister; it enjoys all powers, rights, and privileges as are vested in the High Court, and a summons signed by its members is equivalent to a formal process issued by the High Court for enforcing the attendance of witnesses and the production of documents. The purpose of the Commission being the prevention of profiteering both in wholesale and in retail prices, it is necessarily armed with full powers of investigation. In reaching a decision as to whether or no overcharging is taking place, the Commission is involved in a judicial process. Witnesses are called, documents produced, and the issue decided in a judicial spirit. The ultimate authority enforcing the decision is the Minister for Industry and Commerce. He may fix the maximum retail or wholesale price for any specified commodity, either for the whole of the Free State or for any particular area. From his decision there is no appeal. From the point of view of administration the advantages of this procedure are evident. The Commission is not, as the Law Courts, bound by precedent. They decide each case on its merits; they may take account of circumstances inadmissible as evidence in a Court of Law. At the same time, one notable assumption is involved; namely, that officers of the administration are adequately equipped to decide on judicial issues. It is impossible to suppose other than that, by training and environment, their sympathies lie on the side of the Executive. The administrator of to-day is required to couple enthusiasm for his work with a capacity to arbitrate impartially on issues which vitally affect it. It is probable, however, that the increasing publicity which is being centred on the work of administrative tribunals will help to eliminate a great number of the difficulties confronting them. "It is a queer sort of justice," writes Lord Hewart,[1] "that will not bear the light of publicity." It is for the administrative tribunals to refute such an innuendo, by rendering their proceedings as public as possible.

We now turn to specialized Courts of a more informal

[1] *The New Despotism*, p. 49.

character, created by statute and whose members are appointed for the purpose of determining justiciable issues arising in connection with the work of a Government department. The ministerial tribunals and judicial and quasi-judicial functions exercised by the ministers themselves deserve particular attention, in that the tendency is for them to increase in number and importance.

MINISTERIAL TRIBUNALS

These ministerial tribunals are appointed for the express purpose of determining issues arising out of the work of a department. The procedure, in a large majority of these appeals, is such as the minister may by regulation determine. Under the Housing (Building Facilities Act), 1924, the Minister for Local Government and Public Health is empowered to decide certain judicial issues by order. Whenever a right of appeal is allowed from such orders "the appeal shall be . . . to a standing tribunal of appeal, consisting of three persons to be appointed by the President of the Executive Council, and such tribunal shall have the power to confirm or annul the order appealed against or to make such other order in the matter as the Minister could have made under this Act and the decision of the tribunal of appeal in the matter shall be final and not subject to appeal or to review by any Court." Similar provisions respecting an appeal to the Housing Tribunal are to be found in the Housing Acts of 1931 and 1933.

The Dairy Produce Act, 1924, permits, in certain cases, an appeal from an executive order to an arbitrator, appointed by the Executive Council, and in the same manner a panel of referees is established under the Livestock Breeding Act, 1925. In the latter case the minister is not in any way bound to accept the decision of the panel of referees. The administrative tribunals established under the Old Age Pensions Act, 1924, represent a continuation of the practice of the former régime.[1]

[1] Cf. Old Age Pensions Act, 1908.

An appeal lies in the first instance to the local Pension Committee, and their decision is subject to a similar appeal to the central pension authority. In the same way the judicial functions performed in relation to Unemployment Insurance and by the National Health Insurance Commission need not detain us.[1] They are of great importance, but in broad outline the practice is a legacy of English rule and does not, therefore, in any way illustrate the development of quasi-judicial bodies under Irish Government.

The Civil Service (Transferred Officers) Compensation Act, 1929, provides a concluding and very instructive example of such ministerial tribunals. It is an Act supplementing Article 10 of the Treaty, and making provision for the final determination of all claims for compensation made by persons transferred from the service of British Government to that of the Provisional Government, or its successor. To determine these claims, a Civil Service Compensation Board is appointed. The Board is to consist of (*a*) a Chairman—who must be a judge—appointed by the Executive Council; (*b*) a panel of five persons appointed by the Minister for Finance; (*c*) a panel of twenty-five persons named in the Act. The Board enjoys full power and jurisdiction to entertain and decide all matters intended by the Act and is not subject to restraint in the exercise of their jurisdiction by any Court. "The decision of the Board on any claim for compensation under Article 10 of the Treaty . . . shall be a final and conclusive determination of such claim and shall not be subject to appeal to or review by any court, authority, or tribunal whatsoever." This provision indicates the most important principle involved in jurisdiction by administrative Courts. The vital feature of the whole arrangement is that there is no appeal to the ordinary Courts of Law.

Besides these judicial functions, performed by ministerial tribunals, there are also functions of a similar nature exercised by the ministers themselves. One example will suffice in that

[1] See Robson, *Justice and Administrative Law*, pp. 118–130, for a discussion of the principles involved.

The Ministers. Their Administrative Rôle

the principle at stake is the same as in the statutes quoted already. In respect of certain new buildings a reduction in ratio was permitted under the Local Government Act, 1925,[1] and it was, in consequence, a matter of importance to decide what was and what was not a new building under the terms of the Act. On that account it is provided that if any doubt, dispute, or question shall arise as to whether a building is a new building . . . such doubt, dispute, or question shall be determined by the minister, whose decision shall be final. Moreover, in every Licensing Act the minister exercises a judicial power from which there is no appeal.

It is difficult to classify such judicial tribunals as have been mentioned. They may be described as administrative or ministerial tribunals, but they differ very widely indeed in respect both of constitution and of powers. In the Free State it is still true to say that in the majority of cases a judicial decision by an administrative person or body is subject to appeal to the Court. On the other hand, there is a growing tendency to invest such decision with a final authority. This constitutes a very striking breach with the Rule of Law. Obviously it requires careful scrutiny. While little fault has as yet been found with the administration of judicial functions within their sphere, there remains the great danger that as the powers of the administrative bodies increase in scope and extent their functions will be perfunctorily or carelessly discharged. Another danger lies in a somewhat different direction. A new policy of social improvement carried out by the State (such as Housing) which involves interference with vested rights is usually, and probably rightly, accompanied by the erection of an administrative tribunal to deal with questions connected therewith. There is a danger, as Dr. Robson[2] has suggested, that their jurisdiction will be extended to deal with matters arising out of the increasing control of the State over economic affairs. It seems that the constitution of the present administrative

[1] Section 69.
[2] *Justice and Administrative Law*, pp. 298 et seq.

tribunals is peculiarly unsuited to bureaucratic adjudication in matters of this kind.

POWERS OF INQUIRY

In addition to the legislative and judicial powers vested in the ministers, they also enjoy extensive rights of inquiry. These rights are important in that they enable the departments to secure first-hand knowledge of the conditions for which legislation is required. The extent of such powers of inquiry is usually indicated in the conferring statute. The Creamery Act of 1928 provides an excellent example in enacting that "every person in charge of a creamery within the meaning of this Act, shall, upon being so required . . . by an officer of the Department, produce to such officer all records, books and other documents in his custody, relating to such creamery and permit such inspector to examine and take copies of or extracts from the same." Refusal or failure to comply is an offence under the statute and renders the offender liable, on summary conviction, to a fine not exceeding five pounds. Similar provisions are to be found in a large number of statutes.[1] They illustrate, perhaps more than any other of the ministerial powers whose nature we have indicated, the completeness of the breach with the *laissez-faire* individualism of the nineteenth century. Their very existence is a recognition of the claim of the State to control productive activity and it is probable that without such powers the extensive reorganization of industry, and particularly agriculture, could not have been carried out with equal efficiency. For if the departments are to be invested with a wide discretion in functions of a primarily legislative character, it is a necessary preliminary that they should be empowered to secure accurate statistical information.

---

[1] E.g. Dairy Produce Act, 1931; Control of Manufactures Act, 1932; Road Transport Act, 1932; Dairy Produce (Price Stabilization) Act, 1932

The Ministers. Their Administrative Rôle

THE DICTATORSHIP OF THE DEPARTMENTS

An analysis of the administrative powers of ministers indicates that in the modern State administration cannot be defined as the process of applying law enacted by the Legislature. Its demesne is far wider; it is in itself a creative force. This is to be seen particularly in the practice of delegating legislative power to the ministries; a practice whose tendency is to increase even though already it is estimated that the volume of delegated legislation is considerably in excess of that of parliamentary legislation.[1] The discretion of the heads of the departments is the more real in that the ordinary type of delegated legislation is permissive in principle, or, in other words, it is left to the departments to say, not merely how, but also whether or no, they will legislate at all. In addition to a discretionary power in legislation, the departments are invested with certain functions of a judicial or a quasi-judicial character. Furthermore, in times of emergency the Executive Council is empowered not only to legislate on major matters of principle, but also to impose taxation. Again, in times of internal disorder the Executive Council is entitled by certain of the Public Safety Acts to suspend the ordinary guarantees of personal liberty by Proclamation. There is no question but that the hegemony of the Executive is complete.

What, then, are the guarantees to the individual against Executive oppression or injustice? They may be classified under two headings: (*a*) the Courts; (*b*) the responsibility of ministers to the Dáil. The Judiciary, in fact, constitutes the more obvious and effective guarantee. Not only are the Courts in a position to declare *ultra vires* legislation which conflicts with the Constitution, and delegated legislation which exceeds the powers conferred in the delegating Act, but also in a large majority of cases an appeal is allowed to the Courts from the decisions of ministerial tribunals. The appeal to the Courts is generally entertained on a question of law. There are certain

[1] No precise statistics are available.

objections in principle to an appeal on a question of fact.[1] The second safeguard is, perhaps, more real than is generally realized. Ministerial responsibility, it is often felt, is a somewhat remote check on departmental tyranny. It must, however, be remembered that the Free State is a small country; that injustices of this kind are speedily brought to light and that deputies make full use of question time in the Dáil for bringing it to the attention of the minister concerned.

It is, of course, quite evident that if the ministry and the departments were desirous of misusing their power to oppress individuals, they would be in a position to do so within legal formulae. Against an intentional bureaucratic tyranny there appears to be no adequate formal safeguard at all. But in such circumstances, the ultimate check is to be found in a healthy public opinion. The latter is of far more importance than legal safeguards, upon which it is possible to lay excessive emphasis. The whole conception of individual rights safeguarded against the State is a legacy of the heyday of the supremacy of individualist ideals. It is fundamentally opposed to the main current of English political thought. In Ireland, with its closer connection with Continental philosophy, the doctrine of rights has found a more responsive outlook. Thus in England the submission of all classes and persons to the rule of law is held to be an all-sufficient guarantee of individual liberty. In Ireland it is supplemented by a constitutional guarantee of rights. The distinction may not appear vital now. None the less, this approximation to Continental thought leads one to suppose that the creation of a system of administrative law is more probable in Ireland than in England. "Administrative law," writes Lord Hewart,[2] "profoundly repugnant as it is to English ideas, is at least a system." That constitutes its most powerful attraction. The present devolution of powers to ministers is somewhat haphazard. Lord Hewart's remark: "that it would be a strange misuse of terms if the name of 'Administrative

---

[1] Cf. *Report of Committee on Ministers' Powers*, p. 108.
[2] *The New Despotism*, p. 13.

Law' were to be applied to that which, upon analysis, proved to be nothing more than administrative lawlessness, is equally applicable to the Free State." A rationalization of existing practice would in itself constitute a most valuable safeguard.

The reasons which led to a rapid growth of ministerial power have already been indicated. The development is one common to post-War democracy and the practice of the Free State has been paralleled by that of Great Britain. The greater rapidity with which this development has evolved in the former country is due to her peculiar needs. The constructive programme of the Cumann na nGaedheal Government has been followed by the new social programme of Fianna Fail. The result is made evident by the large legislative output of the Oireachtas. On an average more than forty statutes have been promulgated each year—a very large number in a small country. The volume of the legislative output has led inevitably to a greater reliance being placed on subordinate legislation.

From the point of view of the individual there seems no question but that in broad outline the powers now exercised by the ministers in the Free State are despotic. They constitute a very definite breach with the classic forms of judicial and parliamentary control. The issue, indeed, no longer centres on the question whether or no ministerial authority is despotic. It centres on the question of whether or no the new despotism is a benevolent despotism. And the answer depends largely upon personal political opinions. Approval of the increase of State control leads one to regard it as benevolent; dislike of activities controlled by a State bureaucracy leads one to suppose that its influence is entirely malignant. In general it does, however, appear that the old parliamentary system needs a certain adaptation in order to cope with the complexity of modern affairs. It was peculiarly fitted to a period or a country in which there existed agreement about the fundamental nature and basis of the State. The growth of Socialism[1] has destroyed that agreement in Great Britain. In the Free State also there is a

[1] See, for example, Professor Laski's *Democracy in Crisis*.

sharp cleavage of opinion as to the basis of the State. That cleavage centres on the issue created by the Treaty. From the point of view of internal administration the preoccupation of the Legislature with this purely political aspect of affairs is unfortunate. It has, however, had the important consequence of enlarging the authority and discretion of the departments. Democracy tends to become increasingly autocratic. The real, as opposed to the formal, safeguard lies in an enlightened public opinion; and in the creation of this opinion the local authorities have a rôle of supreme importance to play.

From one standpoint this development of ministerial authority is of peculiar interest to the framers of the Irish Constitution. It constitutes in itself a retrospective justification of the conceptions underlying the "extern" ministries. For the assumption which resulted in their creation was that the parliamentary system, as interpreted by the jurists of the last century, and as practised in England, was inadequate to meet modern needs. The practice of devolving powers upon the ministers shows that this assumption has been justified. The mere fact that the extern ministries involved an institutional change in the Cabinet obscured the fact that a probably greater breach of the parliamentary system might be effected by constitutional practice. The present system, it is true, perpetuates the illusion of legislative control. But in fact, even within its own sphere, the Legislature is dominated by the Executive. Of this the volume of delegated legislation on matters of principle provides an all-sufficient testimony. Such a breach with traditional parliamentary practice would not have followed from the creation of the extern ministries. They were intended to preserve the reality of parliamentary control. By institutional innovation, it was felt that constitutional continuity might be maintained. With their disappearance there vanished the last possibility of counteracting the advance of the new despotism.

CHAPTER XII

INTERNAL ADMINISTRATION

THE powers of the Executive throw an ever-increasing responsibility upon the Civil Service. The progressive socialization of production and of the public services makes the State, to an exceptional extent, dependent upon the quality of its officials. The assumption that the less the control of the political executive over the appointment of permanent officials, the better it is for the administration, has been accepted. It is one of the more obvious difficulties confronting a new State that there are no trained officials at its disposal. In the case of the Free State, this difficulty was in part countered by the transference of a considerable proportion of the Civil Servants of the previous régime to that of the Provisional Government. The position of the British Civil Servants was safeguarded under the Treaty[1] wherein the Government of the Irish Free State agreed to pay fair compensation to judges, officials, members of the police forces, and other public servants, who are discharged or retire in consequence of the change of Government. The exact proportion of the Civil Servants who transferred their services to the new administration is obviously a matter of some importance. Accurate statistics are not, however, readily available in that many were transferred, not in 1922, but at a considerably later date.

THE CIVIL SERVICE

The organization of the new Civil Service was regulated in a series of statutory enactments. Under the Acts[2] of 1923 and

[1] Art. 10. It was supplemented by a subsequent agreement in June 1929.
[2] Civil Service Regulation Act, 1923. Civil Service Regulation Act, 1924.

1924 provision was made for the appointment by the Executive Council of a Civil Service Commission. It was to be composed of not more than three members. Its purpose was to inquire into the qualifications of applicants for positions to which the Act applied, and a certificate of qualification issued by the Commissioners was to be a necessary preliminary to appointment. From these provisions officers appointed on the advice of the Executive Council, or that of the Comptroller and Auditor-General, or members of the Police Force, and those appointed to certain specified subordinate posts, were exempted.

In the lower grades of the Civil Service admission is determined by competitive examination. It was originally the practice for similar examinations to be held in respect of the higher grades, but subsequently this was abolished. A University honours degree, or its equivalent, is now required, but there is a written examination in Irish. The Civil Service Commissioners were authorized to dispense with the ordinary regulations governing admission to the Civil Service in cases when the Minister for Finance or the minister in charge of the department affected, declared either that the qualifications for the position to be filled were of a professional character or that it was in the public interest that they should not be enforced. The latter proviso enabled the Government to appoint members of the Dáil administration and of the Irish Republican Army.

The department in whose hands is vested the control of the Civil Service is the Department of Finance. Its position in this respect is one of peculiar authority, in that there are no external bodies with power to adopt resolutions respecting the privileges and salaries of Civil Servants. In 1919 a Civil Service Joint Council was established under the British régime. Its existence was terminated by the Free State Government. An Advisory Council under the Chairmanship of the Secretary of the Department of Finance has since been established, but its function is to recommend and not to decide. Moreover, the Government has consistently refused to permit the creation of a Civil Service Arbitration Board on the English model. All power is retained in the hands of the Minister for Finance.

THE DEPARTMENTS OF STATE

The departments in the Free State are remarkably responsive to public opinion. This is due, on the one hand, to the close contact between the officers of the administration and the outside public. In a small country, as the Free State, it has been found possible to maintain by frequent informal consultation an interchange of views between the departmental officers, who prepare the legislation, and those whose interests are most liable to be affected. In addition, the ministers are available for a very large number of personal interviews, though it is frequently maintained that excessive dependence is placed upon the views and opinions of the capital city. On the other hand, a new State is not liable to pay exaggerated respect to bureaucratic or departmental tradition. Of that the age of the ministers and their subordinates is a guarantee. Happy, indeed, is the Civil Service which has no history.

The Report of the Machinery of Government Committee in 1918 directed attention to the fact that in Great Britain "there is much overlapping in the functions of the Departments," and added that this is primarily due to the gradual evolution of these departments in compliance with current needs. The definition of functions of the Free State departments was carried out in the Ministers and Secretaries Act of 1924, in which due attention was paid to the Report of the 1918 Committee. A rationalization of departmental function, of which the first step is to be found in the creation of a Department of the President, was undertaken. The departments, eleven in number, are as follows:

Department of the President of the Executive Council.
Department of Finance.
Department of Justice.

Department of Local Government and Public Health.
Department of Education.
Department of Agriculture.
Department of Industry.
Department of Lands.
Department of Posts and Telegraphs.
Department of Defence.
Department of External Affairs.

The War Cabinet in Great Britain appointed a secretary to the Cabinet charged with the performance and control of its secretarial work. The practice has been continued in the Free State, with this proviso, that it is no longer an individual but a department which performs the secretarial work of the Executive Council. For such is the purpose[1] of the Department of the President. It has the custody of the Seal of the Executive Council, it is responsible for the official publications of the Council, it keeps the records of the meetings of the Council. It is widely felt that the existence of this department, of an established secretariat to the President and the Council, is advantageous both in enabling the preparation of agenda for Cabinet discussions and in the publication of its decisions. On the other hand, the proviso that any services or functions not specifically allocated to any other ministry should be administered by the Department of the President, is open to criticism. A department whose primary purpose is the co-ordination of policy and the unification of administration should not be encumbered with duties of a nondescript or indeterminate character. In England such duties are administered by the Home Office. It is a department more suited to act the rôle of a residuary legatee. The importance of the existence of a Department of the President lies in the fact that it provides a means of putting forward a carefully planned policy. And such a policy is now an essential feature of government. Among the complicated functions now entrusted to our political

[1] See Ministers and Secretaries Act, No. 16 of 1924.

government there comes first, write Mr. and Mrs. Sidney Webb,[1] the whole function of anticipating the future. The future maintenance of the nation in security and self-determination is as important as its momentary affairs. The State has to administer its resources so as to make provision, not merely for the needs of the contemporary generation, but also for those of future generations as far as can usefully be foreseen. And year by year the community must make a decision as to how much of the annual production of commodities and services shall be appropriated for present needs, and how much to anticipation of the future. And in the making of these decisions it has to be determined, though not necessarily expressly formulated, what sort of civilization it is intended that the community of the future shall enjoy. Do we prefer a universally educated people closely approximating to economic equality, or a society of grades and layers highly differentiated in degrees of culture and amounts of wealth; a predominantly urban or a predominantly rural existence; do we, in fact, want in Ireland a population of five million, or one of ten or even twenty million? Such are the questions which Mr. and Mrs. Webb claim, and rightly claim, must be decided by the Governments of to-day. To facilitate their decision the existence of a department concerned with the collection of evidence and statistics is a necessary preliminary. It serves, on the one hand, to correlate the needs of the different departments, on the other to co-ordinate the administration of a political and economic programme when the Council has decided upon its application. So far the tendency has been to stress the secretarial as opposed to this wider aspect of the duties of the presidential department. It is to be hoped that the balance will be redressed.

[1] *A Constitution for the Socialist Commonwealth of Great Britain*, pp. 90–93.

CONSULTATIVE COMMITTEES

In the detailed application of policy very considerable use is made of advisory or consultative committees. This is particularly to be noticed in the work of the departments of Agriculture and Industry and Commerce, but is also to be found in the majority of the other departments. Their purpose is neither to direct nor to control; it is to advise. Of their value there is now no room for doubt. They form a link between the work of a department and the outside public, and if well selected command the respect of the interests most closely affected. "We think," reported Lord Haldane's Committee on the Machinery of Government, "that the more they are regarded as an integral part of the normal organization of a department, the more will Ministers be enabled to command the confidence of Parliament and the public in their administration of the services, which seem likely in an increasing degree to affect the lives of large sections of the community."

UNIFICATION OF FUNCTION

It will be seen from the list of the departments that certain of the recommendations of the Haldane Committee Report were adopted in the Free State. In particular, attention may be drawn to the establishment of the Ministry of Finance and the Ministry of Justice. In both cases the unification of services has been abundantly justified. The same principle underlies the division of functions between the other departments. They are distributed by services. Thus the Ministry of Education deals directly with the educational needs of all persons. Under the former régime responsibility has been divided, and education in Ireland was controlled by independent Boards of Commissioners, dealing with Primary, Secondary, and Technical education. A similar co-ordination of function is to be noted in the Ministry of Local Government and Public Health. In this respect the Department of Agriculture merits particular

Internal Administration 223

attention. In 1899 the Agricultural and Technical Instruction Act set up what was in effect a Department of Agriculture for Ireland. Associated with this department were certain statutory bodies, a Council of Agriculture, an Agricultural Board, a Board of Technical Instruction, and County Committees of Agriculture and Technical Instruction. The department, in conjunction with the Co-operative Movement, brought about a remarkable revival of interest in Irish agriculture. Its constitution was democratic, and farming interests controlled both the Central Board and Local Councils and Committees. Its value was unquestioned, and it is no insignificant tribute to its work that even in the troubled times preceding the establishment of the Free State it retained its popularity. The Ministers and Secretaries Act, 1924, provided for the establishment of a Department of Lands and Agriculture. The title was later changed to that of Department of Agriculture, and this alteration signified a redistribution of function. The Agriculture department is concerned solely with services relating to agricultural development, and does not deal with land distribution and settlement.[1] The Department of Agriculture and Technical Instruction set up in 1899 was dissolved by the Agriculture Act, 1931. The dissolution involved the disappearance of the Council of Agriculture and the Agricultural Board, neither of which, in fact, had met for several years. The Council of Agriculture is replaced under the Act of 1931 by consultative Councils, which the minister is empowered to establish. The County Committees of Agriculture have, with certain modifications, been continued under the Agriculture Act. But the system is regularized. Under the Act of 1931 there must be a Committee of Agriculture in every county. It may consist wholly of members of the County Council, or its members may be drawn from outside. The number of members is fixed. To the County Committees are delegated, subject to departmental supervision, the administration of services

[1] This work is done by the Land Commission, included in the Department of Lands.

for which the county can be made the unit and from which the ratepayers derive advantages. These services include various forms of technical instruction and livestock and crop improvement schemes. The expenditure of the County Committees provides an estimate of the importance of their work. In 1930-31 the following were the amounts expended by the Committees for the purposes of agricultural and livestock schemes.

    (a) Expenditure from Department Grants .. £82,078
    (b) Expenditure from Local Rates £55,167

The changed system of agricultural administration serves to illustrate the change in governmental outlook between the new and the old régime. Admittedly the old Department of Agriculture was created to answer needs very different from those confronting the new national State of 1924. At the same time, however, it is to be noticed that the emphasis was then placed on co-operative and individual effort. The emphasis is now placed on governmental inspiration; on governmental control. The difference is important in that it stresses the new dependence that is placed upon the Civil Service. In no department is a specialized knowledge of conditions throughout the country more essential for the drafting of creative legislation and for the control of marketing conditions than in that of Agriculture.

CHAPTER XIII

LOCAL GOVERNMENT

IN the Free State all the powers of government reside in the executive and legislative organs at Dublin. There are no competing authorities. The extent, even the existence, of local autonomy depends upon statutory law. The powers that the local bodies exercise can be obliterated at will by the Oireachtas. It was the aim of the Constituent Assembly that the government of Ireland should be decentralized. That intention has not been fulfilled, owing to the successive national difficulties with which the country has had to cope. It has been found necessary to invest the minister with greater powers of control than was at first deemed desirable. These powers have been freely exercised. There is no possibility of conflict between central and local government. The former is the undisputed master. It is evident that the minister must retain a power generally to control the local authorities. There are matters, in housing, in health (for example), in which a standard of minimum attainment must be enforced. At the same time the existence of a department charged with the specific duty of supervising local government tempts the minister to extend the boundaries of his jurisdiction.

LOCAL GOVERNMENT IN TRANSITION

Before defining the statutory position of the Ministry of Local Government, it is necessary to refer to the course of events prior to the Anglo-Irish Treaty. The Local Government Department of Dáil Eireann was created in 1919. Mr. Cosgrave was the minister in charge. The department was most active in organizing opposition to the existing administration. The Imperial Parliament passed measures to cope with the growing resistance. Under the Local Government (Ireland) Act, 1919, the principle of Proportional Representation was applied to local government elections. These were held in the following year, but the new method of election effected no radical change in the position. A considerable majority of the newly elected local bodies refused to recognize the control of the Local Government Board, and made declarations of allegiance to Dáil Eireann. In several instances legal proceedings were instituted against local bodies who refused to submit their accounts to the auditors of the Local Government Board. Orders of Mandamus were granted by the Courts but could not be enforced. Extensive reforms, in particular affecting the Poor Law administration, were undertaken by Dáil Eireann contemporaneously with the campaign against British rule. Subsequent to the signature of the Treaty on December 6, 1921, the functions of the Local Government Board were performed by the Provisional Government, and the two administrations were co-ordinated.[1]

RECONSTRUCTION AND REFORM

In April 1922 the Ministry of Local Government was established by the Provisional Government. Its functions and duties were defined in the Ministers and Secretaries Act, 1924.[2] The purpose of this Act was to constitute the departments of the new State in accordance with the Constitution. It was not primarily concerned with a reorganization of local government, which was then urgently required. This need was answered by the Local Government Act of 1925,[3] which constitutes the basis of the existing system. Under the British system local administration had been in the charge of the Local Government Board for Ireland, a body composed of four Commissioners with the Chief Secretary as Chairman. When the new ministry was set up under the Provisional Government in 1922, it took over,

[1] Cf. First Report of the Department of Local Government and Public Health, 1922–25.
[2] No. 16 of 1924.
[3] No. 5 of 25.

in addition to the functions of the Local Government Board, other services which had been under the direct supervision of the Lord-Lieutenant. Among the latter were included the functions hitherto administered by the Inspectors of Lunatic Asylums in Ireland, the Inspector of Reformatories and Industrial Schools, and the Registrar-General of Births, Deaths, and Marriages. In October 1922, by Order[1] of the Provisional Government, the powers and duties in relation to roads, bridges, and ferries, and traffic thereon, was transferred to the ministry from the then Ministry of Economic Affairs. Certain changes were effected under the Ministers and Secretaries Act. The National Health Insurance Committee was included in the department, whilst the control of reformatories and industrial schools was transferred to the Ministry of Education. Under this Act the department was constituted under its present title—the Department for Local Government and Public Health. Its functions are carefully defined. They comprise "the administration of public services in connection with local government, public health, relief of the poor, care of the insane, health insurance, elections to each House of the Oireachtas, elections to local bodies and authorities, registration of voters, maintenance of public roads and highways, registration of births, deaths, and marriages, and vital statistics and all powers . . . connected with the same."[2]

In the administration of these functions the department (like all Gaul) is divided into three parts. The first and most important of these divisions is subdivided into sections dealing with local administration, poor law, public health, roads, housing, old age pensions, trade and local finance.[3] The two remaining divisions deal with National Health Insurance Commission and the General Register Office.

The Ministers and Secretaries Act provides the central machinery which controls the local authorities. The Local

---
[1] Order of October 4, 1922.
[2] No. 16 of 1924, Section 3.
[3] See Flynn, *Parliamentary Companion*, for details.

Government Act of 1925 secures a comprehensive reorganization of the local bodies themselves. The old system was swept aside and a radical reform carried through. In the first place the Rural Districts were abolished as administrative units.[1] The Rural District was a subdivision of the county, governed by a Rural District Council, whose members were ex-officio guardians of the poor. It was constituted under the Local Government (Ireland) Act of 1898. Its existence encouraged administrative confusion and led to a needless disintegration of function among a welter of local authorities. For example, at the time of the passage of this Act there were in the county three local authorities concerned in differing degrees with public health administration. They were the County Boards, the County Councils, and the Rural District Councils.[2] A system of dual control between the County Councils and the Rural District Councils existed also in road administration. It was to prevent this overlapping of function, and to secure a unified control of public health administration, that the reforms were considered both necessary and desirable. Under the Act of 1925 a new enlarged rural sanitary district, called the "County Health District," was created. As a rule this County Health District extends over the whole county, with the Urban District excluded. In some cases the county is divided into two or more health districts. The sanitary authority for a County Health District is the County Council. The duties involved, being of a specialized nature and requiring frequent meetings, the County Council performs them through a Board of Health composed of ten members of the Council. The expenses of a Board of Health are supplied by the County Council, who raise the necessary money by means of a poor rate. The latter also are required to appoint a County Medical Officer of Health to secure the effective administration of the sanitary code. With certain exceptions[3] the county health

---

[1] Local Government Act, No. 5 of 1925, part 1.
[2] See Second Report of Department, 1925–27, pp. 1–6.
[3] E.g. Cork County and Waterford County.

authority is also the public assistance authority. It is called the Board of Health and Public Assistance.

POOR RELIEF

The reform of the system for the relief of the poor was from the first taken up by Dáil Eireann. The Irish Poor Law dated from 1838. Till 1847 it was an offshoot of the British system, and was controlled by the English Poor Law Commissioners. In that year a body of Poor Law Commissioners was set up in Ireland, but in turn they were superseded by the Local Government Board of 1872. It was felt that the English system of relief was peculiarly unsuited to Irish needs. There had been a continuous demand for reform. The principal objection lay in the fact that poor persons of practically all classes were relieved in workhouses. The outdoor relief afforded was comparatively small. In this connection it is important to remember that at the time when the Poor Laws were introduced the country was passing through the great famine. In consequence the workhouse became associated in the minds of the people with the sufferings of that period.[1] The dislike of the workhouses grounded on this historic basis survived long after the hardships, which had called it into being, had disappeared. At the same time, among the respectable poor, relief in a workhouse carried with it an enduring stigma. In brief, public assistance had become a hardship to those it was intended to help. In order to carry out a reform, it was necessary to enlarge the Union area. The workhouse had been built at a time when the population of the country was almost twice what it is to-day. It became too large for present needs. A wider administrative area was found in the county. In the Local Government (Temporary Provisions) Act, 1923,[2] schemes promulgated by the county authorities, with special reference to their particular requirements, were sanctioned by the Oireachtas.

[1] See Report of Ministry, 1922–25.
[2] These schemes are open to criticism but were passed in very unsettled times. Each county put forward its own.

The principal provisions were (i) the abolition of relief in workhouses in each Poor Law Union; (ii) the centralization of the administration under one authority in each county; (iii) the establishment of central county institutions in which the poor of the county could be relieved; (iv) allowing those requiring relief to be relieved either in or out of the central institution as might be deemed advisable. The County Board of Health is entrusted with the administration of this relief.

The Act of 1923 provided the basis of the new system of poor relief, though in certain respects it has been considerably modified. Public assistance is organized on a county basis, the Poor Law Unions within each county (except in Dublin City and County) have been amalgamated, Boards of Guardians have been abolished, and workhouses closed as such. County Homes have been established for the aged, infirm, and chronic invalids, and County and District Hospitals for the sick. Home assistance is the normal method of poor relief. In August 1927 a Commission appointed to inquire into the Poor Law presented their report. While it is evident that there remained much room for improvement, particularly in respect of the County Homes, the Commission considered that the changes had been distinctly for the better.

The closing of a large number of superfluous workhouses was agreed to be beneficial. The Commission, moreover, reported that institutional relief should be granted only where it is impossible, impracticable, or wasteful to give assistance otherwise. At the same time the difficulties in controlling and supervising home assistance are widely recognized. The Commission, noting that there is now no "workhouse test" to fall back on, observes that "to avoid abuse . . . requires careful scrutiny of each applicant's case and courage and determination to resist undue pressure to afford relief under circumstances that may not altogether warrant its being given." In many districts there is considerable dissatisfaction with the administration of home assistance. It is felt that it is not always the deserving poor who receive the sums spent on poor relief. It is to be noted that it is the Board of Health, composed of ten members, who administer the relief. On the one hand it is claimed that the number is too large for efficient administration. On the other it is suggested that it is too small for security. There is, it is felt, safety in numbers. It is difficult to bribe a large body. From this point of view it is maintained that the whole County Council should compose the Board of Health. Under the present system there have been definite cases of corruption and maladministration, but that does not, perhaps, involve any essential weakness in the system itself.

THE LOCAL COUNCILS AND THEIR OFFICIALS

In the Free State there are twenty-seven administrative Counties, and four County Boroughs, namely Dublin, Cork, Limerick, and Waterford. Each such district elects a Council to administer the duties devolving upon local authorities. The Council is the sole rating authority within its area. There are, besides, sixty-five urban sanitary districts, comprising four County Boroughs, six Municipal Boroughs, two towns constituted under special Acts, and fifty-three under the Towns Improvement Act, 1854. Local government elections are held according to the principles of Proportional Representation. The franchise extends to practically all persons of either sex who are of full age and have during a qualifying period occupied as owners or tenants any land or premises in the area whose rateable value is £10. Any married woman of 30 years or over, residing in premises in respect of which the husband is entitled to be registered as a local government elector, is also qualified for the franchise.[1] Women are eligible for election upon the same conditions as men. A comparison with the numbers of Dáil electors registered in any given year shows more clearly the nature of these provisions. In 1929 (for example) the number of registered Dáil electors was 1,717,684, that of registered

[1] But the husband of a woman entitled to be registered as a local government elector is not by that fact so entitled.

local government electors was 1,041,030.[1] Elections to local authorities (with certain exceptions) take place trienially. It has frequently happened, however, that the local elections have been postponed by the Oireachtas. Since 1922 no fewer than four Local Election Postponement Acts have been placed on the Statute Book.

The elected members of local authorities are unpaid, though provision is made for a contribution towards travelling expenses. Attendance to local business fluctuates according to the character of the person elected. But Professor Laski is not inaccurate in suggesting[2] that "local government based on the unpaid member has, the world over, somehow seemed to accrete to itself a variety of persons—small contractors, publicans, shopkeepers, and the like—whose disinterested zeal for the public welfare has been less apparent in the quality of the work done than in their pronouncement of intention." Attendance at County Councils and general attention to local business is on the part of (probably) a majority of members extremely spasmodic. There is in consequence a tendency for the execution of local business to devolve more and more upon the Chairman of the Council. If he is an able and efficient man, the majority are only too willing to permit him to direct local affairs. Generally speaking, the principal executive, technical, and professional offices at the service of the local authorities are filled by the department. The local bodies, it is true, appoint such officers, but before making the appointment they must request the Local Appointments Commissioners to recommend to them a suitable person. This procedure must be followed in the case of certain prescribed offices which cannot be filled by promotion. The Commissioners are a central body who select persons for appointment by examinations or other means. The local authority must accept the nominee of the Commissioners.[3] This practice has been considerably enlarged

[1] 1929. See Report of Ministry of Local Government.
[2] *Grammar of Politics*, p. 461.
[3] Refusal to accept a nominee by the Mayo Co. Council led to the dissolution of the Council.

since its introduction in 1926.[1] Previous to that date the minister[2] from time to time prescribed by order appointments which were to come under his review. The power, compared with that of the Commissioners board, was merely negative. It prevented the appointment of obviously unsuitable persons. It did not secure the recruitment of competent officers. "No doubt," as the report of the ministry reads,[3] "many local bodies had brought into their services officers of high competence; but, with the expansion of the functions of local authorities, it became more and more evident that the appointment of local officials could no longer be exposed to the evils of patronage, of family, local and political influences." The system established in 1926 rests on a more positive basis. In the year ending March 1930 the Commissioners selected 276 persons for various local offices.[4] The success of this method of appointment is seen in the offices since added to those to which the Act of 1926 applied. Under the Cosgrave régime, that is till 1932, the Local Appointments Commissioners were instructed by the Government to send down the name of only *one* selected person to the local authority. In 1932 the Fianna Fail Government instructed that the names of three candidates were to be sent and the local authority had thus the privilege of exercising a limited choice. In 1933 the former procedure was reverted to. It is claimed that this reversion was prompted because of the bribery and canvassing prevailing in some parts of the country. Many, but not all, of the local bodies maintain that it is an undue restriction upon their liberty.

LOCAL FINANCE

The main duties of the local authorities may be divided under the headings of public health, housing, poor relief, and

[1] Local Authorities (Officers and Employees) Act, 1926.
[2] Local Government (Temporary Provisions) Act, 1923. The principal Order, the Local Offices, and Employments Order, 1924.
[3] Report of Ministry of Local Government and Public Health, 1929–30, p. 14.
[4] Ibid.

road maintenance. In all these functions it is apparent that, if the will of the Oireachtas is to be enforced, the minister must exercise a careful supervision. He must see that a certain standard of minimum achievement is attained. He enjoys extensive powers for this purpose, and on that account it is probable that there is a considerable underestimation of the importance of the local authorities. A brief review of local finance is necessary to readjust the balance. The local authorities derive their local revenue from rates on property, charged on the occupiers. The total annual value of rateable property in the Free State in 1929 was £11,572,731. Local expenditure is between nine and ten millions sterling. Were all local revenue to be drawn from rates the charge would be almost twenty shillings in the pound. The local area receives, however, subventions from the central government. The following figures[1] show the proportion of revenue derived from each source:

	1923–24	1925–26	1927–28	1930–31	1931–32
Local Revenue from Rates	71·69	62·33	56·6	55·4	51·7
Local Revenue from Central Exchequer	22·56	32·02	37·7[2]	38·2	42·3

In 1932–33 actually more than half of the amount of local expenditure was defrayed by the central government. To this we shall return in dealing with National Finance. Here it is sufficient to remark that local expenditure amounted to between nine and ten millions for the year 1931–32, as compared with a total national expenditure of over twenty-four and a half millions.[3] The proportion is therefore about two to five. This system of dual supply is probably inevitable. It is open, however, to the objection that there is no unified system

---

[1] Taken from an article by T. J. Kiernan in the *Saorstat Eireann*. Official Handbook.

[2] The small balance is derived from undescribed sources.

[3] Cf. Returns of Local Taxation, 1931–32.

of controlling expenditure. The main method of raising revenue in the localities is by a rate levied on the annual rateable value of property. Under the Local Government Act of 1927,[1] poor rate is now to be made in respect of every hereditament and tenement in the county, without distinguishing between agricultural land and other hereditaments. Under this improved method one rate is made on each holding for general and separate charges and is applotted on the total valuation of the holding. The amount of the rate in the pound on agricultural land to which the total agricultural grant would be equivalent is then ascertained. The latter rate is applotted on the valuation of agricultural land in each holding and allowed to the ratepayer as an abatement.

The difficulties attending local administration in the early years of the Free State was reflected, not surprisingly, in the difficulties involved in the collection of rates; the ratepayers were strongly tempted to avail themselves of the prevalent unrest to escape payment of their liabilities. At the end of the year 1922–23 the arrears of rates outstanding amounted to £1,740,000. In succeeding years the figure has dropped rapidly, and the amount of arrears now varies between £400,000 and £600,000 each year, and not all these rates are irrecoverable. A proportion of them is collected in the succeeding year. The amount outstanding varies from year to year, but there is none the less a marked improvement in payment, which reached its maximum in 1929–30, when 86 per cent. of the total warrants were lodged within the year.[2] It is to be noticed that a special grant is made by the Government to relieve agriculturists of the full burden of the local charges. The annual sum thus paid being £1,198,022 increased by £750,000 in 1931–32, which represents a flat rate of 3s. 4d. in the pound on the valuation of agricultural land.[3] A further result of the difficulties through

[1] Sec. 6.
[2] See Local Government Reports for details of these figures.
[3] Cf. Article by T. J. Keirnan, *Saorstat Eireann*. Official Handbook.

which the local authorities passed is to be found in the sums raised by loans. At the same time the indebtedness of local bodies has remained fairly stationary. In 1922 it was £15,005,380 and on March 31, 1932, it stood at £15,710,711. Local loans have to receive the sanction of the minister.

THE GROWTH OF COLLECTIVE BARGAINING

The device of joint action is peculiarly well suited to the needs of local authorities. In that direction two interesting steps were taken in 1926 and 1927. In the former year the Local Authorities (Mutual Assurance) Act was passed. Considerable attention had been devoted by the Council of the General Council of County Councils to the position of the local authorities in respect of insurance. It had been felt for some time that the amounts of the premiums payable were excessive, when measured with the insurable risks involved. The Act[1] of 1926 enables local authorities to join in forming a company to provide for their mutual insurance against damage to their property by fire, or their liability to pay compensation to their employees. It is interesting to recall that Mr. Robson, writing in 1931 on local government in England, suggests that "a common service such as the insurance of municipal buildings against losses by fire might profitably be undertaken at once by local authorities, acting in co-operation."[2] In the Free State the principle of co-operative action was carried further by the Local Authorities (Combined Purchasing) Act, 1925. The object of the Act is to enable local authorities to obtain commodities of standard quality at the lowest possible price. The minister appoints official contractors after obtaining competitive tenders. Lists of contractors are then published annually and the local authorities are thereby in a position to obtain their requirements from contractors at list prices.[3] The principle of these

---

[1] Cf. Local Government Report, 1925–26.
[2] *The Development of Local Government*, p. 20.
[3] Local Government Report, 1927–28, pp. 28–29

Acts is one that is capable of indefinite development. The Report of the ministry declares[1] that the value of this scheme, giving as it does to each authority the advantages of joint purchasing, has been "abundantly demonstrated in the early years by a comparison of the prices paid by authorities purchasing independently with the prices of official contractors. The material for comparisons," it continues; "decreases as the amount of independent purchasing falls, but there can be little doubt that the scheme is not less effective now in saving public money than it was in the early years."

THE CONTROL OF THE MINISTER

We must consider the nature of the ultimate control exercised by the minister. In the difficult times which followed the establishment of the Free State there was, not surprisingly, a demand for powers to enable the removal of such local authorities as had shown themselves unfitted for the discharge of their public duties. Accordingly a provision was inserted in the Local Government (Temporary Provisions) Act of 1923[2] to the effect that the minister may at any time order a local inquiry into the performance of its duties by any local authority. If, after such an inquiry the minister is satisfied that the duties of the local authority are not being duly and effectually discharged, or that it wilfully neglects to comply with any lawful order, direction, or regulation, or that it fails to comply with any judgment, order or decree of a competent court, or refuses after due notice to allow its accounts to be audited by an auditor of the minister, he may dissolve such local authority. He may then either order a new election or transfer the duties of the local authority to any person or persons. These ministerial powers have been ratified in a permanent form in the Local Government Act of 1925. It is also provided therein that if Commissioners be appointed after the dissolution of a local authority their

[1] 1928–29, p. 33.   [2] See 12 of the Act.

period of office shall not exceed three years, after which a new election of members is to be held. The discretion in the hands of the minister is wide. Whenever he makes an order "dissolving a local authority he may appoint such and so many persons as he shall think fit to perform the duties of each local authority, and may from time to time remove any or all such persons and appoint others in their place and may fix the tenure of office, duties, and remuneration of all such persons." It is added, "The Minister may from time to time by order do all such things and make all such regulations as in his opinion shall be necessary for giving full effect to any order made by him under this section."[1]

The powers thus granted to the Minister for Local Government and Public Health have been extensively used. The functions of local authorities offending against the Act are customarily transferred to local commissioners, appointed by the minister. In 1923, for example, five local authorities were dissolved by order of the minister. In 1924 the number rose to thirteen. In subsequent years the number has dwindled rapidly as the country became more settled. The following are the figures, since the Local Government Act came into force:

Year	Number of Local Authorities Dissolved	Year	Number of Local Authorities Dissolved
1923	5	1929	1
1924	13	1930	3
1925	4	1931	1
1926	3	1932	0
1927	0	1933	1
1928	2		

It is a mistake to suppose that the inhabitants in the respective localities are opposed to this exercise of ministerial authority. On the contrary, in some cases there is widespread regret when the Commissioner's term of office expires. In 1929

[1] Local Government Act (No. 5 of 1925), Sec. 72.

(for example) the term of office of the Commissioner who administered the affairs of the Ennis Urban District expired. The necessary steps were taken locally to hold an election for a new Council, but the people of Ennis nominated no candidate, in order to indicate their desire that the Commissioner should remain for a longer period in charge of the administration. In the ordinary course the matter was referred to the Clare County Council, who requested the minister to appoint the Commissioner for a further term. The request was complied with after the necessary fresh legislation[1] had been passed. A similar position subsequently arose in Trim. When, on the expiry of the Commissioner's term of office, no candidate was nominated, the matter was reported to the Meath County Council. The latter decided "in view of the reluctance of the electors of the Trim Urban Council to depart from the system of administration by Commissioners," to take no action. As in the case of Ennis, fresh statutory powers were obtained.[2] These events show in the first place that local jealousy of central interference is not widely felt. More important still, it indicates the difficulty experienced in the smaller local areas to secure an efficient administrative Council. There is indeed a certain volume of opinion which considers that local autonomy has been carried too far, and that in the case of smaller urban areas the self-governing powers should be revoked.

The power of dissolving local authorities is the supreme weapon placed in the hands of the minister. In itself it precludes the possibility of a conflict between the central and local government. But it remains a means by which a spasmodic, rather than a continuous, control may be exercised. Ministerial supervision is secured in other directions. Every action of the local authorities is done subject to the sanction of the minister. It is provided by legislation[3] that the exercise and performance of all powers, duties, or functions by statutory bodies shall be

[1] Ennis Urban District Council (Dissolution) Act, 1929.
[2] Trim Urban Council (Dissolution) Act, 1929.
[3] Ministers and Secretaries Act, No. 16 of 1924.

and remain subject to the direction and control of the minister, and the ministers shall be responsible for their administration of public services. It is indeed the responsibility of the minister which is the foundation of his authority.

The Board of Health and Public Assistance is to be regarded as performing the most important functions of local government. It is a sphere in which the control of the minister is peculiarly necessary. It is provided in the Act of 1925 that "it shall be the duty of the Minister in the exercise and performance of his powers and duties to take all such steps as may be desirable to secure the preparation, effective carrying-out, and co-ordination of measures conducive to the health of the people. . . ."[1] It is evident that in education, in health, in housing, whatever the local will, it is impossible for the State to permit local achievement to fall below a certain standard of minimum attainment. The standard is defined by the Legislature, and the minister retains full power to inspect and if need be to control. In the Housing Act of 1932 (for example) provision is made to the effect that if a local authority does not carry out adequately the work proposed, the minister may send down an engineer appointed by the department to perform it. Two aspects of the relations between the central government and local bodies are illustrated by this clause. It shows in the first place that in certain social services the locality must maintain a minimum level of efficiency. It shows, secondly, that local authorities are not in a position to disregard or to mitigate the purposes of State legislation, save in so far as provision is definitely made for it. Such powers are within the proper sphere of the central government. They could not with safety be abandoned. They involve a further power, namely, the reservation to the central government of a right of inspection and report, even in matters of a character essentially local.

Once more, in the all-important sphere of local finance, the minister holds a dominating position. His consent must

---

[1] Local Government Act, No. 5, Sec. 18, 1925.

be obtained before a local loan is floated.¹ He may by order make rules for regulating (i) "the estimating and raising of the expenses of boards of health, (ii) the accounts, audits and annual estimates of boards of health, in such a manner that units of cost for comparative and control purposes can be established."² In the general management of local finance the local bodies have an almost complete control. They compare revenue and expenditure; they strike the local rate. But even in purely internal finance there are limits which the local bodies may not pass. There are certain broad outlines within which they must keep. In January 1933 the Waterford County Council adopted an estimate for roads so greatly reduced that the minister refused to sanction it. He directed them to strike a proper estimate. A special meeting was called and the Council adopted a rate which met with the minister's approval.³ In the same manner refusal to strike a rate leads ultimately to the institution of legal proceedings against the recalcitrant County Council.

These are certain leading questions relating to the audit of the accounts of local authorities which cannot be overlooked. The subject is not merely one of technical routine; but is rather one upon which rests a most important aspect of local government. The position in Great Britain is remarkable. "Beneath the guise of what is called auditing," writes Dr. Robson[4] in a controversial passage, "a struggle for the substance of financial control has been proceeding apace for the last three or four decades. A state of affairs has now been reached when it may be said without exaggeration that the District Audit system constitutes not only a serious menace to the freedom of the local electorate and to the authority of the demo-

---

[1] Also under Local Government Act, 1927, Sec. 4. "A board of health shall not, without the previous consent of the County Council, exercise any power to borrow."

[2] Local Government Act, 1925 (No. 5), Sec. 86, which contains a summary of ministerial powers.

[3] Vide *Irish Times*, March 12, 1933.

[4] *Development of Local Government*, p. 337.

cratically elected local Council, but also a danger to the fundamental conception of ministerial responsibility on which our method of parliamentary government is supposed to rest."
In the Free State, local accounts are reviewed by the auditors of the Department of Local Government and Public Health. The position of the auditor has been strengthened since the passage of the Local Government Act of 1925. Previously, in many instances of questionable expenditure where there was an absence of negligence or misconduct the only course open to the auditor, precluded by law from allowing illegal expenditure, was to surcharge the signatories of the advice note as the persons causing the payment to be made. Such persons were frequently in a position to claim that they had acted in a purely ministerial capacity. Under the Act of 1925 it has now, however, become possible to fix with greater accuracy the personal responsibility "of members of a local authority or their servants for actions which involve illegal, unnecessary, or extravagant payments or which lead to avoidable losses."[1] The Act[2] provides that when a proposal is made at a meeting of a local authority to do anything in consequence of which an illegal payment is to be made or a loss or deficiency is likely to result, it shall be the duty of the responsible officer of the local authority to make objection, and if a decision is taken on such a proposal the names of the members present voting for and against such a decision and abstaining from voting are to be recorded. The power of the auditor under the Local Government (Ireland) Act of 1902 to charge against "persons accounting" the amount of any deficiency or loss occasioned by his negligence or misconduct is extended by the Act of 1925, so as to apply to any member or officer of a local authority. Audit by the central authority has always been the rule in Ireland, and the accounts of almost every local authority of whatsoever kind are audited by the Government auditors.

We have indicated the nature of the control exercised by the minister over local bodies. It remains to be asked whether

[1] Local Government Report, p. 49, 1925–27.   [2] Sec. 61.

or no it is excessive. A categorical answer it is, perhaps, impossible to give, for the successive crises which the Free State has weathered have led to a centralization of power. It is probable that a lessening in the importance of national issues would lead to a greater freedom for the local authorities. In the Free State, not merely is it the rule that the local bodies may exercise only those powers for which a special warranty in statute exists, but also there is a ministry charged with the particular duty of supervising local government. It is not surprising in consequence that a greater uniformity holds sway in the administration of local affairs than is perhaps either necessary or desirable. Local experiment is, after all, the very soul of local government. And while it is right that the department should investigate, compare, and suggest experiments, there is a danger that it will prefer uniformity to local initiative.

THE CITY MANAGERS

The most instructive experiment carried out by local bodies within recent years has been the appointment of General Managers in certain of the large cities. The ministers' power of dissolving local authorities drew attention to the merits of administration by Commissioners. This was particularly the case in Dublin and Cork where the Commissioner system was seen to best advantage. When the Commissioner's statutory three-year term of office was drawing to its close the trend of opinion was in favour of a continuation of the system, with the Commissioner working in conjunction with the elected Council. The term of the Commissioner's office was extended in order that a Commission of Inquiry might present a report. The Commission devoted its attention to the question of how the merits of the old system of an elected municipal Council might be co-related to the new demand for individual responsibility for efficient municipal government. In Dublin the position was complicated by intricate questions of area, finance, and town planning, so that the Bill to deal with Greater Dublin was not passed till 1930. In the case of Cork County Borough, these complications did not exist. The Cork City Management Bill became law in February 1929.[1] It is interesting to notice that the first step was taken by a local Committee formed in 1926.

The system set out in the Cork City Management Act is briefly as follows. The Manager exercises and performs for the Corporation all powers and duties not specifically reserved for the Council. The Manager holds office until he dies, resigns, or is removed. The Council may, by a resolution passed by a two-thirds majority, suspend him, and he may be removed with the sanction of the minister. He is required to furnish to the Lord Mayor all available information concerning transactions of the Corporation, and at the beginning of every month he is to furnish to the Lord Mayor and all members of the Council a statement of the financial position of the Corporation. He enjoys full control over all officers and servants of the Corporation subject to any Act or regulations in force. At the same time the control of the Council is safeguarded. The Manager must act by signed order in all cases where an elected body would act by resolution, and such signed orders are to be entered in a register available for inspection by members of the Council. In respect of financial matters, the Manager may authorize the making of payments, but the Lord Mayor may at any time require that such payments shall be submitted to him for his signature. It is the Manager's duty to prepare the annual financial estimates and to submit them to the Council at their rates meeting, to be adopted with or without amendment or modification. In conjunction with the creation of this form of city government the inherent defects of the old system were eliminated. The ward system of election was reformed by reducing the Council to a number that would conveniently be elected by the city as a whole. At the same time the old practice under which municipal affairs were dealt with in the first instance by some fifteen Committees of the

[1] No. 1 of 1929.

Council before being submitted to the Council as a whole was abolished.¹ The number itself constituted a guarantee for inefficiency. Dublin and Dun Laoghaire have followed the example of Cork and appointed City Managers.

In Germany the elected local councils fulfil a similar function in that their duty is not themselves to administer, but to supervise the trained permanent officials. "The economy and practical success of the method," writes Lord Bryce,² "are unquestioned, but some observers deem it too bureaucratic." The new system of local government adopted in the County Boroughs of Dublin and Cork and in the Borough of Dun Laoghaire merits consideration, in that it presents a practical solution of the difficulties of local authorities. An extension of the system to all County and Borough Councils is regarded, by many persons, of all shades of political opinion, as a very desirable and very likely reform.³

THE INTRUSION OF THE POLITICAL PARTY

There is a very distinct tendency towards the intrusion of the parties into the arena of local government. Candidates are now being nominated by the party conventions, and questions are decided on party lines.⁴ The Centre Party—the Farmers and Ratepayers League—were particularly noticeable in emphasizing this tendency. It is at the same time a tendency that is entirely regrettable. The cleavage of parties is decided by national issues. It has no fundamental relation to the needs of local policy. Local questions are distorted for party ends. The minds of the electors are diverted from the personal merits of the candidates. Moreover, when elected members of the Council get together as parties within these

---

[1] See *Local Government Report*, 1928–29, pp. 15–20, for full account.   [2] *Modern Democracies*, vol. ii, p. 484.

[3] In small boroughs the expense in salary would, no doubt, render it impracticable unless agreement was reached to appoint one Manager for several boroughs.

[4] Cf. the elections the Dublin Municipal Council, 1933.

bodies, such patronage as lies in the gift of the Council is liable to be misused for party purposes. The practice retains, however, one saving grace. It draws men of ability into local affairs. It gives them a chance of showing their quality and thereby opens a door to success in national politics. On an average nearly one-third of every Dáil is composed of men who have acquired previous experience in local government.

The nature of the restricted franchise in local government has been noted. It appears at first sight somewhat paradoxical that a man should find that less qualifications are required to vote at a national than at a local election. The present system excludes a very considerable proportion of the national electors from voting at the local elections. The figures in the register of 1929 were: Dáil electors, 1,717,684; local government electors, 1,041,030. It is not surprising, therefore, that one of the large parties introduced a Bill to reform the local government franchise. The position, it is to be remembered, is not similar to that of ten years ago. In 1923–24, the amount of local revenue derived from the central government subventions was only 22·56 per cent. of its total revenue. By 1928–29 the proportion received from the national exchequer was 37·7 per cent. On these grounds it might be argued that as in 1923–24 the ratepayers supplied by far the greater part of the local revenue, they alone were entitled to vote. Ten years later the position is radically changed. As the central government supplies more than half of the revenue which is raised by national taxation, it is only reasonable that the national taxpayer should become a local government elector. Otherwise one has taxation without representation. There would, however, on this line of argument, be necessarily an exclusion of all receiving relief from local bodies. On May 10, 1933, the Fianna Fail Government introduced a Local Government Bill in which it is provided that "Every person (without distinction of sex) who on any qualifying date is a citizen of Saorstat Eireann, and has attained the age of twenty-one years, and is not subject to any legal incapacity, shall be entitled to be registered in the register of electors prepared in relation to that qualifying date, as a local government elector in the local government area in which he was ordinarily resident on the said qualifying date."

THE DECLINE OF CIVIC PATRIOTISM

The most obvious weaknesses in the structure of Irish local government were removed in the early years of the Free State. The multiplicity of councils which previously existed had extremely disadvantageous results. A welter of small authorities, with overlapping functions, could lead to nothing but inefficient administration. The most outstanding example of the weakness of small areas was, as has been suggested, in the sphere of public health. Small authorities showed themselves lacking in either the means or the will to carry out the functions with which they had been entrusted. . . . And in normal times these small authorities, with their local vested interests, might well have defied reform. But the troubled times which accompanied the emergence of the Free State enabled the central government to uproot them with comparative ease. There can be no doubt but that the nature of local government has changed very considerably in last few decades. The altered circumstances require a corresponding modification of the local areas. The larger area has been found in the county. There is a prevalent impression that large areas of administration are opposed to the true principles of local government and in themselves undemocratic. This outlook is quite unsubstantiated by the course of events. Local government is not menaced by a larger area of jurisdiction, but by excessive centralization. And it is the inefficiency of small areas that encourages centralization.

Local self-government secures a benefit of real value in encouraging the development of local centres of thought and action. Citizens of the Free State have had reason to dread the excessive predominance of its capital city. The provincial cities, instead of becoming representative of local opinion, tend to take their ideas submissively from Dublin. It is of importance to the standard of national politics that the quality of local politics should be revivified. Men engaged in local politics need to be inspired with something of the burning local patriotism so well portrayed by G. K. Chesterton in the *Napoleon of Notting Hill*. Only if this spirit is prevalent in the local units of self-government is there any hope that sufficient vigilance will be exercised. For nothing is of more importance than that the work of the local bodies should be closely and continuously scrutinized. It is to be much regretted that, generally speaking, so little interest is taken in the functioning of local administration. New conditions may well call for a comprehensive reconstruction of local government machinery. It is extremely doubtful whether the extent of the powers at present possessed by local authorities in all the various spheres of local government are sufficient to meet modern demands. While a survey of local functions in the social services, in health, housing, education, and town-planning would be a necessary preliminary to a decision on the sufficiency or insufficiency of local powers, yet the fact remains that in the majority of cases such powers as exist are by no means fully exercised. Within the range of existent powers local activity could be enormously intensified. Mr. and Mrs. Sidney Webb[1] suggest that in Great Britain "already more than fifteen hundred million pounds' worth of national capital is being administered in this country by the local authorities; and if these authorities were even as energetic and enterprising as the best among them now are, the amount would probably be doubled or trebled." In the Free State the position is similar and the figures quoted indicate how greatly the range of direct local administration could be increased within existent powers. The interesting steps taken in the Combined Purchasing and Mutual Assurance Acts suggest how local administration would be enlarged were it to become the rule for local authorities, in their position of

[1] Mr. and Mrs. Webb, *A Constitution for the Socialist Commonwealth of Great Britain*, p. 238.

associations of consumers, to free themselves from their present subjection to rings and price agreements among contractors, by producing for themselves like the co-operative societies as many as possible of the commodities they require. Were this practice adopted it is estimated as much as one-half of the whole of the industries and services would fall within the sphere of local government.[1]

Another aspect of the development of local government is to be noticed in the possibility of expansion among the services administered by local bodies. The distribution of coal and the handling of the milk supply are cases which come under consideration.[2] The milk supply in the large cities (particularly in Dublin) has been severely criticized as costly, unhygienic, and badly distributed. In the financial resolutions for 1933 a grant of £100,000 was provided for the distribution[3] of free milk to necessitous children. It is suggested that, while the local authorities should not enjoy a monopoly, they should be permitted to undertake the collective provision of a more adequate and cheaper supply.[4]

In Irish local government nothing is more evident than that the growth of local patriotism needs to be fostered. The history of administration by Commissioners indicates that local pride is not sufficiently developed to resent a government imposed from above. Local emulation and rivalry in efficiency should become characteristic. Without local pride or local shame, local institutions will remain undeveloped. In the Free State, statistics showing the extent of local and municipal achievement would be invaluable. As Mr. and Mrs. Webb[5]

[1] Mr. and Mrs. Webb, *A Constitution for the Socialist Commonwealth of Great Britain*, p. 238.
[2] Cf. Robson, op. cit., p. 202.
[3] It was distributed by the local authorities.
[4] Waterford City attempted an experiment of this kind. When milk price was high the Council sold milk in competition with private dealers. While at first successful, the falling price of milk led to the conclusion of the experiment.
[5] *Socialist Commonwealth of Great Britain*, pp. 239–240.

suggest, we need to see all the local authorities regularly compared, in sets, according to their population, as to the average percentage of children at school, the proportion each year passed forward to higher stages of education, the physical records at each age, the sickness-rate as well as the death-rate; the number, per thousand population, of books in the public libraries, attendances at picture-galleries, concerts, recreation-grounds; acres of parks and open spaces available, the relation between the total population and the provision of hospitals, convalescent homes, mental asylums, homes for the aged . . . the relative success of the several administrations in cost per unit of production . . . and so on. And it is to be remembered that local government in Ireland is in a favourable position in that the country remains predominantly agricultural. Whilst centralization has been the tendency since 1922, it has been much accentuated by the vital issues with which the country has been faced. A slackening of this tension, combined with a growth in local patriotism, would lead to a revival of the influence of local bodies. It was, after all, in small communities that democracy first arose; from them the theories of its philosophers were derived; and it is upon their adaptability to changing circumstances that hopes for the future of democratic government must ultimately rest.

CHAPTER XIV

FINANCE AND FINANCIAL RELATIONS

THE problem of finance provided the most important of the practical issues in Anglo-Irish politics prior to 1921. Sir Horace Plunkett stated the position clearly when he wrote[1] that "the tendency of recent political thought among constitutional Nationalists has been towards a form of government resembling as closely as possible that of the Dominions, and, since the geographical position of Ireland imposes obvious restrictions in respect of naval and military affairs, the claim for Dominion Home Rule was concentrated upon a demand for unrestricted fiscal powers." And, moreover, apart entirely from the claims of national sovereignty, a strong financial case was made for complete fiscal autonomy, a case whose substantial accuracy was vindicated by the Report of the 1912 Committee on Irish Finance. In their report the members of that Committee held[2] "that the experience of the last few years amply confirms the theory that a financial partnership with Great Britain does lead in Ireland to a scale of expenditure beyond the requirements and beyond the resources of the country itself." And the Committee recommended,[3] subject to reservations in certain matters of detail, that "the power of levying and imposing all taxation in Ireland should rest with the Irish Government." It was a recommendation which the British Government never endorsed in practice until events in Ireland compelled a radical revision of its whole attitude towards Irish affairs.

[1] Report of the Proceedings of the Irish Convention, p. 5.
[2] Page 6.
[3] Report of the Proceedings of the Irish Convention, p. 28. Professor Adams, who has written the Foreword to this book, was a member of this Committee.

THE FINANCIAL AGREEMENTS WITH GREAT BRITAIN

The financial status secured by the Anglo-Irish Treaty destroyed the fiscal unity of the United Kingdom. Dominion status involved the creation of a new and quite independent financial machinery. At the same time the previous dependence of Irish finance on that of Whitehall made necessary certain provisions of great practical importance. These were included in Article 5 of the Treaty. So much subsequent controversy has arisen in respect of the interpretation of this Article that it merits being quoted in full: It reads as follows:

"The Irish Free State shall assume liability for the service of the Public Debt of the United Kingdom as existing at the date hereof and towards the payment of war pensions as existing at that date in such proportion as may be fair and equitable, having regard to any just claims on the part of Ireland by way of set-off or counter-claim, the amount of such sums being determined in default of agreement by the arbitration of one or more independent persons being citizens of the British Empire."

This Article, whilst equitable in intention, is lamentably lacking in precision. Neither the liability of the Free State Government in respect of a proportionate share of the Public Debt and War Pensions, nor that of the British Government in respect of the Irish counter-claim was fixed with any attempt at accurate definition. Indeed, the Article appeared likely to become a source of friction. Fortunately this was averted by subsequent negotiations which modified the terms contained in the Treaty. In the Agreement on the Boundary question, signed at London on December 3, 1925, by the representatives of the Governments of Great Britain, Northern Ireland, and the Free State, the latter was released from its obligations under Article 5 of the Treaty. In return for this valuable concession it assumed all liability undertaken by the British Government in respect of malicious damage done since the Assembly of the first Dáil in January 1919.[1] This Agreement, which was of first importance, was ratified by legislation in both the British and Free State Parliaments.[2] In 1926[3] a subsequent Agreement, termed the "Heads of the Ultimate Financial Settlement" between Great Britain and Free State, finally determined the then outstanding financial questions raised by the dissolution of the fiscal unity of the United Kingdom. It was arranged, *inter alia*, that the question of double income tax should be settled generally on a residence basis, and the two Governments agreed to introduce legislation necessary for this purpose.

The weakness of the financial settlement contained in the Treaty lay in its lack of definition. This became evident in the subsequent Anglo-Irish dispute on the question of payment of the Land Annuities. The latter are half-yearly payments collected from the tenant farmers who, with State assistance, bought their land under a succession of Land Acts, particularly the Wyndham Act of 1903. They are in effect "payments on the instalment system by the Irish tenant for the land he has bought." These payments, amounting to over £3,000,000 a year, are collected by the Land Commission and, till the present dispute, they passed through the Free State Ministry for Finance and the National Debt Commissioners before being ultimately received by the holders of Irish Land Stock. In the Treaty these payments were not specifically mentioned. Were or were they not included under the heading of "Public Debt"? It is a question that does not admit of a categorical reply. It can and has been argued with equal logic that they were and that they were not included under that term. The matter is of practical importance in that if the answer is that they were included then the Financial Settlement of December 1925 released the Free State from its obligation to pay. On the other hand, it is apparent that the British Government at any

[1] Cf. Damage to Property (Compensation) (Amendment) Act, 1926 (No. 19 of 1926) for matters of detail agreed to.
[2] In Ireland (Confirmation of Agreement) Act, 1925, Amd. Treaty (Confirmation of Amending Agreement) Act, 1925 (No. 40 of 1925).
[3] March 16th.

rate did not at that time consider the annuities as a part of the Public Debt. For the annuities were the subject of two further financial agreements. In the first, that of February 12, 1923, the Free State Government undertook "to pay at agreed intervals to the appropriate fund the full amount of the annuities accruing due from time to time, making themselves responsible for the actual collection from the tenant purchaser." And in the Heads of the Ultimate Financial Settlement the Free State agreed to pay the full amounts of the annuities accruing due under the Irish Land Acts, 1891–1909, "without any deduction whatsoever, whether on account of Income Tax or otherwise."[1] Besides the annuities payments, several less important monies are involved both in these settlements and the subsequent dispute. But the vital thing to notice about these agreements is that neither of the documents was ratified by the Oireachtas. That of 1923 was signed for the Free State by President Cosgrave and for the British Government by John W. Hills. It was not presented to the Dáil until April 1932 when the dispute had already arisen. The Agreement of 1926 was presented to the Dáil on November 16, 1926. It was not formally ratified. President de Valera relies on the basic constitutional doctrine, that agreements entered into by a minister must be approved by Parliament. The British Government appeal with some inconsistency, as Professor Keith[2] remarks, to International Law to support its claim that the financial settlements required no ratification.[3] From this dispute two facts emerge. In the first place it is evident that a mistake of the first magnitude was made in not making the validity of the Agreements clear by casting them into Treaty form and specifically insisting on a formal parliamentary sanction. In the second place, the dispute emphasizes the necessity for agreement between the British and Free State

---

[1] March 16, 1926.
[2] *Constitutional Law of the British Dominions*, p. vii.
[3] See Correspondence between the two Governments on this Question, published in Cmd. 4056.

Governments on some form of super-national tribunal whose impartiality is unquestioned by either party.

THE DEPARTMENT OF FINANCE

The great advance in constitutional status attained in 1921 is indicated by the creation of the Department of Finance. In the Home Rule Acts only a very limited control over fiscal policy was to be granted to the Irish Government, and the conception of the fiscal unity of the British Isles was once more upheld in the correspondence prior to the signature of the Treaty. The Prime Minister wrote[1] that it was necessary that the British and Irish Governments should agree to impose "no protective duties or other restrictions upon the flow of transport trade and commerce between all parts of these islands." This position had to be abandoned. The Government of the Free State was invested with full control over its fiscal policy. Consequently, upon the reorganization of administration carried out in 1924 under the Ministries and Secretaries Act a Department of Finance was established. Its functions were comprehensively defined. In broad outline, the intention was to secure unity of financial administration by investing in the department all duties and services connected therewith.

The Department of Finance occupies a pre-eminent position among various organs of government. In that the annual estimates are proposed by the Minister for Finance, the estimates of the other departments must previously receive his sanction. In the autumn of each year each department tabulates its proposed expenditure for the following year. This estimate is sent to the Department of Finance. Each item is carefully scrutinized and the need for every new proposal involving expenditure must be fully proved by the department concerned before it can be sanctioned by the Department of Finance. A very great deal depends upon the scrutiny thus exercised. The control of the Ministry of Finance is the only real check upon unnecessary or wasteful expenditure by the departments.

[1] Letter of July 20, 1921. Cmd. 1502.

It has proved invaluable. Since the ministry must balance receipts against expenditure it has a very practical conception of what the State can afford. Almost invariably the estimates of the departments need to be cut down. And, as we have seen, the control of the ministry is rendered the more significant by the fact that the debates in the Dáil never result in any considerable reduction in the Estimates.

REVENUE AND EXPENDITURE

The task facing the Free State Government in 1922–23 was one of peculiar difficulty, and in no sphere was this more apparent than in that of Finance. The revolution and subsequent Civil War involved the State in heavy liabilities in respect of compensation as well as disorganizing the financial administration. The Government aimed at restoring stability by adopting a conservative financial policy. In the three years 1922–23 to 1924–25, not only was normal expenditure fully met by revenue, but also abnormal expenditure, which amounted over this period of three years to more than £26,000,000, was covered as to £17,500,000 by surplus and abnormal revenue —£8,500,000 was met by borrowing.

Subsequent to 1925 the financial reorganization was completed. It is interesting to indicate the broad outlines of the financial policy that has been pursued. The following figures show the relation of revenue to expenditure since 1922:[1]

Year	Revenue	Expenditure
	£	£
1922–23	27,863,000	29,595,718
1923–24	31,414,255	38,687,006
1924–25	26,948,114	27,937,834
1925–26	25,439,097	26,693,488
1926–27	25,060,379	27,392,787
1927–28	24,123,270	26,180,381
1928–29	24,221,046	25,435,734
1929–30	24,172,639	25,072,711
1930–31	24,365,197	25,266,584
1931–32	24,658,150	24,661,000
1933–34	30,229,182	28,874,298

[1] Cf. Statistical Abstract, 1932.

Finance and Financial Relations 257

In the early years an examination of the individual items reveals a very considerable expenditure on the Army Compensation and Pensions. A rapid reduction was effected in these abnormal items. The saving thus secured enabled an extension of the social services and more considerable grants to Agriculture. Thus in 1923-24 Education represented 11·66 per cent., in 1927-28 14·46 per cent. of the total expenditure. The needs of Agriculture, the staple occupation of the people, are placed in the forefront of financial policy. The Report of the Commission of Inquiry into De-Rating declared that "it is plain that the agriculturists' share of the benefits of public expenditure is far greater than their contribution to taxation. . . ."[1] The accession of the Fianna Fail Party to office has led to rapid increase in the expenditure on the social services.

An analysis of the principal sources of revenue reveals a striking dependence on indirect taxation. That dependence has increased steadily since 1922. In 1925, for example, the proportion of the total revenue raised by indirect taxation was 60 per cent. In 1930 it was approximately 66 per cent., whilst in the following year it reached almost 70 per cent. The protectionist policy, accepted by both the large parties, has been applied with an ever-increasing intensity since the creation of the Free State. The unshaken ascendancy of the doctrines of economic nationalism makes it probable that the percentage of revenue derived from indirect taxation will tend, for a period at any rate, to increase rather than decline. Of the revenue raised by direct taxation between 60 and 70 per cent. is derived from income tax.

The importance of local finance has already been indicated. Local expenditure amounts to approximately 40 per cent. of national expenditure. Local taxation has tended to rise, more especially in recent years. This is due primarily to an extension of social services and improved relief schemes. Local expenditure amounts to between nine and ten millions and of that

[1] Pp. 127-128.

amount nearly 40 per cent. is received in grants from the central Exchequer. The latter makes a special grant each year to relieve agriculturists from the full burden of the local rates.

Even a brief outline of the finance of the Free State indicates the change in Irish financial policy that has resulted from the destruction of the fiscal unity of the United Kingdom. The dependence on indirect taxation, notably on Customs, would not have been possible under the provisions of the Home Rule Acts. It gives a retrospective justification to the insistence of the Nationalist members of the Convention on the supreme importance of the Customs issue. An interesting comparative analysis as to the manner in which the Free State has exercised her fiscal independence has been carried out by Dr. Kiernan.[1] He compares the financial position of Norway with that of the Free State in the year 1928–29. The population of Norway is approximately 2,810,000, that of the Free State 2,971,992. In Norway 1,864,371 persons lived in rural districts, in the Free State 1,815,496. Norway's total expenditure was £32,640,601, that of the Free State £27,731,352. Norway's debt charge amounted to 18·84 per cent. of her total expenditure, the Free State's to only 6·61. Expenditure on social services was more considerable in Norway, where £5,595,461 was spent on Education against the Free State's £4,080,389, and where approximately £7,000,000 was spent on Public Works and Social Services, as against the Free State's £5,000,000. The Free State spent more on Agriculture, £1,090,472 as against Norway's £875,706, but the balance was redressed in Trade and Industry, upon which Norway spent £703,432, as against £354,734.

[1] *Saorstat Eireann*. Official Handbook.

CHAPTER XV

EXTERNAL AFFAIRS

During the last half-century the large rôle played in politics at Westminster by the division of opinion between the supporters of Home Rule and the supporters of the settlement achieved by the Act of Union, led many to suppose that the difference between them was one of kind. In fact, as the ultimate solution of the Irish Question has shown, it was one only of degree. In no sphere is this more plainly illustrated than in that of the control of foreign affairs. Both Unionists and Home Rulers were agreed that in such matters the British Foreign Office was to be the sole authority. This was a position quite unacceptable to the Sinn Fein Party. In 1919 Dáil Eireann created a Ministry of Foreign Affairs, and thereby emphasized the completeness of the breach with the Home Rule solution. The nature of the settlement achieved in 1921 was indicated by the continuation of this ministry. Its function and new title—the Ministry for External Affairs—were confirmed by the Ministers and Secretaries Act. In the first place, the department is the normal channel for inter-imperial communications; in the second it deals with international relations.

INTER-IMPERIAL RELATIONS

In the Treaty it was provided that "Ireland shall have the same constitutional status in the Community of Nations known as the British Empire, as the Dominion of Canada, the Commonwealth of Australia, the Dominion of New Zealand, and the Union of South Africa . . . and shall be styled and known as the Irish Free State." It is added, more particularly, that "the position of the Irish Free State in relation to the Imperial Parliament and Government and otherwise shall be that of the Dominion of Canada, and the law, practice, and constitutional usage governing the relationship of the Crown or the representative of the Crown and of the Imperial Parliament to the Dominion of Canada shall govern their relationship to the Irish Free State."[1] One aspect of these Articles needs consideration. It is the inadequacy of the analogy that is drawn. In other words, an agreement may declare that Ireland shall have the same constitutional status as the Dominions, but the fact remains that both its past and its future development is bound to be radically different. "From the point of view of the Dominions," writes Sir Cecil Hurst, "the important thing to note is the evolution from a position of dependence to one of freedom from control. These great communities have all the time been climbing a ladder. Now they have reached the top; but the climbing practice is common to all the communities which form part of the Empire. Each of them is gradually ... as it develops in strength and capacity passing upward from the stage in which the community is wholly subject to control exercised from London, to that in which the measure of control diminishes and so on to that in which the control has ceased entirely. The Dominions of to-day were but Crown Colonies in the past. The Crown Colonies of to-day will be Dominions in days to come. There is nothing static about the British Empire."[2] This excellent summary of Dominion development illustrates the wide divergence in position between the Irish Free State and the Dominions. The all-important difference is that Ireland has advanced to self-government not by a process of evolution but by an act of revolution. And this fact, in effect, negatives the reality and the accuracy of the analogy with the law and constitutional practice of the Dominion of Canada. Two assumptions underlay the definition of the status of the Free State in the Anglo-Irish Treaty. On the one hand, it was assumed that a Dominion which had come into being in a manner quite opposed to that of the other Dominions

[1] The Treaty, Arts. 1 and 2.
[2] *Great Britain and The Dominions*, Harris Foundation Lectures, 1927, pp. 12–13.

could be placed upon a similar constitutional basis. On the other hand, it was assumed that having acquired this status, the Free State would evolve along lines similar to those of the Dominions. A brief examination of Anglo-Irish relations subsequent to the Treaty will reveal the fact that neither of these assumptions has been justified.

British statesmen were too wise to attempt to insert a definition of Dominion status in the Treaty. "What," asked Mr. Lloyd George,[1] "does Dominion status mean? It is difficult," he answered, "and dangerous to give a definition. When I made a statement at the request of the Imperial Conference to this House as to what had passed at our gathering, I pointed out the anxiety of all the Dominion delegates not to have any rigid definition." And in respect of Ireland the Prime Minister added: "All we can say is that whatever measure of freedom Dominion status gives to Canada, Australia, New Zealand, or South Africa, that will be extended to Ireland, and there will be the guarantee, contained in the mere fact that the status is the same, that wherever there is an attempt at encroaching upon the rights of Ireland every Dominion will begin to feel that its own position is put in jeopardy. This is a guarantee which is of infinite value to Ireland." But in the Dáil, as we have already suggested, there was little belief in the Treaty as the final basis of settlement, and more important still, with the exception of Mr. Kevin O'Higgins, there was no clearly expressed support given to the conception of the evolutionary development of the Dominions.

More than a decade has now elapsed since the foundation of the Free State. During that period the whole tendency in Inter-Imperial affairs has been towards the securing of complete autonomy both in law and in practice by the British Dominions. Their new status was defined in the Report[2] of the 1926 Imperial Conference. "They are autonomous communities within the British Empire, equal in status, in no way subordinate

[1] *Parliamentary Debates*, 1921, December 14th.
[2] Cmd. 2768, 1926.

one to another in any aspect of their domestic or external affairs, though united by a common allegiance to the Crown and freely associated as members of the British Commonwealth of Nations." Later it is added that, "Equality of status, so far as Britain and the Dominions are concerned, is thus the root principle governing our Inter-Imperial relations. But the principles of equality and similarity, appropriate to status, do not universally extend to function. Here we require something more than immutable dogmas. For example, to deal with questions of diplomacy and questions of defence we require also flexible machinery—machinery which can from time to time be adapted to the changing circumstances of the world." In this manner the special responsibility of Great Britain is still emphasized in a manner unacceptable to Irish opinion. It was felt that the doctrine of equality of status was being, stealthily as it were, deprived of practical effect. The phrase "immutable dogmas" was doubtless an allusion to the emphasis placed by the Free State delegates upon the need for a realization of the full meaning of the principle of co-equality. They had no wish that "questions of diplomacy and questions of defence" should be referred to in the context, for the purpose of demonstrating the unity of the British Commonwealth of Nations in the field of international relations. Indeed, as we shall see, the position defined in the Report was undermined by the Free State Government within the next few years. Since 1926 further advances have been made in the adjustment of Inter-Imperial relations, but they represent a formal restatement of the position attained in 1926 rather than new progress. It might, indeed, be said that with the Reports of the Imperial Conferences of 1926 and 1930 and the Statute of Westminster, the British Dominions have reached complete independence. Their constitutional evolution has reached its ultimate goal. What the Balfour declaration propounded in 1926 as the principle to guide Inter-Imperial relations has by the Statute of Westminster received legal recognition. For this development in Inter-Imperial constitutional law and practice, the Free State is in no small measure responsible. "We had one purpose in 1926," said Mr. McGilligan,[1] the Minister for External Affairs, "and that was that there must be uprooted from the whole system of this State the British Government; and in substitution for that there was accepted the British Monarch. He is a king who functions entirely, so far as Irish affairs are concerned, at the will of the Irish Government, and that was the summing up of the whole aim and the whole result of the Conferences of 1926, 1929, and 1930: that one had to get completely rid of any power, either actual or feared, that the British Government had in relation to this country. In substitution for that under the Treaty there was accepted the monarchy, as I say, a monarchy in every respect in relation to Irish affairs, subject to the control of an Irish Government." The achievement of the successive Imperial Conferences has been to reconcile the autonomy of the Dominions with the unity of the Commonwealth. For, though difficult to define in juridical terminology, there remains a unity which is symbolized, however vaguely, by the Crown. In the final message of "fidelity and devotion" addressed by the Imperial Conference of 1926 to "His Majesty the King, Emperor of India," we read: "The foundation of our work has been the sure knowledge that to each of us, as to all your Majesty's subjects, the Crown is the abiding symbol and emblem of the Unity of the British Commonwealth of Nations."[2]

It would be a mistake to regard this message as mere verbiage. It is unquestioned that, in the working of British political institutions, the Crown remains the most important as "a symbol and emblem of unity." But the union thus symbolized is a personal union. And in a personal union the States concerned are separate international persons. Such a union in no way conflicts with the declaration that the Dominions "are autonomous communities within the British Empire equal in status. . . ." And to the conception of a purely personal union, Irish opinion is not opposed. But it is hostile to the conception of an indi-

[1] *Dáil Debates*, July 16, 1931.   [2] Cmd. 2768.

visible Crown. "The unity of the Crown," said Mr. Amery, the Secretary of State for the Dominions, in a speech made in 1926, "is a cardinal point in the Constitution of the British Empire." And he added, "The Crown in the British Empire is one and undivided." It is a doctrine which the Free State could not accept. The constitutional framework of the Free State is established upon the fundamental conception of the several monarchy functioning through a series of constitutional and legal fictions, upon different advices given by the Cabinets of the respective States of the Commonwealth. The idea of an indivisible Crown appears indefensible. On the one hand, theoretically it is unsatisfactory. It involves us in a welter of legal conundrums in such matters as treaties between the Dominions and the right of the Dominions to secede. How can the Dominions make treaties with each other if the unity of the Crown is a cardinal point in the Constitution of the British Empire? On the other hand, in practice it is no less objectionable. Any attempt to hold the Commonwealth together on the basis of an indivisible Crown appears foredoomed to failure. In respect of the Free State, or one might go further and say in respect of the whole of Ireland, it would be nothing less than disastrous. If one postulates the unity of the Crown, then that Crown is (as regards Ireland) an alien Crown. But a large part of the external policy of the Free State is based upon the conception of the Kingdom of Ireland. The Crown of the Irish Free State is quite distinct from the Crown of Great Britain. And, moreover—and it is a fact of vital importance—the notion of the Kingdom of Ireland is one which presents the most practical possibility of unity among Irishmen themselves. It was upon this conception that Kevin O'Higgins built his whole policy, and it approaches closely to the idea of "external association" put forward by Mr. de Valera in 1921-22.

The nature of the reforms in the legal structure of the Commonwealth has been indicated in dealing with the executive and legislative functions of the representative of the Crown and with the Privy Council appeals. It will be noticed, however, that while the passage of such reforms has in all probability been hastened by the admission of the Free State to Dominion status, the Minister for External Affairs was accurate in maintaining that the old legal framework of the Empire "has been brought to an end by four years of assiduous concentrated collaboration between the lawyers and statesmen of the States of the Commonwealth." But it is obviously easier to secure unanimous co-operation in the negative task of destroying legal machinery opposed to contemporary thought than to unite in realizing a positive ideal. For as the Imperial Conference Report of 1926 stated, "no account, however accurate, of the negative relations in which Great Britain and the Dominions stand to each other can do more than express a portion of the truth. The British Empire is not founded upon negations. It depends essentially, if not formally, on positive ideals. Free institutions are its life-blood. Free co-operation is its instrument. Peace, security, and progress are among its objects. . . . And though every Dominion is now, and must always remain, the sole judge of the nature and extent of its co-operation, no common cause will, in our opinion, be thereby imperilled." Now it has been a frequent imperialist criticism that the Irish Free State has (since its foundation till 1932) kept the letter but ignored the spirit of the Treaty Settlement. And it has this much justification that the Irish Government has paid far more attention to the negative formulae than to "the positive ideals" upon which the Commonwealth depends.

In 1931 the Minister[1] for External Affairs said in the Dáil, "Deputies will agree with me when I say that there can be no two views on the question that when this country accepted the status of Canada in certain respects in 1921 the status of Canada then accepted was not a stereotyped legal formula.[2] Therein

[1] Mr. P. McGilligan, *Dáil Debates*, July 16, 1931.
[2] This is, of course, quite correct and was substantiated by several statements of Mr. Lloyd George in 1921–22. In his note of November 14, 1933, Mr. Thomas implicitly contradicted the essential

lies the kernel of the whole Treaty position and the key to the progress that has gone on . . . since 1926." These words on the surface imply an acceptance of that evolutionary progress which represents the genius of the British Commonwealth development. In reality, however, as the remainder of the speech shows, the minister was thinking solely of the negative aspect—namely the progress that has been made in destroying the legal formulae of the old colonial Empire. But now that the Dominions have reached the goal of their constitutional evolution, a more positive co-operation is required. It is most unlikely to come from the Irish Government, whatever party may happen to be in power until its constitutional status commands a more widespread satisfaction amongst the people.

The underlying conception of the British Constitution and of the British Commonwealth of Nations has been that of evolutionary development. This political doctrine has not found a ready acceptance in Ireland.

(i) In the first place, the principle is not illustrated by Irish history. Unlike the Dominions, Ireland did not evolve towards Dominion status. It is and it always was, in the eyes of its people, a sovereign and independent nation. Neither the Norman invasion nor the Act of Union could deprive it either of its sovereignty or its nationhood. The legislative Union with England was never accepted by the Irish people. Hence it is that there exists a peculiar controversy as to whether the settlement reached in 1921 should or should not be termed a Treaty. The British view is that certain powers were delegated to that part of Ireland to be known as the Irish Free State by Act of Parliament. The Irish view is that it is an international Treaty negotiated by the United Kingdom on the one hand and

feature of the Treaty Settlement in questioning the right of the Free State Legislature to amend its Constitution in matters affecting the status of the Crown and the Privy Council. As Professor Keith quite rightly pointed out, the amendments afforded "neither moral nor legal ground for criticism." See *Manchester Guardian*, December 6, 1933.

Irish nation on the other. The two conflicting interpretations of the 1921 settlement have given foundation to quite conflicting and irreconcilable views respecting the international status of the Free State. To this we shall recur. Here it is sufficient to point out how wide is the gulf between the history and development of the Free State and the political evolution of the other Dominions.

(ii) The position of the Irish Free State in relation to the Imperial Parliament and Government was based[1] on the law, practice, and constitutional usage of the Dominion of Canada. This proviso was inserted partly to provide a guarantee both of independence and future political development to the Free State and partly to avoid the danger of giving a precise definition of Dominion status. It presented the most obvious and the most simple solution. "There is nothing static," Sir Cecil Hurst has said, "about the British Empire." It was dangerous therefore to make a precise statement of Dominion status. It was, of course, also dangerous not to make it. There is no analogy at all between the past political and constitutional development of Canada and the past political and constitutional development of the Irish Free State. The prospect that they would evolve along similar lines is therefore somewhat remote. Yet that is what the Treaty Settlement contemplated. And so long as it was a question of destroying the legal relics of the old British Empire it was justified. But it is difficult to suppose that the future evolution of Canada and of the Free State is likely to be similar.

(iii) Finally, the whole underlying principle of the development of the British Commonwealth has been challenged by an influential section of Irish thought. The Balfour Declaration (already quoted) was a formula which showed that the British Dominions had reached the goal of their constitutional development. They were autonomous communities within the British Empire. This declaration, as Professor Zimmern[2] has said, is

[1] The Treaty, Art. 2.
[2] "L'Empire Britannique après la Conférence d'Ottawa." Extract from the *Revue de l'Université de Bruxelles*, 1933, p. 277.

"analogous to the Declaration of Independence of the United States in 1776, but with a political philosophy quite different, derived from a Burke rather than from a Rousseau, from Common rather than from Roman Law." This distinction is of great interest. For since 1916 Irish political thought has tended to draw its inspiration from Rousseau rather than from Burke. We have already referred to that conception of an inalienable and always existent national sovereignty which held sway in revolutionary Ireland and whose origins are to be found in the teachings of Rousseau. It rests upon a political theory directly opposed to the main current of English thought. That is why negotiation and agreement between the two countries proved and still proves so difficult. They speak in different political languages. In the Proclamation of the Irish Republic in 1916 "the right of the people of Ireland to the ownership of Ireland and to the unfettered control of Irish destinies" was declared to be "sovereign and indefeasible." The dependence on national Right was reaffirmed in the Democratic Programme of 1919. It is once more peculiarly evident in the correspondence which passed between Mr. de Valera and the Prime Minister prior to the signature of the Anglo-Irish Treaty. The Irish claims were exceedingly difficult to refute. To do so it was necessary to question their basic assumption, and no doubt Mr. Lloyd George felt that a correspondence of that nature was not suitable for a philosophic controversy on the issue of national rights. The question recurred in respect of the oath to be taken by members of the Oireachtas under the Treaty. Only an imperfect comprehension of the prevalent Irish political thought can have led the British Government to make the Oath mandatory under the Treaty. For in Ireland the Continental doctrine of national sovereign Rights inevitably regards such an Oath as an infringement of National Sovereignty. In a statement in March 1932, to the Secretary of State for Dominion Affairs, the Irish Government based their case for the abolition of the Oath on "the absolute right" of the people to modify the Constitution. To the contention that the Oath was "an integral part of the Treaty made ten years ago" it was replied that that was no longer the issue, but it was rather one of the right of the people to remove an "intolerable burden."[1] To many English people the latter description seemed somewhat fanciful. It was because their ingrained political thought was quite opposed to a doctrine of Rights. If one allows the present approximation of Irish to Continental political thought, it is at once apparent that in making the Oath mandatory under the Treaty the British Government made a grave blunder. Indeed, it is not too much to say that the disruption of the Treaty Settlement could not have been better planned than it was by the insertion of that provision.

There is a further important issue raised by the influence of Continental thought. A solution of political problems by means of an absolute standard of Rights implies that it is a problem of unvarying elements. If it is one which changes with the successive changes in the history and outlook of man, then logically it must be denied, as Mazzini denied, that the theory of Rights can provide any final answer to the problem. No conceivable answer can be more than tentative and provisional.[2] For the basis of the problem varies continually. The assumption of finality is one which disregards the very nature of the problem it seeks to solve. Among the revolutionaries of the eighteenth century the doctrine of Rights was widely accepted. "And for Right, the Right which is the same at all times," says Professor Vaughan,[3] "they had a consuming passion." Their position was attacked by Burke. On the one hand, he countered the principle of Right with the principle of expediency. He based his thought not on abstract principle, but on the lessons of the past. On the other hand, he argued that the individual with his inalienable abstract rights, as conceived

---

[1] Papers relating to the Parliamentary Oath of Allegiance in the Irish Free State and the Land Purchase Annuities, Cmd. 4056.

[2] Cf. Vaughan, *Studies in the History of Political Philosophy*, vol. ii, pp. 252 et seq.

[3] Op. cit., vol. ii, p. 20.

by the revolutionaries, has no existence whatsoever. The British Commonwealth of to-day is a remarkable product of the political thought of Burke. It is its accepted doctrine that the life of every State is inevitably conditioned by its past, and that Inter-Imperial relations are governed not by speculative and abstract principles but upon the principle of expediency. Hence we have the Dominions regarded as evolving toward the ultimate goal of their political development. This thought is counteracted in Ireland by the influence of the doctrine of Rights. And the acceptance of the standard of a speculative Right involves the view that the elements in the political problem are unchanging. Thus it is that the Commonwealth, with its belief in a dynamic and changing political relation, comes into conflict with the static speculative Rights as conceived in the Free State. In such circumstances comprehension and co-operation are difficult. For the Irish outlook has not, as the French in Canada, served to bridge the gulf between English and Continental thought. This is seen in the arguments which centre round the right of the Dominions to secede. It can and has been argued quite convincingly that the Dominions have a right to secede. It can also be, and has been, argued equally convincingly that the Dominions have not a right to secede.[1] The importance of the issue is more obvious than real, in that when a Dominion desired to secede it is unlikely that it would be encouraged or restrained by the arguments of legalists. But this dispute is interesting here because it shows how Continental thought has influenced imperial questions. In the philosophy of Burke the question would not be whether or no the Dominions have a right to secede, but whether or no in certain particular circumstances it is expedient for a Dominion to secede. And it seems the juster view. It is not a question of an absolute right but a question of expediency. In this dispute we see exemplified the result of pushing arguments to a logical conclusion. We see the "free association

[1] The issue is fully stated in Noel Baker, op. cit., pp. 258 et seq.

in the Commonwealth" and the "autonomous communities" of the Balfour Declaration placed in contradistinction. That would not be possible were the problem approached from the standpoint of English political thought. Indeed, the nature of the British Commonwealth demands that one should not attempt to look too far ahead. But the Irish people endeavour to do so. While Great Britain and the Dominions say "one step enough for me," the Free State asks to "see the distant scene."

INTERNATIONAL AFFAIRS

In International (as opposed to Inter-Imperial) affairs, the activity of the Free State has centred at Geneva. There has, indeed, been a tendency to emphasize the League as the ultimate international authority, and thereby to counter the claim of the British Government that relations *inter se* of the various parts of the British Commonwealth are not to be placed under the auspices of the League. The position is of considerable interest in any examination of the question whether or no the Irish Free State is a full sovereign State in International Law. The issue came to the front in 1924. In that year the Free State Government registered the document commonly known as the Irish Treaty at Geneva. The mere fact of registration was of no significance, in that the Secretary-General had no power to reject the document. There followed in November a note from the British Government, which declared[1] that, "since the Covenant of the League of Nations came into force His Majesty's Government has consistently taken the view that neither it nor any conventions concluded under the auspices of the League are intended to govern relations *inter se* of various parts of the British Commonwealth. His Majesty's Government considers therefore that the terms of Article 18 of the Covenant are not applicable to the Articles of Agreement of December 6, 1921." The Free State Govern-

[1] H.M. Government to League of Nations, November 27, 1924.

ment replied[1] that "the obligations contained in Article 18 are, in their opinion, imposed in the most specific terms on every member of the League, and they are unable to accept the contention that the clear and unequivocal language of that Article is susceptible of any interpretation compatible with the limitations which the British Government now seek to read into it." The view of the British Government was no doubt that later put forward by Sir Cecil Hurst. He writes[2] of Great Britain and the Dominions as territories subject to the same sovereignty and he adds, "If I may put the matter in one short sentence, I would say that the common allegiance to the Crown prevents the relations between the different communities of the Empire from being International relations."[3] The position was discussed at the Imperial Conference of 1926, but the Report is not so clear as is desirable.[4] It led Professor Keith[5] to declare that, "no argument appears to demonstrate convincingly the incorrectness as opposed to the grave inconvenience of the views of the Free State." Moreover, in his speech to the Assembly on the occasion of the admission of the Free State to the League, President Cosgrave spoke of the Settlement of 1921 as an "international treaty." His description was not challenged. The issue was raised once more, and indirectly, in connection with the signature of the Optional Clause of the Statute of the Permanent Court of International Justice in 1929. The British and other Dominion Governments accepted that clause, which renders reference to the Court compulsory in certain circumstances, but reserved "disputes with the Government of any other Member of the League which is a Member of the British Commonwealth of Nations, all of which disputes shall be settled in such manner as the parties have agreed or shall agree." The Irish Free State made no such reservation and made reciprocity the sole condition

[1] I.F.S. Government to League of Nations, December 18, 1924.
[2] Op. cit., p. 55.
[3] This view is opposed by Phelan, *Sovereignty of the Irish Free State*, p. 38.   [4] Cf. Noel Baker, op. cit., pp. 300–318.
[5] *Responsible Government*, vol. ii, p. 911.

of acceptance. It is probably true to say with Professor Keith[1] that in these circumstances the British reservation could not be overridden by the Court. But doubtless it will later require modification. In the letter[2] of November 1924 (already referred to), the British Government dogmatically asserted that neither the Covenant of the League nor any conventions concluded under the auspices of the League "are intended to govern relations *inter se* of the various parts of the British Commonwealth." That position appears already to have been abandoned. If, as the British Government claim, disputes *inter se* between members of the British Commonwealth of Nations are not international questions, and therefore do not admit of international arbitration, why reserve them? And, moreover, it would appear that if in fact disputes of such character may not be settled by international arbitration, it would be because of the validity of the reservations. It would *not* be because of the *inter se* doctrine. In that event the issue has passed from the demesne of Inter-Commonwealth into the demesne of International law. But the fundamental importance of these issues lies not in the legal technicalities involved, but in the attitude and the tendencies which they represent.

There can be no question that the diplomatic autonomy of the Dominions has been enormously enlarged since the Free State came into existence. In the Report of the Proceedings of the Imperial Conference of 1926 it is stated[3] that: "The principles of equality and similarity appropriate to status do not universally extend to function. . . . For example, to deal with questions of diplomacy and questions of defence we require also flexible machinery—machinery which can, from time to time, be adapted to the changing circumstances of the world." The Government of the Free State found this principle unacceptable. It conflicted with its insistence upon the doctrine of equality. The subsequent attitude of the Executive Council

[1] *Constitutional Law of the Dominions*, p. 80.
[2] H.M. Government to League of Nations, November 27, 1924.
[3] Cmd. 2768.

S

reveals the distinction between the Irish point of view and that contained in the Report. In the first place, we must note the appointment by the Irish Free State of diplomatic representatives in the more important capitals of the world. And secondly, the creation of the New Irish Seal deserves attention. The position was previously somewhat anomalous. The Great Seal is used by H.M. Government on certain documents, for example, those granting powers to a plenipotentiary to negotiate. The seal is issued on the warrant of the Lord Chancellor. It has been the practice of the Dominion Governments to have such documents sealed with the Great Seal of the Realm. To this practice the Free State objected. The legal authority for the executive act was thus vested in His Majesty's Government in the United Kingdom. But as His Majesty acts in such matters on the exclusive advice of the Executive Council, it is apparent that the legal authority should be that of the Free State Government. So long, indeed, as a Dominion concluded treaties signed by plenipotentiaries appointed by the King under the Great Seal of the Realm, the necessary intervention of a British minister retains the appearance, at any rate, of Imperial diplomatic unity. The decision of the Free State to dispense with all British intervention formally disposes of this conception of unity. It removes a power which the British Government formerly enjoyed, namely that of securing consideration of any proposed action which might be held injurious to the rights of the United Kingdom. But Professor Keith[1] over-emphasizes the importance attached to this alteration in procedure. when he writes that the arrangement was hailed in Ireland "as marking the definite emergence of a Kingdom of Ireland as a distinct international unit. . . ." There was a Great Seal of Ireland before the Union.

On the occasion of the admission of the Irish Free State to the League, President Cosgrave said, "It is our earnest endeavour to co-operate with our fellow members in every effort calculated to give effect to these ideals, to mitigate, and

[1] *Constitutional Law of the Dominions*, pp. 51–52.

wherever possible to arrest the ancient evils of warfare and oppression; . . . to enable even the weakest of nations to live their own lives and make their own proper contribution to the good of all, free even from the shadow and the fear of external violence, vicious penetration or injurious pressure of any other kind." In the actual work of the League the Irish Free State has played no insignificant rôle, and in September 1930 was elected to one of the non-permanent seats on the Council. Subsequently President de Valera became for a term Acting President of the Council. It is the policy of the Free State Government to emphasize the international aspect of its external relations. It is from the League that it aspires to secure an unqualified recognition of the international character of the Treaty Settlement.

CHAPTER XVI

POLITICAL PARTIES

The practice of modern democratic government depends as much upon conventional practice as upon constitutional or legal provision. Of the truth of this statement, the political parties in the modern State remain abiding witnesses. With all their faults they yet render services to the democratic State which are indispensable. They provide the only effective means available to us of securing the popular decision in a manner capable of interpretation in legal form. But to say that parties are indispensable is not to say that they are perfect. The Constituent Assembly, impressed with the evils of the party system, devoted considerable discussion in an effort to secure their elimination. It was not surprising that it was the imperfections of the party system—that is the two-party system—as it existed in England that attracted most attention. Hence we find the introduction of Proportional Representation and of the extern ministries. The former was the more fundamental in that it provided, or rather was intended to provide, the only possible basis upon which the latter could be securely founded. It was felt that Proportional Representation would lead to the growth of a multiplicity of parties. Subsequent events have not justified this expectation. The status, the interrelation, and the objectives of parties in the Free State consequently have remained analogous to those of the parties in England. It was anticipated, for example, by the framers of the Constitution that the Government of the day would in fact, as well as in form, be elected by the Dáil. But, as we have seen, the essential feature of the two-party system, that is the election of the Government by the people, has reappeared. As in England, therefore, the object for which the parties strive is the simple one of obtaining a majority in the Legislature. For this purpose they must capture public opinion.

Political Parties

And in Ireland, as elsewhere, the rapidity of the party response, upon which Professor Laski has remarked,[1] to rapidly changing social and political conditions is very striking. Of this the evolution of the social democratic programme of Fianna Fail is the most noteworthy, but by no means the only instance.

POLITICAL ISSUES

Political parties in the Free State are based upon the fundamental principle of the two-party system, the election of the Government by the people. The introduction of Proportional Representation has modified but has made no radical alteration in the aims and outlook of the political parties. It has not eradicated those evils with which the Constituent Committee were unfavourably impressed. As Mr. and Mrs. Webb have remarked,[2] "the evolution of party organization, necessary feature of Democracy though it may be, brings with it in a world of busy, uninformed, and apathetic citizens its own distortions of the popular voice, not to be obviated by even the most scientific systems of marshalling the electors and counting their votes." The history of Proportional Representation in the Free State bears out this verdict. It has prevented exaggerated majorities; it has given to the minority in every constituency seats proportional to its votes; it has not, to any substantial extent, affected the radical problem of the decline of representative institutions in popular estimation. For distortions of the people's will exist, not because of inaccuracies in electoral machinery, but because various and often totally irrelevant considerations, or some last-minute issues, influence the electors to an extent quite disproportionate to their true significance.

In one particular respect the development of parties in the Free State has proved quite different to that generally anticipated in 1922. It was expected that a small but probably influential Unionist Party would survive. Minority represen-

[1] Cf. Laski, *Democracy in Crisis*, pp. 67-68. [2] Op. cit., p. 83.

tation was specifically guaranteed by the Irish leaders, and accepted by the British Government, under the impression that it would provide a means to enable the Unionists to form a party in the new Irish Legislature. In the event such a party was never formed. In the Senate, it is true, there is a sprinkling of ex-Unionists, but they have made no concerted attempt to form the nucleus of a minority party in the Dáil.

It was the Civil War which finally rendered impossible the growth of a multiplicity of parties. The issue in the Civil War was the quite simple one of whether or no the country should accept the status offered to it in the Settlement of December 6, 1921. It was an issue in which the argument of expediency was countered by the argument of an inalienable right. In the debate on the Treaty no large body of opinion regarded the Settlement as ideal. On the desirability of the establishment of an independent Irish State opinion was almost unanimous. In the possibility of its immediate realization, opinion was sharply divided. This was the issue which split the Sinn Fein Party in two; which caused the Civil War; and upon which the present division of parties ultimately rests. The question of the approval of the Treaty was put to the Dáil on January 7, 1922. It was carried by 64 votes to 57—a majority of 7. Subsequently Mr. de Valera, who led the Opposition, resigned his office as President, and with him the Cabinet resigned as a body. He was proposed for re-election, but on a division the motion was defeated by 60 to 58. On January 10th Mr. Arthur Griffith, who had acted as Chairman of the Peace Delegation, was proposed. When the question was about to be put from the Chair, Mr. de Valera and his supporters withdrew. Mr. Arthur Griffith was then elected.

It will be noticed from the above figures that in the Dáil the margin of approval for the Treaty was extremely slight. As the subsequent election showed, there was, however, no doubt that the majority had the support of the country behind them. In the election[1] of June 1922 the supporters of the

[1] A total of 128 deputies were returned.

Treaty returned 94 deputies, of which 58 were followers of Griffiths and Collins, 17 Farmers, and 17 Labour; while the anti-Treaty deputies numbered 34. In the election of August 1923, the first held under the new franchise, 102 deputies supporting the Treaty were returned in a house of 153.

For the first five years of the existence of the Free State the principal Opposition party declined to take their seats when elected. Till 1927 the leader of the Opposition was the leader of the Labour Party. So diminished an attendance could not but lead to hasty legislation and hasty action by the Government of the day. The normal minority had no chance whatsoever of being in a majority on any important division. In consequence Government measures and Government proposals were carried without adequate scrutiny. The quality of the enactments passed depended, not upon the quality of the legislative amendments, but upon the quality of their original draughtsmanship. From the point of view of legislation it may therefore be maintained that the abstention of the Fianna Fail Party from the proceedings of the Legislature was inimical to the best interests of the country. Moreover, from the more narrow aspect of the fortunes of the party itself, election results indicate that the policy was not popular in the country. In any event the history of the Free State since 1927 shows that the objectives of Fianna Fail were attained with more celerity by constitutional action within the Legislature than by unconstitutional opposition to the right of that Legislature to speak for the Irish people.

The abstention of the Fianna Fail Party from the Legislature was the result of the imposition of the Oath, and responsible for the bitter controversy which it aroused. It has already been suggested that the issue was more fundamental than the mere subject around which the controversy centred. For the eleven years which intervened between the promulgation of the Constitution and the Removal of Oath Act in 1933 the Fianna Fail Party conducted a vigorous campaign for its abolition. The Oath was not defended on its merits by the

Opposition. President de Valera was substantially justified in saying, "I have not heard anybody defend the Oath on its merits. I have not heard anybody argue that it is right that an obligation of this sort should be imposed. The only arguments against the Bill[1] that I have heard are arguments . . . as to whether or not it is right or permissible for us to do this consonant with the Treaty."[2] It was, in fact, because the Oath raised the whole question of the sanctity of the Treaty Settlement that its removal was placed in the forefront of the Fianna Fail programme. As Senator Douglas—a member of the Constituent Committee—said in opposing the Removal of Oath Bill, "the real issue which we have before us is not the merits or otherwise of the Oath in the Constitution. Far more serious questions are involved, and the passing of this Bill not only raises the question of our Treaty obligations, but may also affect our membership of the British Commonwealth—our trade and commerce, and last but not least, the ultimate political unity of Ireland."[3]

No provision in the Constitution has more profoundly affected the history of Irish political parties than Article 17, which enacts the form of the Oath to be subscribed by every member of the Oireachtas before taking his seat in either House. Till 1927 the opponents of the Treaty refused to take the oath. If, as the leader of this Opposition later remarked, "representative institutions are going to be really effective, they ought to be really representative."[4] In 1927 a more critical position arose. In July of that year Mr. Kevin O'Higgins, Vice-President of the Council, was assassinated, and as a result in the following month an Electoral Amendment Act[5] was passed, which required parliamentary candidates prior to nomination to swear a declaration of their willingness to take the Oath, if elected, and disqualified deputies who failed to

---

[1] Constitution (Removal of Oath) Bill. 1932.
[2] *Senate Debates*, May 25, 1932, cols. 673-674.
[3] Ibid., col. 686.   [4] Ibid., cols. 673-674.
[5] No. 33 of 1927.

do so within a specified period. The alternatives for the Opposition were both uncongenial. The Government by the Act compelled them to decide between permanent exclusion from the Dáil or compliance with Article 17 of the Constitution. In the event the party subscribed to the Oath, holding that the prescribed declaration was no more than an "empty formula," and that the taking of it had no "binding significance in conscience or in law." The decision, however open to criticism, was certainly the only possible one in the circumstances. The more extreme Republicans, under the title of Sinn Fein, refused to subscribe to Article 17.

In the history of political parties in the Free State the year 1927 is of supreme importance. It marked the entry of the bulk of the Opposition into the Legislature. It marked the one serious attempt that was made to form a group Government. It marked finally both the maximum influence wielded by the small parties and their rapid decline. The entry of the Fianna Fail Party into the Dáil revived the Oath controversy. It was becoming increasingly evident that the Oath could not be imposed much longer. The first attempt to eliminate it was an attempt to eliminate by consent. The Labour Party and the National League were prepared to form an administration with the support of Fianna Fail, the central feature of their programme being a modification of the compulsory imposition of the Oath, by agreement with the British Government. The administration was never formed. A vote of "no confidence" in the Cumann na nGaedheal Ministry was defeated by the Speaker's casting vote. The proposed administration is of interest from two points of view. First, we have a pledge to negotiate with the British Government in respect of the modification or removal of the Oath. Negotiation implied that the Oath could not be removed without violation of the 1921 Settlement. This was not the view in 1932. "The position to-day,"[1] said President de Valera in the Senate, "is that it is competent for us without any violation whatever of the Treaty of 1921

[1] *Senate Debates*, May 25, 1932, col. 675.

to remove that Article (17) from the Constitution." Upon these grounds, therefore, the first act of the Fianna Fail Ministry upon their accession to office in 1932 was to introduce a Bill to delete Article 17 of the Constitution. Thus it was that the failure to form an administration pledged to negotiate was followed five years later by the election of an administration pledged to remove the Oath. A second important aspect of the "no confidence" motion of August 16, 1927, was that it led to immediate decline in voting strength of the smaller parties. The material which might have provided the basis of a broad non-party administration was thereby, for the moment at any rate, destroyed. The struggle between the larger parties became the dominant feature of Free State politics and subsidiary interests were overlooked. The following figures indicate the extent to which the position was altered by the entry of the Fianna Fail Party into the Dáil in August 1927. A General Election was held in June of that year and another in September. The results were as follows:

	Seats Won in June 1927	Seats Won in September 1927
Cumann na nGaedheal	46	61
Fianna Fail	44	57
Labour	22	14
Independents	14	12
Farmers	11	6
National League	8	2
Sinn Fein	5	—
Independent Republicans	2	—

In the election of 1932 the same tendency is to be noticed —a further diminution in the representation of the smaller parties.[1]

The decline of the smaller parties coincided with an in-

[1] The figures were Fianna Fail, 72; Cumann na nGaedheal, 57; Independents, 11; Labour, 9; Farmers, 4.

creasing concentration of political interest on the programmes of the larger parties. The acute, and frequently bitter, rivalry between the two parties has resulted in an exceptionally strict party discipline. Of this the most remarkable feature is the requirement that each party candidate, prior to selection, must sign a written statement to the effect that on all occasions he will obey the Party Whip. This demand, an heritage from the old Nationalist Party, allows little room for divergence of opinion on any controversial question within the party itself. As we have already seen, cross-voting in the Dáil is extremely rare. Another and more remarkable feature in the status of the two large parties is that they have the support—often a very qualified support—of organized but entirely unofficial bodies of men. Behind the Fianna Fail Party there lies the Irish Republican Army with an organization quite independent of that of the party itself, whose objective in 1933 is the same as it was in 1921–22—the achievement of an independent Irish Republic. The Cumann na nGaedheal administration attempted to eradicate it, and in certain of the Public Safety Acts membership of the Irish Republican Army was made a criminal offence. These Acts checked the open activity, but certainly did not destroy the organization of the Irish Republican Army. The accession of the Fianna Fail Party to office led to repeal of the Proclamation by which the Public Safety Act was put in force. In the meantime a body called the Army Comrades' Association[1] was formed to guarantee the rights of those opposed to the claims of the Irish Republican Army. The origin and the continued survival of both of these "unofficial armies" is an unfortunate consequence of the Civil War. Estimates of the importance of the rôle played by these societies vary considerably, but it may be asserted with confidence that the tendency is to exaggerate rather than to diminish their significance. Their existence, however, in itself

[1] This body was later known under the more comprehensive title of National Guard, and finally formed a component part of the United Ireland Party.

constitutes a challenge to democratic government in that they are in a position to exercise authority without popular confidence, power without responsibility.

THE UNITED IRELAND PARTY

For the first ten years of the existence of the Free State the Cumann na nGaedheal Party was in office. The remarkable duration of its tenure of power is a tribute to its legislative output and administrative reorganization. During its period of office the policy of the party was considerably modified. The first or evolutionary period of the Free State Government may be said to have lasted till 1927. Till that date there was no large opposition in the Dáil, and the Government programme was carried through with considerable rapidity. The ministry aimed at building up new Irish industries and reviving agriculture. The most notable experiment facilitating the growth of industry was the Shannon Hydro-Electric scheme. Critics of the Government claimed—and with a certain justification—that it had mistaken legislation for progress. Whilst actual statistics show that from 1923 to 1926, 198 statutes were enacted, and that from 1928 to 1931,[1] 191, it is yet true that the legislative output of the earlier period was both more considerable and more fundamental.

From 1927 till the resignation of the Government in 1932 there is a distinct movement to the Right. It is the conservative period of Irish politics. The Cumann na nGaedheal Party places the emphasis on the preservation of the *status quo*, on the development of the State on the foundations already laid. It is the period of the Public Safety Acts. It is the period during which the ex-Unionists give increasing support to President Cosgrave. In external affairs the ministry remained radical. At the Imperial Conferences of 1926 and 1930 the Minister for External Affairs pressed for certain and considerable modifications of the Imperial Constitution and Inter-

[1] These figures are inclusive.

Political Parties

Imperial practice. The minister, speaking in the Dáil[1] on the Statute of Westminster, declared that "by four years of assiduous concentrated collaboration," the whole "legal machinery of the old Colonial Empire" had been taken asunder. It is an opinion, frequently expressed, that the efforts of Cumann na nGaedheal to take the wind out of their opponents' sails, by pressing for a practical elimination of all Inter-Commonwealth ties, proved an electoral weakness. It is quite probably true. A decided stand, emphasizing the benefits of Inter-Imperial co-operation, would lend a more distinctive colour to their external policy. At the same time such a policy would involve an acceptance of expediency as opposed to Right as the standard upon which policy must ultimately rest. For that the present outlook of many of the party's leaders would need to be radically changed. At the same time a policy of Imperial co-operation might bring with it a solution of the Ulster Question. The anomaly of a divided Ireland, the economic wastage involved, and above all national sentiment, place the question in the very forefront of every party programme. The solution of the Cumann na nGaedheal Party was that a well-governed and prosperous Free State would deaden old animosities and lead inevitably to a United Ireland. Moreover, it is to be noted that whatever the policy of the Free State at the Imperial Conferences, the Government maintained during their conservative period of office that the economic organization of Ireland was inextricably bound up with that of Great Britain. Consequently their industrial programme received less attention, and the emphasis was placed on the scope which the British market provided for the almost unlimited development of Irish agriculture.

In September 1933 a fusion of the parties of the Right took place. The new party thus formed was called the United Ireland Party. It was composed of the members of the former Cumann na nGaedheal Party, the Centre Party, and the National Guard. The alliance was brought about by the hostility of these parties

[1] *Dáil Debates*, July 16, 1931.

to the policy of the Fianna Fail Government. Its immediate objective was settlement of the "economic war" by negotiation with the British Cabinet. Its programme emphasized the growing crystallization of party policies on internal, economic, and social issues. United Ireland, in contrast with Fianna Fail, placed the need for safeguarding the interests of ratepayers and taxpayers generally before that of extending the social services. The cleavage of opinion on the Treaty, during the first decade of the existence of the Free State, was, broadly speaking, vertical. Supporters of either side were drawn indiscriminately from all classes of the community. Now that division tends to become horizontal. The wealthier classes, those who bear the onus of direct taxation, are in a large majority antagonized, on the one hand by the losses they have sustained through the Anglo-Irish dispute, on the other by the ever-increasing burden of taxation necessitated by the extension of the social services. At the same time the conservative capitalism of United Ireland alienates both those who benefit most directly by the social services as well as the small-scale farmer or industrialist, who relies on an administrative check to excessive competition. Meanwhile as a testimony to the continued predominance of external over internal issues, United Ireland place as the first article of their manifesto[1] the fact that the party "stands for the voluntary reunion of the Irish nation as the paramount constitutional issue in Irish politics, and considers, that to achieve this end, the first essential is solidarity of purpose among the citizens of the Free State."

THE FIANNA FAIL PARTY

It was not till March 1932 that the Fianna Fail Party attained office. Their strength in the country had increased steadily at every election since 1922. At the election of June 1922, 34 deputies of that party were returned; in August 1923, 39;

[1] Manifesto of September 10, 1933. Signed by General O'Duffy.

in June 1927, 44; in September 1927, 57; in February 1932, 72; in January 1933, 77. This growing support in the country was based upon two central features of the party's programmes, the abolition of the Oath and the retention of Land Annuities. The first action of President de Valera on his accession to office was to introduce the Oath Removal Bill. In a statement communicated to the Secretary of State for the Dominions, it was claimed that the Oath had "been the cause of all the strife and dissension in this country since the signing of the Treaty."[1] In the same communication it was declared that the "Oath is not mandatory in the Treaty," and thus once again the Treaty controversy was revived. In the debate on the Bill the President insisted that its passage was essential in order to maintain law and internal peace. Moreover, he asserted that unless the resolutions of the Imperial Conferences of 1926 and 1930 were meaningless, the Government had a right to amend the Constitution as they wished. The Free State as a Dominion had developed constitutionally, and whatever the position in 1921, it was clear that in 1932 the Free State was not bound in this, a matter of domestic law, by the Treaty. "I hold," said the President, "that this (the Oath Bill) is a test, a real test as to whether the declarations of 1926 and 1930 mean what they say or not."[2] Meanwhile, the more serious issue of the payment of the Land Annuities arose. The nature[3] of these payments has already been indicated. Their retention by the Irish Government led to the outbreak of the economic war, in which the British Government imposed tariffs on all livestock imported from the Free State. The fact is of importance in that it enabled Fianna Fail to put their programme into action more quickly than would otherwise have been possible. It was the deliberate intention of the Free State Government to diminish the existing Anglo-Irish trade in order to terminate the country's economic dependence on Great Britain. They reverted in effect more decisively, and

---

[1] Cmd. 4056.   [2] *Senate Debates*, May 25th, cols. 679-682.
[3] Chapter on Financial Relations.

with more determination, to the economic policy which the Cosgrave Administration had originally supported. The encouragement of industry and the revival of agriculture were placed in the very forefront of the new programme. The economic war, by killing, for the time being at any rate, the cattle trade, facilitated the return to tillage. Fianna Fail aimed at developing agriculture on a basis that would enable it to withstand periodic depressions. To achieve this end, it believed that a diversified agriculture would be most suitable.[1] Industry was encouraged under Government control.[2] At the same time it was the intention of the Government to encourage small-scale as opposed to large-scale industry. The Industrial Revolution in Great Britain was the product of *laissez-faire* individualism. The denunciation of an unequal society by a long succession of contemporary thinkers, from Ruskin and Carlyle to Mill and Matthew Arnold, had not been ignored in Ireland. An alternative form of industrial evolution was thereupon championed. Its central feature is the small industrialist, the small farmer. Wasteful competition is to be eliminated by Government supervision and control. The external policy is similar to the internal. "We believe that we can be self-supporting," said de Valera. It is that belief which underlies the economic programme of Fianna Fail. Ireland would never provide employment for her own population until that object could be achieved; and emigration to America could not be checked until unemployment had ceased at home. In agriculture (for example) the practice of grazing cattle for the English market was to be reversed for one of growing wheat for home consumption, and the increased tillage would give much increased employment.[3]

The economic programme of Fianna Fail goes hand in hand with a comprehensive social programme. Social services have

[1] Cf. Speech of Mr. Lemass at Newcastlewest, September 24, 1933
[2] Cf. Control of Manufactures Act.
[3] It is probable that on this question the Government are over optimistic. Tillage, even if it eventually leads to increased employment, is unlikely to do so for a considerable period.

been extended, relief works inaugurated to tide over the transitional period between the new and old régime. Housing is being carried out on a more considerable scale[1] than that which the Cumann na nGaedheal Party felt the financial position of the country warranted. The policy of division of large estates and "ranches" is somewhat more actively pressed forward than under the preceding régime.[2]

The extension of the social services has led to the belief that Fianna Fail aims at creating a Socialist State. An examination of their proposals does not bear out this point of view. Their objective is not a Socialist State, but a State in which each individual is the owner of property; in which there exists neither great wealth nor abject poverty; in which each individual enjoys the advantages of ownership, without suffering from the menace of *laissez-faire* competition. "The victory of individualism, the triumph of the acquisitive society," writes Professor Laski,[3] "has been almost entirely a Pyrrhic one. It has shown us, in marvellously ingenious fashion, the secret of the arts of production, it has given us no clue to the problem of justice in distribution." Unregulated industrialism is irreconcilable with the doctrine of equality. To Fianna Fail, as to the English Socialists, it is an evil that must be eradicated. Unlike the Socialists that party does not disturb the fundamental thesis that ownership of economic power must remain in private hands. It does not wish to destroy that basis of the old economic order, but rather by State regulation and State control to modify it in order to secure a substantial measure of economic equality. *Laissez-faire* may mean, as Rousseau believed, *laissez-mourir*, but that undermines our belief, not in private property, but in unregulated private competition. Such is the economic faith of Fianna Fail. Many years must elapse before it is possible to pronounce on its success or failure. Here we can only remark on its rare combination of

[1] Cf. Housing Acts, 1932 and 1933.
[2] Cf. Land Bill introduced July 1933.
[3] *Democracy in Crisis*, p. 19.

a revolutionary objective with a conservative appeal; a combination of inestimable value in securing popular confidence. The goal is not a new Utopia, but the revival of an Old World to redress the balance of the New.

THE SMALLER PARTIES

The acuteness of the struggle on the Treaty issue has tended to diminish both the numbers and the significance of the smaller parties. In successive elections their strength has declined. The emergence of the Centre Party in 1932, representing the interests of the Farmers, indicated the desire to break away from the controversies originating in the Treaty and the Civil War, but the votes polled by its candidates showed that it commanded no large measure of support. A non-party administration has been suggested frequently,[1] but the bitterness of party feeling makes it extremely doubtful whether the personnel for such a ministry exists. The Labour Party has enjoyed a prolonged but chequered career. It is, indeed, one of the more remarkable features of Irish political organization that there is no place in it for a large Labour Party. This is partly because of the predominance of external policy, but more particularly because of the new social democratic programme of Fianna Fail which attracts electors who would otherwise be supporters of Labour. The gradual change of opinion is reflected in the changed attitude of Labour towards the Treaty. At first the champions of the Treaty Settlement, the party has now accepted the external policy of Fianna Fail almost in its entirety. Since the creation of the United Ireland Party, Labour is the only surviving small party within the Dáil. The Independents constitute the closest approximation to a Unionist Party, in that the large majority of them are representatives of the extreme Right. They have no party organization, and their electoral appeal tends to be personal rather than a political programme.

[1] E.g. prior to the President's dissolution in January 1933.

CONCLUSION

It was for long held in England that the success of parliamentary democracy was due on the one hand to the existence of a two-party system, on the other to an agreement between the parties about the fundamentals of political action.[1] The accuracy of this diagnosis may well be questioned,[1] but none the less it is held to expose an underlying weakness in the organization of Irish politics. This weakness has attracted more attention than is warranted by party differences. The parties are to a very considerable extent agreed as to the fundamentals of political action. They are agreed in a desire to terminate the anomaly of a divided Ireland. They are agreed in a determination to remove all symbols of external domination. They are agreed as to the need of reviving Irish agriculture[2] and Irish industries. In the manner by which these objectives may be attained they differ. Broadly speaking, the two parties are in unity over the kind of State they want, they differ profoundly as to the merits of the State they have. And behind the differences, both exaggerating and distorting them, lie the memories of the Civil War. Thus it is that among the more violent supporters of either party success at the polls is not always accepted as giving an unquestionable title to office, that the menace of a forcible seizure of political authority cannot be dismissed as a chimera, and that it may not be asserted with absolute confidence that neither party will consider the possibility of revolutionary effort.

[1] Cf. Laski, *Democracy in Crisis*, pp. 30–33.
[2] Cf. Land Act, 1923, and Land Act, 1933. The underlying assumptions and the objectives are the same.

CHAPTER XVII

THE JUDICIAL SYSTEM

"There is no better test of the excellence of a government," wrote Lord Bryce,[1] "than the efficiency of its judicial system, for nothing more nearly touches the welfare and security of the average citizen than his sense that he can rely on the certain and prompt administration of justice." A consequent recognition of its vital significance is less widespread than is desirable. For the influence of the Judiciary is profound rather than striking. On account of its comparative permanence, it is overshadowed in the eyes of the people by the deliberations of the Legislature, by the rise and fall of administrations. In the Free State, however, particular attention has been devoted to the working of the judicial system, partly because of the rôle played by the Dáil Courts in the Anglo-Irish war, and subsequently because of the judicial review of legislation with which the Judiciary is invested by the Constitution.

THE JUDICIARY IN TRANSITION

The last phase of the Anglo-Irish struggle was marked by the gradual overshadowing of the judicial system by the demands of the Military Courts. While the superior and County Courts remained active, the work of the Petty Sessions Courts was paralysed by the collapse of the Executive. The menace of a growing anarchy was counteracted by the creation of the Dáil Judiciary. It was established by decree of the first Dáil in 1919, and provided both an effective weapon against British rule and a judicial system supported by popular opinion. The Judiciary thus set up consisted of (a) Parish Courts, (b) District Courts, (c) a Supreme Court having unlimited original jurisdiction. "The extent of the operation of the system may

[1] *Modern Democracies*, vol. ii, p. 421.

The Judicial System

be judged," writes Mr. Justice Hanna,[1] "from the fact that 900 Parish Courts and 77 District Courts came into operation." Decisions in these Courts were based as much on equity as on the strict letter of law. The Code of Rules provides that "the law as recognized on January 21, 1919, shall, until amended, continue in force except such portion thereof as was clearly motived by religious or political animosity. . . . Without prejudice to the foregoing, pending the enactment of a code by the Dáil, citations may be made to any Court from the early Irish Law Codes, or any commentary upon them in so far as they may be applicable to modern conditions, and from the Code Napoleon or other codes, the Corpus Juris Civilis or works embodying or commenting on Roman Law; but such citations shall not be of binding authority. Save, as aforesaid, no legal text book published in Great Britain shall be cited to any Court."[2]

With the signature of the Truce the work of the Dáil Courts was accomplished. Thereafter the integrity of their proceedings was not unquestioned, and certainly the quality of their justice declined. A considerable period, however, elapsed before it was possible to reorganize the judicial system. The Provisional Government and the succeeding administration had two alternatives before them: either to reconstruct the Dáil Judiciary or to confirm the official Courts which had been handed over by the British to the new State. The latter alternative was chosen. It was decided that the Dáil Courts should be abolished, and provision[3] was made to bring all pending proceedings to a close. At the same time the British Judiciary and system of Courts was entirely remodelled.

THE NEW SYSTEM

A comprehensive reconstruction of the British judicial system did not imply a break from the principles by which it is

[1] *The Statute Law of the Irish Free State*, 1922–28, p. 30.
[2] Quoted in Hanna, op. cit., pp. 30–31.
[3] Dáil Eireann Courts (Winding up) Act, 1923.

inspired. On the contrary, those principles were strengthened and confirmed by a constitutional statement of judicial independence and by a judicial review of legislation. It was the practice, not the principle, of the British Judiciary in Ireland that was felt to require reform. In 1923 a Judicial Committee was appointed to advise the Executive Council in the establishment of the new judicial system. A letter from the President of the Executive Council to the Committee set out the manner in which the members were to approach their task. "In the long struggle for the right to rule in our own country," it reads, "there has been no sphere of the administration lately ended, which impressed itself on the minds of our people as a standing monument of alien government, more than the system, the machinery, and the administration of law and justice, which supplanted in comparatively modern times the laws and institutions till then a part of the living national organism. The body of laws and the system of judicature, so imposed upon this Nation, were English (not even British) in their seed, English in their growth, English in their vitality. Their ritual, their nomenclature were only to be understood by the student of the history of the people of Southern Britain. A remarkable and characteristic product of the genius of that people, the manner of their administration prevented them from striking root in the fertile soil of this Nation."[1] On the report of this Committee, the Government based the Courts of Justice Act, 1923. Certain broad outlines of the new judicial framework had already been laid down in the Constitution. It was therein provided that the new system was to comprise Courts of First Instance and a Court of Final Appeal called the Supreme Court. The former were to include a High Court invested with full original jurisdiction as well as Courts of local and limited jurisdiction.[2] The High Court is the principal Court of First Instance, and in all questions in regard to the validity of any law in respect of the provisions of the Constitution it alone exercises original jurisdiction.[3]

[1] Noted in Hanna, op. cit., p. 17.   [2] Art. 64.   [3] Art. 65.

The Judicial System

The Supreme Court was instituted solely as a Court of Appeal. It is expressly[1] provided with a final decision in matters respecting the constitutionality of legislation.

THE COURTS

Such were the outlines of the judicial system laid down in the Constitution. They served to indicate the underlying motive of the new machinery. Judicial administration was to be decentralized. A brief comparison of the system before and after the formation of the Free State will explain the methods by which this was achieved. The basis of the English system was the Petty Sessions Courts presided over by unpaid magistrates, with the assistance of a paid resident magistrate. It was the Court of Summary Jurisdiction, but its civil jurisdiction had extended only to debts under £2. In the new system this Court is replaced by the District Court, presided over by a paid District Justice, whose qualifications are either those of a practising barrister or solicitor of six years' standing, or service as a judge of the Dáil Courts. This demand for a legal training stands in sharp contrast to the unprofessional status of the resident magistrates. The civil jurisdiction of the District Court is considerably wider than that of the Petty Sessions Court. It is increased to £25 in actions based on contract and £10 damages in actions for tort. On the criminal side its jurisdiction corresponds, broadly speaking, to that of its predecessor, namely, summary jurisdiction for minor offences.

The abolition of the old County Court has led to the most striking change in judicial organization. With its disappearance the county no longer constitutes a judicial area. The newly created Circuit Court is not established on this territorial basis, but is organized in regard to the country as a whole. There are eight circuits—later increased to ten in the Courts of Justice Act, 1928—and each comprises an area whose population is in or about 400,000 inhabitants. The Circuit

[1] Art. 66.

Judge must have either ten years' standing as a barrister or practical judicial experience as a Recorder or County Court Judge under the old, or as a District Judge under the new, régime. The jurisdiction of the Circuit Court is far wider than that of the old County Courts. It extends over all claims for debt and damages up to £300. In equity it covers all cases of administration of assets up to £1,000 or land of which the poor law valuation does not exceed £60. It possesses, moreover, a bankruptcy jurisdiction and a winding-up jurisdiction in proceedings extending to companies where the capital issue does not exceed £10,000. On the criminal side the Circuit Court may try all misdemeanours and felonies excepting murder, high treason, and piracy. It is invested with no jurisdiction in respect of proceedings in habeas corpus, certiorari, quo warranto, prohibition, or mandamus. When it is remembered that the old County Court had a jurisdiction on the common law side in contract and tort up to £50; in land disputes in cases where the Poor Law Valuation did not exceed £30; in equity in respect of property not exceeding £500 in value; whilst its criminal jurisdiction covered all minor offences and misdemeanours triable by a jury at Quarter Sessions, it will be realized to what extent the jurisdiction of the new Court has been enlarged. The Circuit Court is the appellate Court from the District Court. In civil cases the appeal from the Circuit Court is to the High Court, where it is heard by two judges on a rehearing both on fact and law. In criminal proceedings appeals are heard, not by the High Court, but by the Court of Criminal Appeal.

The Central Courts remain to be considered. Appointments to both the Supreme Court and the High Court are open to practising barristers of twelve years' standing, to judges of the former régime, of the Dáil Supreme Court, and of the Dáil Winding-up Courts. The High Court consists of six judges, one of whom holds the office of President of the Court. The Court has original jurisdiction in all matters relating to the constitutionality of legislation. The Judges of the High Court preside at the Central Criminal Court in Dublin, where the more serious criminal cases are tried. The Supreme Court consists of three judges,[1] of whom the President is the Chief Justice. It exercises the appellate jurisdiction enjoyed by the Court of Appeal under the previous system in conjunction with that vested in it by the Constitution. The appellate jurisdiction from the decisions of the High Court may be limited by law, but no statutory limitation of this kind may be imposed in matters involving the validity of legislation.[2]

In conjunction with this reform in the organization of the Courts, certain of the more cumbersome machinery of the old system was discarded. In the first place, all the Grand Juries were abolished, and the indictment is now preferred directly to the jury that tries the case. The doom of the Grand Juries was inevitable. On the one hand they served to complicate judicial procedure, on the other their personnel was drawn very largely from Unionist classes. In the second place the old travelling Assize Courts were abolished. Under the Courts of Justice Act, 1924,[3] it was contemplated that a tribunal analogous to the former Assize Court should be set up for trying criminal cases within the jurisdiction of the High Court. It was intended that the judges of the High Court should act as travelling "Commissioners." The proposal was never put into practice, partly because of the inconvenience and partly because of the unreliability of juries in the provinces.[4] The clause allowing for their institution was repealed by the Courts of Justice Act, 1926.

The nature of the revision of the Irish judicial system indicates that its main objective was the decentralization of justice.[5] In this there is little doubt but that the intention of the Oireachtas has been fulfilled. The advantages of the change are beyond question. The most outstanding success

[1] The number is too small. It should be increased to five.
[2] Constitution, Art. 66.   [3] Sec. 3.
[4] Cf. Hanna, op. cit., p. 21.
[5] In England the machinery of adjudication is (comparatively) centralized. See R. C. K. Ensor, *Courts and Judges*, chap. i.

has been the District Court. Its sessions are frequent. There are no delays, no arrears of cases.[1] Its jurisdiction is wide enough to cope with most issues arising in rural areas at any rate. The District Justices are trained in the law, and their impartiality is safeguarded by the practice of not appointing local men to the office. The extensive jurisdiction of the Circuit Courts permits the decision of the bulk of cases in the provincial Courts. The simplification of the judicial process has given widespread satisfaction.

THE JUDGES

In the history of the development of judicial independence there is no phrase more significant than that in the Act of Settlement, by which judges are to hold office *quam diu se bene gesserent*.[2] For it represents a fundamental truth contained in the theory of the separation of powers; namely, that the Judiciary must be held independent of immediate Executive control. In defining the status of judicial office in the Free State the framers of the Constitution followed the traditional practice of the British Parliament. The judges were to be appointed by the Representative of the Crown on the advice of the Executive Council.[3] A new departure is to be noticed in that this provision applies not merely to the Central, but to all Courts whatsoever. The manner of judicial appointment is one presenting no inconsiderable difficulty in democratic States. Nomination by the Executive has the dual advantage of independence from a party vote and of fixing responsibility. In that it has proved the most successful method of judicial appointment, there is much to be said for extending its operation to all judges. It tends to raise the standard of the lower judicial offices.

Under the Constitution the Judges of Supreme and High Courts hold office during good behaviour. They shall not be

[1] Except on occasion in the Dublin districts.
[2] 12 & 13 Will. III, c. 2, iii.   [3] Art. 68.

removed except for stated misbehaviour or known incapacity, and then only by resolution passed by both Houses. Furthermore, the age of retirement of judges of the various Courts has been fixed by statute under the provisions of the Constitution. "There should be a retiring age," writes Professor Laski,[1] "which might reasonably be fixed at seventy years." That, in effect, with certain variations is what has been done in the Free State. The Justices of the District Courts retire at sixty-five (except in Dublin and Cork), the Circuit Judges at seventy, and the Judges of the High and Supreme Courts at seventy-two.

Under the Constitution Judges of the Central Courts may not be removed except by a vote of both Houses. Under the Courts of Justice Act, 1924, the same privilege was extended to the Circuit Judges. Justices of the District Court may be removed[2] from office for incapacity, or physical or mental infirmity, or misbehaviour in office, by a certificate to that effect under the hands of the Attorney-General and the Chief Justice. A decision thus reached may not be questioned or be made the subject of proceedings in any Court.

The judges are to be independent in the exercise of their functions and "subject only to the Constitution and the Law." This abstract principle is reinforced by the constitutional proviso that a judge shall not be eligible to sit in the Oireachtas, and shall not hold any other office or position of emolument.[3] The existence of an office similar to that of the Lord Chancellor was hereby precluded, as well as the combination of minor judicial posts with a seat in the House. The salary of the Judges of the Central Courts may not be diminished during their term of office.

In detail[4] as in principle, the greatest care was taken to preserve the independence of the Irish Bench. In a country where political feeling runs high, where there existed a long tradition of mistrust towards the Judiciary, such an object was

[1] *Grammar of Politics*, p. 550.   [2] Sec. 75.
[3] Art. 69.   [4] See Court Officers Act, 1927.

by no means easy to achieve. In the first decade of its history the difficulties of the task confronting the Irish Judiciary have been intensified by the enactment of emergency and Public Safety legislation and by the creation of military tribunals to try certain political offences. It remains, however, true to say that there is a growing respect for the Judiciary among all classes of the community and a growing recognition of its significance as an independent organ of government.

THE JURY SYSTEM

Certain modifications of the English system of trial by jury have taken place in the Free State and illustrate the tendency of judicial practice. Under the Constitution[1] no person shall be tried on any criminal charge without a jury, save in the case of charges in respect of minor offences triable by law before a Court of Summary Jurisdiction, and in the case of charges against military law triable by Court Martial. The abolition of the Grand Juries by the Courts of Justice Act, 1924, has already been referred to. More important is the provision[2] which deprives the defendants of the right to trial by jury in certain civil cases. No party to an action in the High Court or the Circuit Court for a liquidated sum or an action for the enforcement or for damages for breach of contract or for the recovery of land is entitled to a jury, unless the judge consider a jury desirable for the proper trial of the action. Finally, the Act provides[3] that in every trial in the High Court or the Circuit Court of a *civil* case before a judge and jury, the jury consists of twelve members and a majority vote of nine of those twelve members is necessary and sufficient to determine the verdict. The verdict of the nine or more members is recorded as the verdict of the jury, without disclosure of the dissentients. A majority verdict involves a very striking departure from the traditional English system, and, as we shall see, it was later extended to certain criminal cases.

[1] Art. 72.   [2] Sec. 94.   [3] Sec. 95.

The Juries Act, 1927, provided for the partial exemption of women from serving on juries. In other words, women are not liable to serve unless they themselves apply to be put on the list. Under previous Acts, women properly qualified were liable to serve. Their subsequent exemption[1] was due largely to two causes; in the first place the majority of those summoned had to be excused for some valid reason of business or domestic life, and secondly, those called upon the panel were usually challenged. The total exclusion of women from the register was thereupon proposed, but was modified on account of the protests of feminist champions to the present system.

The Juries (Protection) Act, 1929, introduced to counter intimidation of jurors in political trials, does modify the principles of trial by jury to a remarkable extent. In all criminal cases the jury panel is to remain secret, the accused is not entitled as of right to a copy of the panels of jurors, the public and the Press may be excluded from such trials, the jurors are to be called, not by name, but by number, and the judge is invested with certain discretionary power whenever a person so charged stands mute when called upon to plead to such charge. Most important of all, it is therein enacted, that in a criminal trial a majority vote of nine members of the jury shall be sufficient to determine the verdict, and the vote of such nine or more members shall be recorded as the verdict of the jury without exposure of the number or identity of the dissentients. An exception is provided in a trial upon a capital charge, when the foreman of the jury shall inform the judge privately of the number of dissentients, and the judge shall report to the Minister of Justice the information so obtained.[2]

THE MINISTRY FOR JUSTICE

In the Irish Free State the principle adopted, in the distribution of the business of government, was that of concen-

---
[1] Cf. Hanna, op. cit., pp. 27–28.
[2] This Act was in force only till September 30, 1933.

trating, so far as possible, the branches of each service in the hands of a single authority. In a rationalization of administrative power a new country enjoys a very great advantage, and that advantage was exploited in the Ministers and Secretaries Act of 1924. Under this Act a Department of Justice was created, and its business comprises the general administration of public services in connection with Law, Justice, Public Order, and Police. This co-ordination of functions was facilitated by the disappearance of the office of Lord Chancellor.

The Department of Justice was known prior to 1924 as the Ministry for Home Affairs. In its functions are comprised a large proportion of the functions previously exercised by the offices of the Lord Chancellor and the Chief Secretary for Ireland, and certain new functions have been added by recent statutes. An attempt has been made to place the non-judicial side of the judicial system in the control of other departments. There is, however, considerable difficulty in separating administrative from judicial functions. In respect of the status and powers of the Minister for Justice certain facts must be noted. The minister is responsible for the administration of Justice. The Court Officers and Orders Act, 1926, established and regulated the offices and officers to be attached to the new Courts. In the Circuit and District Courts such officers are under the control of the minister. Under the Constitution all judges are appointed by the Governor-General on the advice of the Executive Council. In respect of the Judges of the District and Circuits Courts the initiative in regard to their appointment lies with the Minister for Justice. The prerogative of pardon is vested in the Governor-General, who acts on the advice of the Executive Council. In reality it is the Minister for Justice who performs this function, subject to the agreement of his colleagues.

The minister controls the Police Force of the Free State. Prior to the Treaty the ordinary police duties had been discharged in Ireland by the Royal Irish Constabulary. The control[1] of this force was never transferred to the Provisional Government. During the Anglo-Irish struggle the Dáil Ministry established a police force in opposition to the existing body. This force, first called the Republican Police, was later termed the Civic Guards. In 1923 a new force was created[2] which was placed upon a permanent basis in the following year.[3] Some time later[4] the Dublin Metropolitan Police, hitherto an independent body, were absorbed in the Civic Guards. Thus the tradition of entrusting the maintenance of public order in Ireland to a national force was continued. In the circumstances a transference of control to local and municipal bodies would probably have proved disastrous. At the same time Lord Bryce's belief[5] "that the less the police acquire the character of a national army the better," is one to which experience lends no inconsiderable justification. But Lord Bryce added that the case of Ireland was exceptional.

The management of prisons and reformatories is vested in the central Government, and in this there can be but little question that central administration is both more scientific and more economical than that of the local bodies. The Department of Justice exercises a supervision over the entire prison system, but the control of the reformatories has been transferred to the Department of Education.

On the remaining and somewhat heterogeneous duties of the Minister for Justice it is unnecessary to dwell. It is sufficient to remark that they extend from a control of alien immigration to a control over the sale of liquor, over betting and lotteries, that they comprise the regulation of vivisection, and control over the importation of firearms, over the storage of explosives, and over dangerous drugs. The administration of the various Censorship Acts is under its jurisdiction. The

[1] In this respect it differed from the Dublin Metropolitan Police, who were an independent force and were transferred.
[2] Garda Siochana (Temporary Provisions) Act, 1923.
[3] The Garda Siochana Act, 1924.
[4] Police Forces Amalgamation Act, 1925.
[5] *Modern Democracies*, vol. ii, p. 45.

duties of Public Prosecutor are vested in the sub-department of the Attorney-General.

In respect of the Ministry for Justice it is of great interest to notice that it represents the achievement of reforms so frequently urged upon the Home Office in England. The Committee appointed in 1918 to inquire into the machinery of Government considered "that a strong case is made out for the appointment of a Minister of Justice."[1] One of the more impressive arguments urged in favour of the creation of this new department was the difficulty under the present system of holding the attention of the Government to legal reform. The position is clearly stated by D. N. Pritt, K.C., when he writes "that a Ministry of Justice, the establishment of which is advocated by many persons on other grounds, might find it less difficult to embark on reform than the office of Lord Chancellor as at present constituted." In the Free State the Department of Justice initiates legal reform. In drafting comprehensive measures of reform attention is paid to the opinions of Advisory Committees created for that purpose. In this way specialized knowledge is placed at the disposal of the department. Moreover, the disappearance of the office of Lord Chancellor has led to a considerable simplification of judicial administration.

The creation of the Department of Justice was prompted by a desire to adhere to the underlying principles which separate governmental functions. In attaining this end, no inconsiderable difficulties have been encountered. The administration of justice is one which involves the performance of such heterogeneous functions that unification of services is no easy task. Moreover, there is an unaccountable tendency to regard the Ministry for Justice as a peculiarly suitable instrument for the carrying-out of the odd jobs of administration. The precise influence of the department is difficult to estimate, yet its general survey of judicial functions, and

[1] Report of the Machinery of Government Committee. Cmd. 9230, 1918.

The Judicial System

particularly its ability to hasten reforms to effect a prompt administration of justice in the lower Courts, make its value unquestioned.[1]

THE LAW

Even in an age when an ever-increasing output of legislation is a characteristic development of representative government in every country, it is yet true to say that the output in the Free State is remarkable not merely in volume but also in content. While the law of the Free State is based on English Common and Statute Law, as in operation in Ireland when the Constitution was promulgated, yet since 1922 a body of new Statute Law has been enacted which both implements the Constitution and provides for an extensive governmental control of the social and economic life of the people. In the early years of the Free State the mechanism of a new State was created by statute. That series of enactments ranging from the Electoral Act, 1923, to the Local Government Act, 1925, from the Courts of Justice Act, 1924, to the Ministers and Secretaries Act of the same year, represent the detailed application of political principle to the needs of political practice. The task of providing the machinery of administration in a modern State is by no means simple, and the manner in which it is accomplished is as important as the structure of the Constitution itself. No sooner was the Government firmly established than a volume of legislation controlling economic and social activities was promulgated by the Oireachtas. With the accession of the Fianna Fail Party to office there followed a period of renewed legislative activity. Some very general indication of the volume of legislation is acquired by a consideration of the numbers of statutes enacted. From 1922 till 1931 no fewer than four hundred and thirty-six Acts were promulgated, or, in other words, on an average more than

[1] Cf. Ensor, *Courts and Judges*, pp. 98–103, for a summary of the advantages and disadvantages of a Minister for Justice in Continental countries.

forty Acts were placed on the Statute Book each year. And it is to be remembered, though precise statistics are not available, that there is good reason to suppose that the volume of delegated legislation is considerably in excess of the direct legislation enacted by the Oireachtas.

Since 1922 the basis of Irish law is the Constitution. In a decision of the High Court, Justice Meredith defined the new position: "The Constitution," he said, "must be recognized by these Courts as an original source of jurisdiction, and as regards the whole code of law to be applied it is the one and all sufficient root of title."[1] The extent of the continuance of the former code of law is defined in the Constitution, wherein it is enacted[2] that, "subject to the Constitution, and to the extent that they are not inconsistent therewith, the laws in force in the Irish Free State at the time of the coming into operation of this Constitution shall continue to be of full force and effect until . . . repealed or amended by enactment of the Oireachtas." These statements make the position clear—or rather contrive to make it a good deal clearer than it really is. The precise intention and the legal interpretation of the constitutional provision that has been quoted has given rise to many important legal cases. With these cases we are not directly concerned. For our purpose it is sufficient to remark on the principle which has emerged; namely, that the law of the Irish Free State is based on the Common and Statute Law which was in force in Ireland when the Constitution was promulgated.

MARTIAL LAW

In the Constitution the jurisdiction of the military tribunals over the civil population is defined. Under Article 6 the right of personal liberty may be suspended in times of war or armed rebellion. Under Article 70 it is provided that the jurisdiction

[1] Irish Law Reports, 1925, p. 76, Cahill v. Att.-General.
[2] Art. 73.

of military tribunals shall not be extended to or exercised over the civil population, save in time of war and armed rebellion and for acts committed during that time. The regulations for the exercise of this power are to be prescribed by law—a valuable safeguard. On the other hand, martial law is not to be exercised in any area where *all* the civil courts are open. The Courts presumably reserve to themselves the right to decide whether the situation calls for such an exercise of military force as to justify the appellation of a state of war. But by the successive statutory enactment of Public Safety Acts the importance of this power is diminished. It was held in the Marais case that the fact that for some purposes some tribunals had been permitted to pursue their ordinary course is not conclusive that war is not raging.[1] The position was defined more clearly—and more favourably from the point of view of the Executive—in the Irish Constitution, in which it is provided that martial law is not to be exercised in any area where all the civil courts are open.

In Great Britain "the orthodox doctrine of the present day is that martial law is no law at all, and that the so-called military courts (as dictinct from courts martial established under the Army Act) are no courts at all, but mere committees of officers meeting to inform the mind, and carry out the orders of the Commander-in-Chief."[2] In consequence Parliament passes an Act of Indemnity to cover bona fide actions taken by the military in times of war or disturbance. Such, apparently, would not be the position in the Free State. An Act of Indemnity would not be required. For under the Constitution the jurisdiction of the military tribunals may be exercised over the civil population in times of war or armed rebellion. This constitutes a marked departure from British theory and approximates to that of the state of siege held in Continental countries. It is—in that it invests the jurisdiction of military tribunals over the civilian population in times of war or

[1] Cf. Keir and Lawson, *Cases in Constitutional Law*, pp. 368–404.
[2] Ibid., p. 273.

armed rebellion with a legal sanction—a breach of the Rule of Law.

THE PUBLIC SAFETY ACTS

The Public Safety Acts rest upon a different principle. The jurisdiction of military tribunals and the suspension of personal liberty is only permissible—under the Constitution—in cases of war or armed rebellion. Subsequent to the promulgation of the Constitution, the powers exercised by the Provisional Government in suppressing the armed rebellion against their authority would cease with the cessation of armed hostilities. The Government maintained that, in the interests of the public safety, it remained necessary for them to continue to wield such emergency powers. Open hostilities might have terminated, but secret opposition survived. In these circumstances, the case of Rex (O'Brien) *v.* the Military Governor of the Military Internment Camp, North Dublin Union, and the Minister for Defence, when the Court of Appeal, holding that the state of war had come to an end, ordered the release of the prisoner by writ of habeas corpus directed to the Governor of the Internment Camp and the Minister for Defence, showed clearly the rights of the Executive under the Constitution were no longer valid.

As a result, in August 1923 the first Public Safety Act was passed by the Oireachtas. It gave a statutory extension to the constitutional provisions defining the scope of martial law. An examination of the powers thereby conferred for the maintenance of law and order will indicate the course followed by the successive Public Safety Acts. The Act was described as one "to make provision for the immediate preservation of the Public Safety." It provided that any minister might order the arrest or detention of any person of who, he is satisfied, was engaged in acts connected with the rebellion, or whose detention is a matter of military necessity, or whose continuance at liberty is, in the opinion of the minister, a danger to the public

The Judicial System

safety. The continued detention of any persons, at that time detained in military custody, was made valid, and sentences, being served, which had been imposed by the military authorities were confirmed. The military and civil authorities might arrest and detain persons found committing, or attempting to commit, certain minor supplementary offences. Such persons either were to be charged with a scheduled offence or released within one week, though they may be detained indefinitely by order of the minister. Appeals Courts were to be established by order of the minister as soon as possible to inquire into the cases of interned prisoners who claimed release. The Court reports to the minister the results of their inquiries. Armed revolt and violent actions connected with it were to be punished either by death or penal servitude. The Act was to remain in force for a period of six months.

The primary purpose of this Act was to make the Executive independent of the Judiciary in the exercise of their authority. In other words it was no longer dependent upon the "judicial" existence of a state of war or armed rebellion. On the other hand it is to be noticed that these statutory powers, though devolving an extremely wide discretion upon the Executive, do define the scope of the authority conferred. The nature of the crimes and of the penalties to be inflicted are indicated. This—the first Public Safety Act—may be justified upon the grounds of State necessity. Civil disturbances had to be suppressed, and their continuation led to the re-enactment of the principal provisions in two[1] subsequent Acts. On the other hand the Public Safety Act, 1926, introduced a new principle in penal legislation. It was an "Act to provide for the preservation of public safety and the protection of person and property during national emergencies. . . ." It was not, it is to be noted, an Act for the immediate preservation of the public peace. It was an Act conferring statutory powers upon the Executive to deal with emergencies. The Act was to come

[1] Public Safety (Powers of Arrest and Detention) Temporary Act, 1924; Public Safety (Punishment of Offences) Temporary Act, 1924.

into effect when "at any time the Executive Council is of the opinion that an emergency has arisen. . . ." The Executive was to declare by proclamation when a state of national emergency existed, and a Proclamation so made remains in force for three months. It might be revoked earlier or renewed. The control of the Legislature is safeguarded. If the Oireachtas stands adjourned it is to be convened under the Proclamation within five days. If within twenty-one days *either* House shall pass a resolution revoking the Proclamation it shall be revoked. The fact that this power of annulling the action of the Executive is placed in the hands of either House, enlarges the extent of legislative control. Under the Act any minister was empowered to detain and arrest persons suspected of being engaged in actions hostile to the Government or disturbing the peace. Responsible officers of the Executive were invested with powers of a similar nature. Provisions for the release or charging of persons so detained within a week—subject to the minister's power to secure further detention—and for the setting up of Appeal Councils were similar to those in the Act of 1924.[1] It will be seen that an Act of this nature, to be put in force by Proclamation of the Executive, involves a serious inroad on the status of the Courts.

There are two subsequent Public Safety Acts with which it is necessary to deal. In the first place we have the Act of 1927, passed as a result of the assassination of the Vice-President of the Council, Mr. Kevin O'Higgins, in July 1927. Its intention was similar to that of the Act of 1924. It was passed to meet a special emergency. The Act was directed primarily against unlawful associations, and for their suppression special tribunals were instituted. The powers

[1] Under the Protection of Community (Special Powers) Act, 1926, the Executive Council has power by Proclamation to declare a state of national emergency, the Proclamation to remain in force for one month. While the Proclamation is in force the Executive Council may make regulations controlling the prices and regulating the supply of certain necessaries of life as food and fuel and such regulations are to be laid on the table of the Oireachtas.

vested in the Executive Council need not concern us here. They will be considered in connection with the Act of 1931 in which they are more fully developed. As in the Act of 1926 the Executive were given power to establish by Proclamation extraordinary Courts. The latter were invested with power to try all offences under the Act, and were to consist of higher military officers, with the addition of one person certified by the Attorney-General to have legal knowledge and experience. There was no appeal. These special Courts had power to inflict the death penalty or penal servitude for life, for unlawful possession of firearms, under the Firearms Act, 1925. In spite of extensive powers conferred there were certain safeguards which disappear in the subsequent Act. In the first place there was an attempt to define with some care the nature of the offences and the penalties to be inflicted. In the second the issue of the Proclamation involved the summoning of the Oireachtas, either House being empowered to revoke the Proclamation by resolution. On the other hand, in this Act we find introduced the most objectionable feature of the Public Safety Acts. It was therein provided that "every provision in this Act in contravention of any of the provisions of the Constitution . . . shall operate and have effect as an amendment thereof." Provisions of this nature make a mockery of constitutional guarantees.

It was enacted that the Public Safety Act, 1927, should remain in force for five years, but it was repealed[1] at the close of the following year. A renewal of disturbances in 1931 led to the last Public Safety Act.[2] It was "an Act to amend the Constitution by inserting therein an Article making better provision for safeguarding the rights of the people and containing provisions for meeting a prevalence of disorder." In other words a long Public Safety Act was inserted[3] in the Constitution with the object of preventing any judicial pro-

[1] Public Safety Act, 1928.
[2] Constitution (Amendment No. 17) Act, 1931.
[3] As Article 2A.

ceedings in respect of the powers conferred on the Executive. If the method adopted in the Act of 1926 was open to criticism, still more is the practice and precedent of this Act to be deplored. Even apart from the clumsy nature of such legislation the definition of Executive power, which should be an integral part of emergency laws, is not required and cannot be enforced, in that the Judiciary is deprived of its control over the provisions of the Constitution. It is also provided that every subsequent Article of the Constitution (the Public Safety Act being Article 2A) shall be read and construed subject to its provisions, and in the event of any inconsistency the inserted Article shall prevail. As in the previous Public Safety Act its provisions are brought into force by order of the Executive Council. There are certain powers conferred by this Act on the Executive which deserve attention. The most striking innovation was caused by the intimidation of jurors, particularly in rural districts. It involved the establishment of a tribunal consisting of five members, all of high military rank, appointed and removable at will by the Governor-General acting on the advice of the Executive Council. The tribunal was invested with full and absolute power to control its own procedure, and to make out such punishment as it thinks fit for contempt of Court. Its jurisdiction is wide. It is empowered to try, to convict, or to acquit all persons charged with offences under the Treasonable Offences Act, 1925, the Juries (Protection) Act, 1929, the Firearms Act, 1925, or with seditious libel, or with any particular offence under the Act itself or with any offence whatsoever in respect of which a minister certifies that to the best of his belief "such offence was done with the object of impairing or impeding the machinery of government or the administration of justice." When the tribunal finds any person guilty, it may, in lieu of the punishment provided by law, sentence such persons to suffer any greater penalty, including the death penalty if deemed to *be necessary or expedient*. Witnesses before the tribunal were granted special protection, and no action lies against a person in respect of evidence given before the tribunal. On application by the Civic Guards the trial of a person charged with an offence under this Act may, by order of the tribunal, be transferred from the Civil Courts to its own jurisdiction. The Executive Council have full power of pardoning any persons convicted by the tribunal. No appeal lies from any sentence or order whatsoever of the tribunal, nor may any of its proceedings be removed by certiorari to any other Court. The Police (and Defence Force in certain cases) are invested with power of arresting and detaining any person on suspicion. They are given full powers of search and interrogation. The statement of a member of the Civic Guards or Defence Forces, in any Court of Justice, as to his action and the reason for it under these provisions is conclusive evidence, incapable of being rebutted or questioned by cross-examination. Every member of an unlawful association is guilty of an offence triable before the tribunal. It is provided "that an order made by the Executive Council declaring a specified association is an unlawful association shall be conclusive evidence . . . that such association is an unlawful association." The Executive Council may prohibit public meetings likely in their opinion to lead to "a breach of the peace or to be prejudicial to the maintenance of law and order." There are similar provisions in respect of the suppression of publications and the closure of premises used for unlawful purposes.

Under this Act the Legislature is vested with no powers of control. Orders of the ministers need not be placed upon the table of either House. In addition, in certain exceptional provisions the Executive is invested with powers which could be used to control the Legislature. In the first place whenever the Executive Council is satisfied that a member of either House has died in consequence of, or is prevented by physical incapacity caused directly or indirectly by an unlawful act, or by unlawful imprisonment, or by threats or intimidation from taking part in the sittings of the Oireachtas, the Governor-General, acting on the advice of the Executive Council, may, "having regard to the known opinions of the member so deceased or so prevented," *appoint* a person to take his place for a certain limited period. Furthermore, in these circumstances the Governor-General, on the advice of the Executive Council, may adjourn either or both Houses for a period not exceeding two months.

This Act was passed by the Oireachtas after a bitter debate in the Dáil and was subsequently put in force by order of the Executive Council. The order was suspended by the Fianna Fail Party on their accession to office in March 1932, but the Act itself, surprisingly enough, was not repealed. It was once more put in force by Order of the Executive Council—a Fianna Fail Executive—in August 1933.

A review of the Public Safety Acts enables one to divide them into two categories, namely, those designed to meet a special emergency and limited in the time of their operation, and those, while passed to deal with a particular emergency, conferring statutory powers upon the Executive which it may at any time call into operation by Proclamation. The former type may be justified upon the grounds of State necessity. The first business of the Government in the face of disorder is to maintain the peace and public order. The latter cannot be justified upon such grounds. They confer powers upon the Executive which the Executive ought not, if the Constitution is to have any force at all, to exercise. To insert a Public Safety Act, which infringes every principle of the Constitution in that Constitution, does not, save in the narrow legal sense, make it any other than a gross violation of the Constitution. The Public Safety Act, 1931, allows for the suspension of the most important constitutional guarantees in an emergency, of whose existence the Executive Council is the sole judge. There is much to be said for basing the discretion which the Executive must exercise in times of national emergency on a statutory basis, but the whole benefit of that practice disappears when the powers conferred are so wide as to be almost absolute. On the two occasions when the Act was enforced it was used far less despotically than was anticipated. But on the other hand, the very existence of such statutory powers at the disposal of the Executive is a menace to personal liberty and free speech and an encouragement to dictatorial action. Repressive legislation was a recurrent feature of English rule in Ireland, and it is one of the saddest legacies of the Civil War that it was found necessary to revive it after 1921.

JUDICIAL REVIEW OF LEGISLATION

"There is no feature of American government," writes Professor Young,[1] "which has been so generally admired abroad, nor which is now undergoing such drastic criticism at home, as the Federal Judiciary." Certainly it was on American precedent that the framers of the Irish Constitution modelled the judicial power. The conception of the supremacy of the Constitution, even the very conception of the existence of a Constituent power, is dependent upon the idea of the super-legality of constitutional laws in comparison with ordinary legislation. Since the close of the eighteenth century there has been a growing recognition of the fundamental import of the text of the Constitution. But that recognition has rarely been pushed to its logical conclusion. For the conception of the super-legality of the Constitution involves the institution of a means whereby the validity of legislation may be controlled. The Federal Judiciary of the United States provides a control of this kind, and in the Free State its purpose and principles have been reaffirmed. As the history of France and Switzerland has shown, this power of judicial review is a by no means inevitable concomitant of a written Constitution.

As in the United States, judicial control is enforced for each concrete case brought before the Court, and the Court does not apply the law or that part of it which it considers constitutes an infringement of the Constitution. The judgment of the Court only applies to the given case, and irrespective

[1] *The New American Government and its Work*, p. 275.

of the judicial decision the law remains in force. The validity of any given law may not be questioned in a "test" case. A concrete issue must be brought before the Court. It has been suggested[1] that, in view of the powers vested by the Constitution in the Irish Judiciary, the High Court and the Supreme Court might declare Acts of the Oireachtas which exceed the constitutional authority of the Legislature null and void. While there is nothing in the Constitution that is directly opposed to such an interpretation, yet its adoption remains exceedingly improbable. It would involve a decisive breach with American precedent.

The constitutional basis of the Irish Judiciary is more clearly defined than that of the United States. The right of the American judges to decide on the constitutionality of ordinary legislation is not expressly placed in their hands by the Constitution. In the Free State Constitution it is enacted[2] that "the judicial power of the High Court shall extend to the validity of any law having regard to the provisions of the Constitution. In all cases in which such matters shall come into question the High Court alone shall exercise original jurisdiction." In actual fact it is evident that a pronouncement of invalidity made by the Courts would render an Act of the Oireachtas void. Only on one occasion[3] has the Court decided on a case involving the constitutionality of legislation. In that instance but little light was cast on the import of the power of judicial review, in that the Act in question[4] was held to be, not invalid, but merely incapable of immediate application. It had no effect as a law on the day in question, owing to the omission of certain constitutional[5] requirements. A new Bill remedying this defect was immediately passed by the Oireachtas.

Owing to certain amendments in the Constitution the power

---

[1] B. O'Brien, *The Irish Constitution*, pp. 117–118. [2] Art. 65.
[3] Rex (O'Brien) *v.* the Military Governor of the Military Internment Camp, North Dublin Union, and the Minister for Defence.
[4] Public Safety Act, No. 28 of 1923. [5] Under Art. 47.

of judicial review envisaged by the framers of the Constitution has been considerably diminished. There were two fields in which this power was held to be of supreme significance. The first was the validity of legislation in regard to the provisions of the Constitution. For the exercise of this control a rigid Constitution was an essential preliminary. But by subsequent amendment the Constitution can be amended by ordinary legislation for sixteen years after its promulgation. As a result, if any doubt is felt as to the validity of a proposed measure, it is silenced either by the insertion of a saving clause to the effect that any provisions of the Constitution conflicting with the proposed legislation are void, or by the enactment of the proposed measure as a constitutional amendment. An example of the former method is to be found in the Public Safety Act, 1927, and of the latter in the seventeenth Constitution Amendment Act, 1931. In the latter case a lengthy statute—a Public Safety Act—is inserted in the Constitution to reduce the possibility of judicial proceedings. The state of affairs which encourages such clumsy legislation is unfortunate.

Formerly another important aspect of the power of judicial review was to be found in the case of the enactment of legislation repugnant to the Treaty. Under Article 50 of the Constitution, it was provided that "Amendments to this Constitution within the terms of the scheduled Treaty may be made by the Oireachtas. . . ." If this clause were taken in conjunction with Section 2 of the Constituent Act, it would appear that if the Courts found an Act repugnant to the terms of the Treaty, such a decision would bind the Oireachtas to introduce legislation to repeal the Act to the extent of such repugnancy. Under the Constitution (Removal of Oath) Act, 1933, both the repugnacy clause in the Constitution and Section 2 of the Constituent Act have been repealed; and such power is therefore no longer vested in the Courts. Indeed, before the enactment of this Act, the Courts were placed in a remarkable position. Till then the municipal law of the Free State was dependent upon the terms of the Treaty. The

Courts were in a position to declare legislation invalid because it contravened the Treaty. It was a power which, had it been exercised, could scarcely have failed to damage the prestige of the Courts by drawing them into the arena of political strife. "Domestic Courts," said the President in the Senate,[1] "ought not to be asked to decide on matters of that kind." It is a judgment with which all who value the high reputation of the Courts will agree.

It has been suggested that so far the power of the Courts to adjudicate upon the constitutionality of legislation has been fraught with no immediate significance, in that circumstances have deprived the Constitution of its rigidity, and there has followed the elimination of the "repugnancy clause." As a result interest will probably centre upon the interpretation of the declaratory Articles of the Constitution. In that event the rôle reserved for the Courts is one of profound importance. That school of jurists, of whom Professor Dicey was the most distinguished representative, regarded as one of the outstanding merits of the English Constitution the fact that under it one cannot say that one right is guaranteed more than another. There is no such thing as a fundamental constitutional law. "To say," wrote Professor Dicey, "that the Constitution 'guaranteed' one class of rights more than another would be to an Englishman an unnatural or a senseless form of speech." Professor Dicey did less than justice to the merits of rights constitutionally guaranteed. For if such rights are not so safeguarded, the Executive is in a position to encroach upon the fundamentals of personal liberty. The history of government in the Free State gives one no reason to suppose that this danger is not a very real one. In this respect, however, the whole merit of a judicial review is diminished till after 1938. Subsequent to that date—if the present provisions remain in force—neither the Executive nor the Legislature will be in a position to infringe the constitutional rights of the private citizen by passing Acts which avoid the possibility of judicial

[1] *Senate Debates*, May 25, 1932, col. 682.

review. In the United States, it is said that the Federal Judiciary legislates in placing its own particular interpretation upon the provisions both of the Constitution and of ordinary legislation. In the Free State the danger lies in the other direction, namely, that Executive and Legislature tend to reduce to nullity the power of the Judiciary to decide on the validity of legislation.

It is interesting to speculate whether or no the declaration of fundamental rights in the Irish Constitution is of a higher legality than remaining provisions of the Constitution. Would the Courts be in position, for example, to declare *ultra vires* a constitutional amendment which infringed the right of free expression or of freedom of conscience? Apparently not; yet it is evident such provisions are of more fundamental import than those defining the outline of government. The idea was well expressed by L. Duguit[1] who built up a hierarchy of legality. "At the top," he wrote, "there is the supreme law, superior to all the other, the declaration of Rights. Below it there are the rigid constitutional laws, which are subordinate to it but superior to ordinary laws. Finally, the latter cannot enact any provision contrary to the Declaration or the laws of the Constitution. The system constitutes a powerful protection for the individual against arbitrary legislation. . . ."A certain tendency towards a similar conception is to be noticed in the Public Safety Act, 1931, which was enacted as a constitutional amendment and inserted after Article 2. It was therein provided that "Article 3 and every subsequent Article of this Constitution shall be read and construed subject to the provisions of this Article, and in the case of any inconsistency . . . this Article shall prevail."[2] Here we have a differentiation between the legality of Articles of the Constitution, and the amendment by which it was so enacted was inserted —significantly enough—among the fundamental declarations.

[1] Duguit, *Traité de Droit Constitutionnel*, iii, p. 641.
[2] Cf. Attorney-General *v.* O'Duffy and Others for legal interpretation of this Act.

THE APPEAL TO THE PRIVY COUNCIL

Attention has already been drawn to the paradox contained in Article 65 of the Constitution, which declares that "the decision of the Supreme Court shall in all cases be final and shall not be reviewed or capable of being reviewed by any other Court, Tribunal, or Authority whatsoever," but adds, "provided that nothing in this Constitution shall impair the right of any person to petition His Majesty for special leave to appeal from the Supreme Court to His Majesty in Council or the right of His Majesty to grant such leave." The manner in which this inconsequent provision, allowing the appeal, is inserted shows how profoundly the Irish Free State Government objected to its inclusion. The right of appeal from Dominion and Colonial Courts to the Judicial Committee of the Privy Council is a survival of part of the Royal Prerogative. It rests on the medieval conception of an ultimate reserve of justice vested in the person of the King. The Judicial Committee of the Privy Council has the right to admit an appeal from any Dominion Court, but it is limited in certain cases by the refusal of the Judicial Committee to admit it; in others by the provisions of Dominion Statutes.[1] The existence of this Appeal Court "dates from the time when all the King's Courts throughout the Empire were part of a single system, and when it was desired through the right of appeal to one supreme tribunal to maintain the uniformity in all the King's dominions of the English Common law."[2] Such an object is now impossible of achievement.

It was the intention of the British Government to secure the maintenance of the right of appeal to the Privy Council, and by making Canada the model of Irish status it was thought the result would assuredly be attained.[3] But it is obvious that

[1] E.g. under the Australian Constitution the interpretation of the Constitution is reserved to the Australian High Court of Appeal.

[2] P. J. Noel Baker, *The Present Juridical Status of the British Dominions in International Law.*

[3] Cf. Keith, *Constitutional Law of the British Dominions*, p. 277.

The Judicial System

the judicial position in Canada is in no sense analogous to that of the Free State. A country governed upon a Federal basis is more likely to find the existence of an appeal tribunal advantageous than is a unitary State. It was ultimately in a large measure agreed that in this respect the status of the Free State should approximate to that of South Africa. The practice governing Privy Council Appeals would, declared Mr. Kevin O'Higgins,[1] "be strictly analogous to the practice observed in the case of South Africa rather than in the case of other non-unitary Dominions." Certainly the provisions of the Constitution bear out this view-point. No appeal is allowed to the Privy Council as of right. No appeal may be made except from the Supreme Court. It was intended that, so far as possible, finality should be vested in the decisions of the Supreme Court. Only in exceptional cases, it was felt, should the Privy Council give the right to appeal. This position was at first accepted on all sides. In 1923 three petitions for leave to appeal came before the Privy Council. Two of the three were dismissed and the third was withdrawn by consent. In his preliminary statement Lord Haldane declared that the Free State must "in a large measure dispose of her own justice." He was supported by Lord Buckmaster, who said that "the statute has made it quite plain upon the face of it, that as far as possible finality and supremacy are to be given to the Irish Courts."[2] No appeal being allowed as of right, it is for the Privy Council to exercise its discretion in accordance with this restrictive interpretation.

On this account it was all the more surprising that leave to appeal was granted in 1925 in the case of Lynham *v.* Butler. If, as the Privy Council suggested, it was normally the intention of the Constitution that the decision of the Supreme Court should be final, then it would surely have been logical to refuse leave to appeal in a case which centred on the interpretation of an Irish Land Act—a matter entirely of domestic concern. The case came first before the High Court. An appeal was

[1] *Dáil Debates*, vol. 14, col. 117. [2] [1926] I.R. 402.

made to the Supreme Court, which confirmed the previous decision. A petition was thereupon made to the Privy Council for leave to appeal. It was granted. In the Free State the admission of the appeal was regarded as a violation of a constitutional agreement. Prompt action was taken. A Bill was introduced and passed by both Houses without a division declaring[1] that the interpretation placed upon the Land Act, 1923, by the Irish Courts was and "be deemed always to have been" the law. As a result of this protest the case was withdrawn, and was never decided by the Judicial Committee of the Privy Council. It provides an interesting illustration of the manner in which an appeal to or a decision by the Judicial Committee may be rendered null and void.

In the same year leave to appeal was given in the case of Wigg and Cochrane v. the Attorney-General. The issue centred upon the position of British Civil Servants who retired in consequence of the change of Government. It involved an interpretation of Article 10 of the Treaty. The decision of the Judicial Committee reversed that of the Irish Supreme Court, and created a position not contemplated by the signatories to the Treaty. On its side the Irish Government declined to give effect to the decision of the Judicial Committee. In a subsequent debate in the House of Lords, Lord Birkenhead stated[2] that the Lord Chancellor, who had presided on the occasion of the appeal, "authorized the Prime Minister to state that in his opinion the conclusion which had been drawn was probably wrong in law." The dispute[3] was ultimately settled by agreement between the two Governments. The case was damaging to the prestige of the Judicial Committee and lent justification to the criticisms of opponents to the appeal.

In 1930 a leave to appeal was granted in the case of the

[1] Land Act, 1926.
[2] *Parl. Debates, House of Lords*, 1928, vol. 70, col. 838.
[3] A similar admission was made by Lords Dunedin and Haldane. In the Commons Mr. Amery, a signatory to the Treaty, declared the decision of the Privy Council to be contrary to the intentions of the signatories.

Performing Rights Society v. the Bray Urban District Council. The plaintiffs claimed an injunction to restrain the Council from the performance of music in which the Society claimed copyright under the Act of 1911. The Supreme Court, reversing the decision of the trial judges, held that the Copyright Act ceased to apply to the Free State when it became, under the Treaty, a Dominion. This disclosed a lacuna in the Irish Free State Law of Copyright. It was partially remedied by a new statute,[1] which the Oireachtas passed to protect the holders of copyright. Owing, however, to the provisions of the Constitution[2] declaring "that the Oireachtas shall have no power to declare Acts to be infringements of the law which were not so at the date of their commission," the Supreme Court held that no remedy would lie for infringement prior to 1929. While the new Copyright Act did not restrict the plaintiffs'[3] right to appeal, it did forestall the judgment of the Judicial Committee of the Privy Council.

Only one conclusion can be drawn from a consideration of these cases, namely, the uselessness of the appeal to the Judicial Committee. In Lynham v. Butler the Irish Government made it plain that the enforcing of an unwelcome appeal upon a Dominion was not a practicable proposition. A legislative interpretation of the disputed issue provided a simple and constitutional solution.[4] And it is, moreover, to be noticed that since the foundation of the Free State judgment has only been delivered in two cases. In the first—the Wigg Cochrane case—effect was not given by the Irish Government to the decision of the Judicial Committee. In the second—that of Performing Rights Society v. the Bray Urban District Council—legislation by the Oireachtas preceded the judgment of the Judicial Committee. These cases illustrate the complete ineffectiveness of the Appeal Court when resolutely opposed by a Dominion Government.

[1] The Copyright (Preservation) Act, 1929.   [2] Art. 43.
[3] The plaintiffs did, in fact, apply for leave to appeal and obtained it.
[4] The issue is fully set out in H. Hughes, *National Sovereignty and Judicial Autonomy in the British Commonwealth of Nations*, pp. 80–85.

"Law without loyalty cannot strengthen the bonds of Empire," declared Lord Balfour, and a realization of this truth has led successive Imperial Conferences to diminish the attention paid to the strict letter of the law and to increase that paid to the wishes of the Dominion Governments. The Report[1] of the 1926 Imperial Conference declared that it was clear "that it was no part of the policy of His Majesty's Government that questions affecting judicial appeals should be determined otherwise than in accordance with the wishes of the part of the Empire primarily affected." It was added that "where changes in the existing system were proposed, which, while primarily affecting one part, raised issues in which other parts were also concerned, such changes ought only to be carried out after consultation and discussion." Unilateral legislation would not (were this Report accepted) be sufficient to abolish the appeal. It will be seen that the Free State, whilst securing a recognition of a more liberal interpretation of the right to seek leave to appeal, did not secure the abolition of the appeal altogether. Their right to raise the question at a later Conference was specifically allowed. At the Conference of 1930 their object was not achieved. The right to seek leave to appeal was not formally abolished. At the same time the Executive Council encouraged the view that it might be possible to eliminate it by unilateral legislation. A Bill to this effect was prepared, but was not introduced into the Dáil. The attitude of the Irish Government has always been one of undisguised hostility. It was well summed up by Mr. Kevin O'Higgins, who described it as "a bad Court—a useless Court and an unnecessary Court."[2] But the British Government remained immovable. Negotiation failed to secure a modification of its attitude. Consequently in 1933 the Executive Council abolished the appeal by unilateral legislation. A Bill[3] was introduced into the Dáil, deleting the proviso in Article 66

[1] Cmd. 2768, 1926.
[2] *Dáil Debates*, 1926, vol. 14, col. 339.
[3] Constitution (Amendment No. 22) Act.

The Judicial System

which declares that nothing in the Constitution shall impair the right of any person to petition for leave to appeal, and substitutes the proviso that "no appeal shall lie from a decision of the Supreme Court or any other Court in the Irish Free State to His Majesty in Council, and it shall not be lawful for any person to petition His Majesty for leave to bring any such appeal."[1]

A review of the cases in which leave to appeal to the Judicial Committee of the Privy Council has been granted, by indicating the futility of its exercise in present conditions, lends no little justification to the unilateral legislation carried by the Executive Council. The effectiveness of a judicial decision depends, and ultimately must depend, upon the support of public opinion. A Court of Appeal whose privileges are jealously circumscribed, whose decisions are mistrusted, whose very existence is regarded (whether rightly or wrongly makes little difference) as a relic of alien domination, is not likely to serve any useful judicial purpose. But the Imperial Conference of 1930 considered that they could not dispose of the divergencies of opinion between the Free State and the British Government by simply recommending the dropping of the appeal.[2] The prospect of such a step in 1930 was the occasion of a strong protest from certain leaders of the Protestant minority in Southern Ireland. The appeal, it was urged, was essential to preserve the rights in religious matters accorded by the Treaty. The position from this standpoint was put forward in a letter signed by the Primate of the Church of Ireland and the Archbishop of Dublin. "We do not impute," they wrote, "to the present Government of the Irish Free State any desire to invade our rights, either of property or religious liberty, but the present Government will not always

---

[1] This new proviso was inserted because of the claim that, unless specifically prohibited, such an appeal would lie to H.M. in Council in virtue of Royal Prerogative.

[2] See Keith, *Constitutional Law of the British Dominions*, pp. 279–280.

be in office, and Ireland is a country in which religious distinctions and prejudices exercise a dominating influence of a kind of which those not living in Ireland can have little or no experience. The position of the minority, a minority viewed with jealous hostility by elements of the population far from negligible, needs therefore the protection of such a safeguard for its fundamental treaty rights as is provided by the portion of Article 66 which we have quoted.

"The minority in the Free State have loyally accepted the new order of things in Ireland; but we would remind you that memories in Ireland are long and that the removal from the Constitution of the safeguard referred to, or the consent of Great Britain to its exercise only with the consent of the Supreme Court in Ireland (as has been suggested), or any similar abrogation or limitation, while it may gratify the desire of Irishmen for independence, will inevitably weaken the security enjoyed by members of a vulnerable minority, and as time passes lead most certainly to infringements of their liberty which they would be powerless to withstand."

The accuracy of several statements in this letter might well be questioned, but it is unnecessary to do so in order to refute the underlying principle by which it is prompted. The Privy Council Appeal is not, and is not intended to be, a safeguard for minorities. The right of appeal which still exists in the Dominions is a safeguard not particularly for minorities but for all litigants. As a safeguard for a minority against the tyranny or oppression of a majority it is valueless. It is, in the first place, restricted in its exercise within narrow limits; it is no longer intended that it should be used in defiance of the wishes of the Dominion Government concerned: the Dominion Government is not likely to adhere to its judgment; it has no means of enforcing its decisions. For these reasons H. Hughes declares that the appeal "is not a practical safeguard for minorities; it is, on the contrary, a trap for them; it misdirects and confounds their energies and substance; it is, even, a wedge which divides minorities; and in some cases it deprives them of the measure of political and executive authority, which they might otherwise reasonably expect to exercise."[1]

[1] *Judicial Autonomy in the British Commonwealth of Nations*, p. 109.

CHAPTER XVIII

THE POLITICAL AND CONSTITUTIONAL DEVELOPMENT OF THE IRISH FREE STATE

For good or for evil, the principle of nationality has played a dominant rôle in the history of Ireland for the last two centuries or more. The most remarkable single advance which it has achieved was the Settlement of 1921. Though the extent of that advance was somewhat obscured by the disastrous Partition of Ireland with which it was accompanied, yet in fact it did secure national self-government for the greater part of the island. As a basis for the final solution of the Irish Question the Treaty remains unsatisfactory. For, apart altogether from the inadequacy of certain of its provisions in detailed application, it rested upon assumptions unwarranted by an historical analysis of the problem.[1] Meanwhile, within the Free State, the merits of the Treaty Settlement have remained the predominant political issue. From this prolonged party strife one fact has emerged, namely, that even if the Dominion status accepted in the Treaty is uncongenial to the majority of the citizens of the Free State, yet by means of that Settlement their aspirations may be more readily achieved than was anticipated in 1921.

The Constitution is permeated by two influences. On the one hand, it represents the protest of national sentiment against alien domination; on the other, the characteristic individualism of the Irish outlook. For it is at times when the established order of things is crumbling, when the crust of tradition is broken, that we must look for the triumph of the individualist creed. It is then that wide vistas of possibility appear to lie before individual effort and individual enterprise. Such an epoch was the period of the last Irish revolt against English rule. The protest against foreign government promoted a

[1] Vide chap. xv.

revival of individualism. At first it was used as a weapon of criticism; later it was accepted as a political dogma. In conjunction with the Nationalism from which its motive power was derived, its influence was the most striking in moulding the framework of the Constitution.

The decade which has elapsed since the enactment of the Constitution has shown quite clearly that, while the vitality of the Nationalist protest has in no way declined, the supremacy of individualist thought has been severely shaken. An analysis of the amendments to the Constitution reveals, on the one hand, with what rapidity the formalism of the Dominion's Constitution has been reinterpreted in accordance with the dictates of Nationalism, and on the other, the extent to which the safeguards for individual rights have been destroyed or rendered ineffective. Both tendencies were accentuated by the failure of the Constituent Assembly to subject the Legislature to the overriding authority of the Constitution.

While the present identification of the constituent with the legislative power has served to lessen the authority of the Constitution, yet in another direction its status has been raised. Until 1933 the Anglo-Irish Treaty was invested—by a statute of the Free State[1]—with the highest legality. Amendments of the Constitution repugnant to its provisions were, to the extent of such repugnancy, null and void. But the Constitution (Removal of Oath) Act of that year repealed the repugnancy clause of the Constituent Act as well as the similar provision contained in Article 50 of the Constitution. The Anglo-Irish Treaty was thereby divested of the character of municipal law. Consequently the Constitution is now the only text by reference to which legislation may be declared invalid by the Courts.

More than a decade has now elapsed since the work of the Constituent Committee was completed, and it is interesting to remark on certain of their intentions which were never or only partially realized. The fundamental miscalculation centred

[1] No. 1 of 1922.

upon their estimate of the probable results of Proportional Representation. Whilst the Committee does not appear to have been entirely convinced that Proportional Representation would produce a multiplicity of parties, they yet framed a Constitution whose whole balance was bound to be destroyed without the emergence of numerous parties. In the event Proportional Representation permitted the evolution of what is, in effect, a two-party system. Consequently the framework of government is radically different from that set out in the Constitution. The Constituent Assembly aimed at elevating the status of the Legislature; in fact, its authority has steadily declined. The Assembly aspired to loosen the control of the Executive by the appointment of ministers individually responsible to the Legislature; in the event the proposals had no prospect of success. It was intended that the Legislature should be the master of the Executive; in fact, it is the servant. The deciding factor in the course of events was unquestionably the failure of Proportional Representation to create the anticipated multiplicity of parties. For the existence of many parties would have led to the formation of group ministries; group ministries would have involved a weak Executive and instability of Governments; which in turn would have resulted in the success of the extern ministries. The main objective of the Constituent Assembly would thereby have been achieved. The Legislature would be the most influential organ of government. But Proportional Representation, surprising its adherents and confounding its critics, produced a two-party system.

The predominance of the Executive depends, since majorities are frequently small, upon the rigidity of the party machine. As a result the debates in the Dáil are deprived of any but a very indirect influence upon the passage of legislation. The normal minority is never in a majority. But wide and extensive as are the powers of the Executive, it is none the less wrong to suppose that this *de facto* control of the Legislature implies a final cession of the authority of the representatives of the people. For, in the last analysis, it is the Executive which

The Political Development of the Free State 331

proposes, the Legislature which disposes. When, in fact, the position is reversed; when democracy proposes and dictatorship disposes, then Representative Government has failed. But that time is not yet. And we venture to think that the people of Ireland will retain and develop their democratic institutions in the face of the gravest difficulties. Meanwhile, within the Legislature, the decisive control of the Council facilitates the passage of legislation. On an average more than forty statutes are passed each year. The prevalence of the legislative illusion is widespread. Legislation is regarded as the universal panacea. Deputies with what the American poet Walt Whitman has termed "the never-ending audacity of elected persons," assume without careful scrutiny upon the adequacy of the remedies they provide.

It is becoming increasingly evident that in certain aspects the government of the Irish Free State stands in sharp distinction to its Constitution. The most striking feature of the former is the extent of State control, whilst the latter is founded upon the principles of individualist democracy. To diminish the cleavage the Referendum and Initiative have been deleted from the Constitution and certain of the Declaratory Articles rendered ineffective. It would appear, indeed, that the Constitution, whilst suitable for a static polity based on a rural economy, is at variance with the spirit and the needs of a modern progressive State. Strict adherence to the principle of the Constitution would imply a return to *laissez-faire* individualism. It may be questioned whether such a return is desirable. Certainly it is not practicable. The complexity of the needs of modern government require that the Executive should exercise powers formerly held to be quite outside its sphere. In the Constitution there is little recognition of the new dependence upon the executive organs of government. Thus it is that the need for a governmental control of economic life, for a wide extension of the social services, and for a planned polity has led to the rapid development of extra-constitutional powers. The departments enjoy full powers of inquiry into private enterprise, and are in a position to control private production. The volume of subordinate legislation enacted by the departments is in excess of that of the Oireachtas. Ministers and ministerial tribunals constitute an administrative system of justice from which there is frequently no appeal to the ordinary Courts of law. The existence of the New Despotism is unquestionable. It remains to standardize its procedure and to decide how far the traditional checks of parliamentary democracy shall be preserved. Meanwhile, the whole development of Irish government is towards an increase in departmental authority. No programme of social reform or social improvement (such as Housing or Land Distribution) is now put into effect without the creation of an administrative tribunal to deal with justiciable issues arising out of its operation. And such tribunals appear certain to fulfil a yet more important rôle in the future. For executive justice, like departmental legislation, constitutes no temporary violation of the democratic individualism of the Constitution, but rather is indissolubly united to modern social and economic evolution and is likely to assume an ever-increasing significance during the present century.

It must not be supposed that the extension of executive power necessarily involves a breach with democratic principle. Rather it implies a change of emphasis, a reversion from individualist to social democracy. "It is abundantly clear," write Mr. and Mrs. Webb,[1] "that what is wrong with the world to-day is not too much Democracy, but too little, not too many thoroughly democratic institutions but too few." In the complex conditions of modern government the ideals of democracy are to be attained, not by restricting the action of the Executive, but by associating the people as fully as possible in the work of government.

The external relations of the Irish Free State are in a state of transition, and no doubt in respect of its Dominion status

[1] *A Constitution for the Socialist Commonwealth of Great Britain*, p. 89.

considerable changes are to be anticipated. The central issue remains, is it possible to reconcile national sovereignty with "free association" in the British Commonwealth of Nations? In the case of the Free State the solution has been delayed because of the cleavage between a political philosophy founded on Continental thought and the English political outlook. But the problem remains one of supreme interest and not merely in respect of Dominion status. For the day of the sovereign-national State, acknowledging no higher claim than that of national interest or national right, has passed. Its continued existence is prejudicial to interests of the World Community. For the sovereign State involves in the field of international relations "a war of all against all." "In all times," wrote Thomas Hobbes,[1] "Kings and Persons of Sovereigne authority, because of their Independency, are in continual jealousies, and in the state and posture of Gladiators; having their weapons pointing . . . on one another. . . ." It was the great service of Mazzini to political thought[2] that, while recognizing as no writer before him had done what may be termed the personality of the nation, he yet denied that nationality is a final and absolute principle. He persistently subordinated it to the larger claims of humanity. He drew a sharp distinction between the true nationality and the false. "In labouring for our own country on the right principle," wrote Mazzini,[3] "we labour for humanity. Our country is the fulcrum of the lever we have to wield for the common good." "Nationality," he adds, "is sacred to me because I see in it the instrument of Labour for the good and progress of all men." The problem to be solved by the Free State to-day in the sphere of External Affairs is that of realizing its true nationality. The achievement of a solution, whether it be found within the existing framework of the British Commonwealth of Nations or no, would be a matter of more than imperial, it would be of international significance.

[1] *Leviathan*, chap. xiii.
[2] Cf. Vaughan, *Studies in the History of Political Philosophy*, vol. ii.
[3] *The Duties of Man*, chap. v.

APPENDIX

LIST OF AUTHORITIES

DR. KOHN'S work on the Constitution of the Irish Free State is the only comprehensive survey of the subject that has yet appeared. It was published in November 1932. The author is primarily concerned with the legal aspect and legal development of the Constitution.

General Authorities

Flynn, W. J. Free State Parliamentary Companion, 1932.
Gwynn, D. The Irish Free State, 1922–27.
Kohn, L. The Constitution of the Irish Free State, 1932.
O'Brien, B. The Irish Constitution, 1929.
Rynne, M. Die Volkerrechtliche Stellung Irlands, 1930.

Statutes and Official Publications

Constitution of the Irish Free State (Saorstát Eireann) Act, 1922.
The Articles of Agreement for a Treaty between Great Britain and Ireland are scheduled to the above Act.
Acts of the Oireachtas.
Dáil Debates.
Iris Oifigiúil, 1923.
Seanad Debates.

The Free State Parliamentary Companion is an invaluable work of reference, containing, amongst other information, the most important Statutes relative to the Constitution and Government of the Free State.

In the following list only the more important Statutes are included. Amendments to the Constitution are not included. They will be found in revised copies of the Constitution contained, for example, in the Standing Orders of either House, or in Flynn's Parliamentary Companion.

CHAPTERS I AND II

Collins, Michael. The Path to Freedom.
Arguments for the Treaty, 1921.
Correspondence Relating to the Proposals of H.M. Government for an Irish Settlement. Cmd. 1470. Cmd. 1502. Cmd. 1539. Cmd. 1561.
Government of Ireland Act, 1914 (4 & 5 Geo. V).
Government of Ireland Act, 1920 (10 & 11 Geo. V).
Griffith, A. The Resurrection of Hungary. A pamphlet, 1905.
Gwynn, S. Life of John Redmond.
Henry, R. M. The Evolution of Sinn Fein.
Irish Year Book, 1922.
O'Hegarty, P. The Victory of Sinn Fein.
Pearse, P. H. Collected Works, 1917.
Philips, A. Revolution in Ireland, 1906–22.
Plunkett, Sir H. Ireland in the New Century, 1904.
Report of the Proceedings of the Irish Convention, 1918. Cmd. 9019.
Treaty Debate in Dáil Eireann. Official Report.

CHAPTER III

Draft Constitution of June 1922. Published as Cmd. 1668, and is also to be found in *Irish Year Book*, 1922.
Irish Free State Constitution Act. 13 Geo. V, c. i, Session 2.
Select Constitutions of the World, prepared for presentation to Dáil Eireann by Order of the Provisional Government. Dublin, 1922.

CHAPTER IV

Headlam-Morley, A. The New Democratic Constitutions of Europe, 1929.
Mirkine-Guetzevitch, B. Les Constitutions de L'Europe Nouvelle. Paris, 1929.

CHAPTER V

Electoral Act, (No. 12 of 1923).
Electoral Amendment (No. 2) Act (No. 33 of 1927).
Electoral (Seanad Elections) Act (No. 34 of 1925).
Pamphlets of the Proportional Representation Society.
Report of the Royal Commission on Electoral Systems, 1910.

List of Authorities

CHAPTERS VI AND VII

Constitution (Removal of Oath) Act, 1932.
Standing Orders of Dáil Eireann.
Standing Orders of Seanad Eireann.
Statute of Westminster, 1931.

CHAPTER IX

Baker, Noel. The Present Juridical Status of the British Dominions in International Law.
Keith, A. B. The Sovereignty of the British Dominions, 1929.
Summary of Proceedings of the Imperial Conference of 1930. Cmd. 3717.
Summary of Proceedings of the Imperial Conference of 1926. Cmd. 2768.

CHAPTERS X AND XI

Civil Service (Transferred Officers) Compensation Act (36 of 1929).
Control of Manufactures Act, 1932.
Control of Prices Act (33 of 1932).
Creamery Act (26 of 1928).
Dairy Produce Act (29 of 1931).
Dairy Produce (Price Stabilization) Act, 1932.
Emergency Imposition of Duties Act, 1932.
Finance (Customs Duties) (No. 3) Act, 1932.
Housing Act, 1933.
Housing Act (50 of 1931).
Land Act (42 of 1923).
Land Act (31 of 1929).
Land Act (11 of 1931).
Land Law (Commission) Act (27 of 1923).
Live Stock Breeding Act (3 of 1925).
Railways Act (29 of 1924).
Road Transport Act, 1932.
School Attendance Act (3 of 1926).
Report of Committee on Ministers' Powers. Cmd. 4060.

CHAPTER XII

Agreement Interpreting and Supplementing Article Ten of the Articles of Agreement for a Treaty, 1929.

Civil Service Regulation Act, 1923.

Civil Service Regulation Act, 1924.

Ministers and Secretaries Act, 1924.

Report of the Machinery of Government Committee, 1918. Cd. 9230.

CHAPTER XIII

Local Authorities (Combined Purchasing) Act (20 of 1925).

Local Authorities (Mutual Assurance) Act (21 of 1928).

Local Elections Act (39 of 1927).

Local Government Act (5 of 1925).

Local Government (Temporary Provisions) Act (9 of 1923).

Reports of Department of Local Government and Public Health, 1925.

Returns of Local Taxation, 1931–32 (P. No. 1066).

CHAPTER XIV

Agreements Amending the Treaty in 1923, 1925, and 1926.

Commission of Inquiry into De-Rating. Reports (P. No. 373).

Currency Act (32 of 1927).

Estimates for Public Services, 1933.

Saorstát Eireann. Official Handbook, 1932.

Statistical Abstract, 1932.

CHAPTER XV

Baker, N. The Present Juridical Status of the British Dominions in International Law.

Great Britain and the Dominions. Harris Foundation Lectures, 1927.

Keith, A. B. Responsible Government in the Dominions, 1928.
Constitutional Law of the Dominions.
The Sovereignty of the British Dominions, 1929.
Speeches and Documents on the British Dominions, 1918–31.

Papers relating to the Parliamentary Oath of Allegiance in the Irish Free State and the Land Purchase Annuities. Cmd. 4056.

Phelan, E. J. The Sovereignty of the Irish Free State, 1927.
The British Empire and the World Community, 1931.

Zimmern, A. The Third British Empire.

List of Authorities

CHAPTER XVII

Courts of Justice Act (10 of 1924).
Dáil Eireann Courts (Winding Up) Act (36 of 1923).
Hanna, H. Statute Law of the Irish Free State, 1929.
Hughes, H. National Sovereignty and Judicial Autonomy in the British Commonwealth of Nations.
Juries (Protection) Act (33 of 1929).
Land Act (11 of 1926).
Ministers and Secretaries Act (16 of 1924).
Public Safety Act (31 of 1927).
Public Safety (Emergency Powers) Act (28 of 1923).

CASES REFERRED TO:

Cahill *v.* Attorney-General, [1925] I.R. 70.
Hull *v.* McKenna, [1926] I.R. 402.
Lynham *v.* Butler, [1926] I.R. 402.
Performing Right Society *v.* Bray Urban District Council, [1928] I.R. 506.
Wigg and Cochrane *v.* Attorney-General, [1925] I.R. 149; [1927] I.R. 285.

INDEX

Administrative Tribunals, 207 et seq.
Agriculture, Dept. of, 223
American Senate. *See* United States
Amery, Mr., 264
Anglo-Irish Treaty, 26, 29, 34, 45, 148, 179, 252, 261, 280, 287, 290, 329
Anthony, Deputy, 72 *footnote*, 132 *footnote*
Army Comrades' Association, 283
Austria, 137

Bagehot, W., 148, 152
Baker, N., 41
Balfour declaration, 17, 262, 268, 271
Barton, R. C., 30
Belfast, Parliamentary Government in, 19
Bills, Procedure on, 120-121
Birkenhead, Lord, 30, 322
Blythe, E., 175, 177
Buckmaster, Lord, 321
Bryce, Lord, 83, 90, 245, 292
Burke, 15, 268, 270

Cabinet System, 71, 101, 128, 147-148, 156, 159-160, 164, 169, 172, 176, 180
Canada, 32, 76, 148, 151, 259, 260, 265-267
Ceannt, E., 20 *footnote*
Centre Party, 69, 70, 245, 290
Chairman, The, 112-120, 184
Chamberlain, A., 30
Chesterton, G. K., 248
Childers, E., 35, 38
Churchill, W., 30, 35, 40-41
Civic Guards, the, 303, 313
Civil Service, the, 217 *et seq.*

Clare, 68
Clarke, T., 20 *footnote*
Collins, M., 26, 30, 35, 38, 39, 44-45
Connolly, J., 20 *footnote*, 99 *footnote*
Constituent Assembly, 43 *et seq.*, 71, 86-87, 90, 92, 94, 106 140, 142, 156, 161, 166
Convention, the, 21-23
Cork, 65
Cosgrave, W. T., 39, 41, 45, 69, 177, 179, 225, 254, 272, 275, 284, 288
Courts, the, 295-298
Craig, Sir J., 30
Crown, the, 92, 147-148, 155, 263-264
Cumann na nGaedheal, 68, 113, 116, 175-176, 184, 215, 266, 281, 283-285, 289
Customs questions, 22
Czechoslovakia, 137

Dáil Eireann, 23-25, 27-30, 34, 39, 46, 49, 55-56, 59 *et seq.*, 74, 78, 88, 92, 94, 99, 102 *et seq.*, 103, 106-107, 125, 154, 158-159, 176-177, 186-187, 226, 259
Davis, T., 16
Declaration of Rights, 51
DeTocqueville, 15
De Valera, E., 26-27, 30, 35, 38, 43, 143, 179, 254, 264, 268, 275, 278, 280-281, 287-288
Devolution Report, 19
Dicey, Professor, 318
Dissolution, power of, 154, 181
Dominion Status, 27, 31, 37-38, 260-261, 267
Douglas, J., 44, 280

Doumer, P., 116
Dual Monarchy, 18
Duffy, G. G., 31, 39 *footnote*
Duggan, E., 30, 39 *footnote*
Duguit, L., 319
Dun Laoghaire, 245

Easter Insurrection (1916), 20–21
Electoral System, 58 *et seq.*
Ennis Urban District, 239
Esthonia, 55, 87, 137
Evans, Sir L. W., 30
Executive Council, 99, 101, 103, 107, 147 *et seq.*, 175, 183, 187, 192

Farmers and Ratepayers League, 70
Farmers' Party, 69, 245
Fianna Fail, 68, 73, 99, 101, 108, 113, 142, 176–177, 179–180, 184, 193, 215, 246, 266, 277, 279, 281–283, 286 *et seq.*, 288, 305, 314
Figgis, D., 44
Finance, control of, 19
Finance, Local, 233–236
Finance and Financial Relations, 251 *et seq.*
Financial Procedure, 132 *et seq.*
Finland and the Finnish Constitution, 54
Fiscal independence, 22
Fiscal Legislation, 18–19
France, C. J., 44
French Cabinets, 93, 182
French Chamber of Deputies, 88–89
French Electoral Act, 70–71
French Electoral System, 99, 116, 153, 181
French Revolution, 15, 84, 87

Galway, 65
George, Rt. Hon. D. Lloyd, 24, 26, 261, 268

Germany, 51, 71, 87, 137, 245
Governor-General, the, 148–149, 150–155, 182, 314
Great Seal, the, 271–275
Greece, 137
Greenwood, Sir Hamar, 30
Griffith, A., 16–18, 30, 34, 38–39, 45, 278
Guyot, Y., 182

Haldane, Lord, 222, 321
Hanna, Justice, 293
Hare, T., 64, 79, 80
Hayes, M., 112–114, 118
Henry, R. M., 16–17
Hewart, Lord, 42, 208, 214
Hills, J. W., 254
Hobbes, T., 333
Hogan, P., 39 *footnote*
Home Rule, 16–19, 24, 255, 259
Hughes, H., 326
Hungarian House of Magnates, 84
Hurst, Sir C., 260, 267, 272

Ilbert, Sir C., 121
Imperial Parliament, 18
Iris Oifigiúil, 177, 205
Irish Agreement Act, Royal assent to, 40
Irish Legislature, 18–19
Irish Parliament, 18
Irish representation at Westminster, 22–23
Irish Republic proclaimed, 20
Irish Republican Army, 283
Irish Republican Brotherhood, 20

Johnson, Deputy, 53, 77
Judges, the, 298–300
Judicial System, the, 292 *et seq.*
Jury System, 300–301

"Kangaroo," the, 119, 130
Keith, Professor, 33, 91, 149, 183, 254, 272–274
Kennedy, H., 44

Index

Kerry, 68
Kiernan, Dr., 258
Kohn, L., 46

Labour Party, 67, 69, 112, 179, 184, 279, 290
Lalor, 16
Laski, Professor, 58–60, 77, 232, 277, 289
Latvia, 137
Law, Bonar, 24
Legislative Committees, 123
Legislature, the, 86 et seq., 105, 192, 276, 330–331
Limerick, 68
List, F., 17
Lithuania, 137
Local Government, 225 et seq.
Lord-Lieutenant, 19
Louth, 65
Lowell, President, 141
Ludlow, 129
Lynch, F., 39 footnote

MacDiarmada, S., 20 footnote
McDonagh, T., 20 footnote
McGilligan, Deputy P., 177, 263
McGrath, J., 39 footnote
Macmillan Report, 191
MacNeill, E., 39 footnote
MacNeill, J., 44, 150
Magyar National Movement, 18
Maitland, Professor, 110
Martial Law, 306–308
Mazzini, 269, 333
Meredith, Justice, 306
Mill, J. S., 52, 58, 80, 190
Milroy, S., 38
Ministerial Tribunals, 209 et seq.
Ministers, the, 172 et seq., 190
Mirabeau, 59, 86
Mirkine-Guetzevitch, B., 51 footnote, 94 footnote
Mitchell, 16
Money Bills, 94–97, 119, 134. See also Finance

Montesquieu, 15
Morissey, Deputy D., 72 footnote, 132 footnote
Mulcahy, R., 39
Murnaghan, J., 44

National Convention, 21
National sovereignty, 16–17, 19–21, 54, 269
Nationalism, 16
Nationalist Party, 19, 22
Northern Ireland, 19, 106
Norway, 83, 102

Oath of Allegiance, 33, 35, 40, 108, 269, 279, 280, 281, 287
O'Brien, B., 186
O'Byrne, J., 44
O'Hegarty, 21
O'Higgins, K., 35, 38–39, 45, 111, 261, 264, 280, 310, 321, 324
Oireachtas, 48, 65, 87–92, 103, 106–109, 111, 121, 141–143, 181, 186, 189–192, 194, 197–198, 200, 202–204, 206, 215, 225, 254, 268, 280, 305–306, 308, 310, 314, 317, 323
O'Rahilly, A., 44
O'Shiel, K., 44

Palmerston, Lord, 72
Parliamentary Procedure, 106
Peace Conference at Versailles, 23, 29
Pearse, P. H., 17 footnote, 20 footnote
Plunket, J., 20 footnote
Plunkett, Sir H., 22, 251
Poland, 50, 53
Police Force, 302–303
Poor Relief, 229–231
President, the, 172, 173 et seq., 175, 180, 186
Prices Commission, 207, 208
Pritt, D. N., 304

Privilege, Parliamentary, 110
Privy Council, the, 320–327
Proportional Representation, 55, 61, 62, 63, 66, 69, 70–73, 81, 161, 187, 276–277, 330
Provisional Government Proclamation, 20–21
Prussian Herrenhaus, 84
Public Safety Acts, 308–315

Railway Tribunal, 207
Redlich, 105
Redmond, J., 19–20, 24
Referendum, the, 87, 91, 137 et seq., 144–145
Repeal Movement, 16
Republicanism, 18, 20
"Resurrection of Hungary," 18
Revolution, 20
Robson, Dr., 165, 211, 236, 241
Rousseau, 43, 87, 137, 268, 289
Royal Irish Constabulary, 302–303

Seanad Eireann, 74–80, 82–85, 88, 92–95, 97-100, 102, 103, 123, 140, 185
Siéyès, Abbé, 59
Single Transferable Vote, 63, 66–69, 79
Sinn Fein, 17–18, 20–21, 23–24, 259, 278, 281
Speaker, the, *see Chairman*
Standing Orders, 127, 129–130
Statute of Westminster, 91

Switzerland and the Swiss Constitution, 101, 140, 145, 156, 160, 162, 165
Tone, 17
Transferable Vote. *See* Single Transferable Vote
Treaty settlement, 18

Ulster, 19–20, 37
Ulster Unionists, 21–22
Unionists, 16, 277
United Ireland Party, 284 *et seq.*
United States Constitution, 57, 99
United States Senate, 101, 145
University Representation, 102

Vaughan, Professor, 270
Vice-Chairman (an Leas Cheann Comhairle), 119
Vice-President, 175
Vico, 15

Waterford County Council, 241
Webb, Mr. and Mrs. S., 221, 248, 249, 277, 332
Westminster, Irish Members at, 128, 132
Wilson, President, 164
Wyndham Act, 253

Young, Prof. A., 84, 315
Yugoslavia, 50, 63

Zimmern, Professor, 268

www.ingramcontent.com/pod-product-compliance
Lightning Source LLC
Chambersburg PA
CBHW032000220426
43664CB00005B/87